Books by Carey McWilliams

Factories in the Field

Ill Fares the Land

Brothers Under the Skin

Prejudice
Japanese-Americans: Symbol of Racial Intolerance

A Mask for Privilege: *Anti-Semitism in America*

A Mask for Privilege:
ANTI-SEMITISM IN AMERICA

A Mask for Privilege:

ANTI-SEMITISM IN AMERICA

By CAREY McWILLIAMS

ᐁ ᐁ I am convinced myself that
there is no more evil thing in this present
world than race prejudice, none at all! I
write deliberately — it is the worst single
thing in life now. It justifies and holds together more baseness, cruelty and abomina-
tion than any sort of error in the world.

— H. G. WELLS

Little, Brown and Company · Boston · 1948

FIRST EDITION

Published March 1948

*Published simultaneously
in Canada by McClelland and Stewart Limited*

PRINTED IN THE UNITED STATES OF AMERICA

For Those Fine Companions
and Irreplaceable Good Fellows

JERRY ROSS McWILLIAMS
and WILSON CAREY McWILLIAMS

Preface

WHEN the United Nations finally voted on November 29, 1947, to partition Palestine, a responsibility without precedent devolved upon the government and people of the United States. The decision to re-establish a Jewish State in Palestine, after the lapse of 2000 years, came in response to the tardy initiative of the United States and the timely concurrence of the Soviet Union and Great Britain. Despite the tortuous vacillation of American policy in the past, a majority of the American people have always favored the idea of a Jewish homeland. When the crucial test came, it was this strong current of popular sentiment that forced the State Department to redeem a promise many times repeated to American Jewry. Having made the motion, so to speak, to re-establish a Jewish State in Palestine, it is now our clear moral responsibility to give this state a chance to fulfill the promise so apparent in what has already been accomplished in Palestine in the way of rehabilitating Jewish life and culture.

But our special moral responsibility now transcends such purely formal considerations: it goes to the question of our integrity as a people. Six million European Jews — one quarter of all the Jews in the world — were liquidated in World War II. For all practical purposes, therefore, Europe has ceased to be a center of gravity in Jewish affairs. To be sure, a million and a quarter Jews still live in Europe: twice the number now to be found in Palestine. But to these survivors Palestine represents the one great hope for the future. Nine out of ten Jews interviewed in the displaced persons camps have expressed an understandable desire to make their home in Palestine. For these survivors, Europe is poisoned by intolerable memories and associations; nor are they blind to resurgent outbursts of anti-Semitism which have embittered their lives since the end of the war. While the physical and economic security of the two million or more Jews in the U.S.S.R. may be taken for granted, it is apparent that the Soviet Union is not a refuge for the surviving Jews of Europe, nor do these survivors look to it as a center of Jewish life and culture. The plain fact is that the United States and Palestine have now become the main pivots of Jewish life — interrelated aspects of a single promise for the future. To such an extent is this true that one simply cannot divorce the hope for Palestine from the fate of Jews in America. "Should America's democracy wither away," asks Israel Knox, "what Jews anywhere could live in safety and security, even in Palestine?" If Palestine is the lamp of Jewish life and culture in the world today, America provides the fuel for this lamp and the shield for its flame. Remove the shield of American support, or seriously weaken the position of American Jewry, and the lamp now being relit in Palestine would certainly be dimmed if not eclipsed. This lamp is the one brave, hopeful beacon in the world today for the surviving Jews of Europe, a people whose claim upon the conscience of America is beyond argument or debate.

World Jewry does not look to Europe for support at this turning point in Jewish history: it looks to America. That Europe has ceased to be a center of gravity in Jewish affairs does not mean, of course, that it can be written off as a place of residence for Jews. A great many Jews will continue to live in Europe, as Jews, and it is reasonable to assume that much of their communal life will be gradually restored. It is even possible to infer that the fever of anti-Semitism may finally have burned itself out in Europe and that the alarming symptoms of the disease to be noted in so many quarters of Europe today are merely the spasms of death. But to grant all this does not alter the significance of the fact that the war has shifted the center of gravity in Jewish affairs from Europe to the United States. While Palestine is the spiritual and cultural center of Jewish life, upon which Jewish hopes and aspirations throughout the world are focused, the largest and most powerful segment of World Jewry is to be found in the United States. The measure of America's power in the world today is the measure of our responsibility to a people who, for 2000 years, have been the victims of man's cruelty to man. If, after all these centuries, the fires of anti-Semitism have finally been extinguished in Europe — which is only a faint inference, the available evidence pointing to a contrary conclusion — then the meaning of the inference may well be that the last great struggle against anti-Semitism will center in the United States.

With America being committed to the protection of the Jewish State in Palestine, various elements in this country will unquestionably seek to exploit this new relationship for their own ends and purposes. Just as England's recent difficulties in Palestine have contributed to the rise of anti-Semitism in Great Britain, so it is possible to assume that elements in America will seek to weaken the American commitment to Palestine by isolationist demagoguery and by various forms of Jew-baiting. Nor can one ignore the fact that a Jewish State in Palestine is being born at a time when anti-Semitism in the United States has entered upon a new and decisive phase. Perhaps the greatest peril to Palestine, therefore, consists in the possibility of anti-Semitism assuming serious proportions here. Should we ever permit this to happen, we would not only have betrayed the hopes and confidence of a desperate people: we would have betrayed American democracy.

The pivotal position which America now occupies in Jewish life should alone dictate the wisdom of undertaking at this time a thoughtful, sober, realistic scrutiny into the nature of anti-Semitism in the United States. As part of this scrutiny, we need to find the answers to a number of questions. Is it true that anti-Semitism lacks deep roots in American life? Deep is a relative term: How deep? What kind of roots? Are these roots withering or sending out new shoots? Again we are told that anti-Semitism is a disease; but what kind of disease? With what symptoms? Why is it that this disease should be regarded, by many of its victims, as essentially incurable? What is there about anti-Semitism that has prompted its characterization as one of the decisive problems of Western civilization? Can it be that secret sources feed meaning and significance into the racist ideology? If so, what are these sources? Is it true that there is some special elixir about the American environment that makes us immune to the virus of anti-Semitism?

I would not suggest that completely satisfactory answers will be found to these questions — which are very large questions indeed — in the following pages. What I have attempted to do is to trace the pattern of anti-Semitism in the United States; to examine as closely as possible the theory that anti-Semitism is without deep roots in American life; to raise certain questions about the nature of the disease and to suggest how it can be most effectively combated. Above all I have tried to challenge complacency and to stimulate curiosity. The order of the chapters has been planned with the thought of raising certain questions in the mind of the reader and of forcing him to seek the answers. The argument is intended to be suggestive rather than dogmatic. I began this work by first seeking to find a workable definition of anti-Semitism. After examining dozens of definitions, I concluded that none of them was satisfactory or in any sense adequate. In fact I discovered, to my amazement, that the inadequacy of social theory in relation to this crucial problem is a scandal for which every social scientist in the United States should feel ashamed. The reader should not, therefore, be inhibited or intimidated: this is a subject, despite its antiquity and the voluminous literature about it, in which amateurs are at no great disadvantage. Since, as the title indicates, it is my conviction that anti-Semitism functions as a mask for privilege, I have sought to remove the mask, to expose the process by which, as Yves R. Simon has written, privileged groups manufacture a system of screens to mask their attempted monopoly of social, economic, and political power.

C. McW.

Contents

Contents

A Mask for Privilege:

ANTI-SEMITISM IN AMERICA

CHAPTER I *The White Frost*

IN THE SUMMER of 1877, Joseph Seligman, the New York banker, was bluntly and noisily refused accommodations for himself and his family at the Grand Union Hotel at Saratoga Springs. Here, simply stated, was one of the first major overt manifestations of anti-Semitism in the United States.[1] This is not to say, of course, that minor incidents had not previously occurred; nor would it be accurate to say that Jews were everywhere treated with perfect equality prior to 1877. But by and large, the record up to this point had been largely free of overt or significant manifestations of anti-Semitism.

That there had been prior "incidents" is, of course, well known. In 1861 the Board of Delegates of American Israelites had succeeded in changing an act of Congress stating that army chaplains must be ministers of "some Christian denomination"; in 1864 the Board brought about the defeat of attempts by church leaders to declare this a Christian country by an amendment to the Constitution; and discrimination against Jewish students had cropped out in 1872 at what is now the College of the City of New York.[2] It is also true that General Grant had issued a rather notorious order on December 20, 1862, expelling "Jews as a class" from his lines, an incident which is described at some length in the *American Jewish Historical Society Publications*, Number 17 (1909), pages 71–79. But none of these incidents aroused the interest that the Seligman case provoked and it will be noted that all of them occurred shortly prior to this case, indicating that it was around this time that the first significant tensions developed.

Both the wide publicity given the Saratoga Springs incident and the wealth of comment which it aroused indicate that this initial manifestation of anti-Semitic prejudice came as a distinct shock to American public opinion. William Cullen Bryant, in an editorial, said that "a prejudice so opposed to the spirit of American institutions" could have only a momentary existence in this country and urged the Seligmans "to view with scientific curiosity, rather than personal annoyance, the survival, in such a remnant, of a medieval prejudice." Today one is impressed with the air of surprise and incredulity reflected in the editorial comments devoted to the incident. That it should have been regarded as utterly anachronistic and completely at variance with contemporary custom is the best proof that incidents of this sort were virtually unknown in 1877. Much the same surprise was occasioned when, at about the same time, a prominent Jewish lawyer was denied membership in the New York Bar Association.[3]

To appreciate the significance of the Saratoga Springs incident, however, the principals must be identified. Joseph Seligman had emigrated from Bavaria in 1837 because, so his biographer states, "he had become dissatisfied with the lack of opportunities for Jews in Germany." With his brothers, he had founded the well-known banking firm of Seligman Brothers in New York. Although they had arrived as penniless immigrants, the Seligmans were well-educated and cultured men and could hardly be regarded as *nouveaux riches*. Henry Ward Beecher, who had summered with the

Seligmans for several seasons prior to 1877, said that they had "behaved in a manner that ought to put to shame many Christian ladies and gentlemen." During one of the darkest hours of the Civil War, Joseph Seligman had undertaken, at his own suggestion, to dispose of a large government bond issue in Europe. The historian William E. Dodd has characterized the successful fulfillment of this mission as scarcely less important to the Union cause than the Battle of Gettysburg. Largely in recognition of these services, Seligman had been offered the post of Secretary of the Treasury by President Grant.

In 1877 the Grand Union Hotel was owned by Judge Hilton, a prominent New York politician, and A. T. Stewart, the well-known New York merchant. Born in Ireland, Stewart had arrived in America as penniless as the Seligmans and, like them, had risen to a position of great wealth and prominence. A notice in the *Dictionary of American Biography* points out that Stewart was notoriously penurious, a shrewd, harsh disciplinarian whose wage policies had once aroused widespread criticism. Legend has it that the coffin containing his remains was stolen and held for ransom by persons who had resented his dictatorial manner. Clearly personifying the new forces that had come to dominate the American scene after the Civil War, it was Stewart, not the Seligmans, who belonged in the *nouveau riche* category. The locale of the incident is also important. The Grand Union Hotel epitomized the parvenu splendor of the gilded age. Through its luxurious grounds strolled the millionaires who had emerged with such abundance in the postwar period.

On June 24, 1877, Henry Ward Beecher preached a

famous sermon on the Saratoga Springs incident at Plymouth Church. "What have the Jews," he said, "of which they need be ashamed, in a Christian Republic where all men are declared to be free and equal? . . . Is it that they are excessively industrious? Let the Yankee cast the first stone. Is it that they are inordinately keen in bargaining? Have they ever stolen ten millions of dollars at a pinch from a city? Are our courts bailing out Jews, or compromising with Jews? Are there Jews lying in our jails, and waiting for mercy, and dispossessing themselves slowly of the enormous wealth which they have stolen? You cannot find one criminal Jew in the whole catalogue. It is said that the Jews are crafty and cunning, and sometimes dishonest in their dealings. Ah! What a phenomenon dishonesty must be in New York! Do they not pay their debts when it is inconvenient? Hear it, O ye Yankees!"

Urging the Seligmans to be patient "under this slight breath, this white frost, this momentary flash of insult," Beecher said that the incident was as the bite of a mosquito to a man in his whole armor. The sermon ended on the note that there should be "no public assemblies called, no resolutions passed, no more unfortunate letters written, no recriminations, no personalities." Was this incident, as Beecher thought, merely a slight breath, a white frost, a momentary flash of anti-Semitism? A mosquito is truly an insignificant insect, but it may be a carrier of malaria.

A decade after the incident occurred, Alice Hyneman Rhine wrote an interesting article for the *Forum* (July 1887) on "Race Prejudice at Summer Resorts." In the course of this article, she said (my emphasis): "This prejudice, in its *outward* expression at least, is a *new* feature in the New World. *Only within the present decade* has there been an anti-Jewish sentiment *openly* displayed in the United States." From Saratoga Springs, Miss Rhine found that the practice of excluding Jews had spread throughout the Catskills and Adirondacks and that, within a decade, the practice had become so well established that it no longer aroused comment.

Surprised that the practice should have spread so quickly, Miss Rhine interviewed a number of resort owners. "Jews swarm everywhere," she was told; "they are lacking in refinement" — in the gilded age! — "as shown by the prominence of patent leather boots, showy trousers, and the conspicuousness and vulgarity of their jewelry." Shades of Diamond Jim Brady! Charging that Jews monopolized the best accommodations, the resort owners in the same breath complained that they were "close and penurious." Unlike some latter-day observers, Miss Rhine thought that the emergence of a pattern of social prejudice at summer resorts was neither trivial nor insignificant. It was precisely at fashionable summer resorts, in her view, that a latent prejudice was most likely to find expression.

No one seems to have noticed that the Saratoga Springs incident had an interesting sequel. Jesse Seligman, one of the brothers, had been a founder of the Union League Club of New York and at one time its vice-president. But he resigned from the club in 1893 when his son was blackballed for membership because he was a Jew. Apparently anti-Semitism was unknown or of little force when the Union League Club was formed. But it is equally apparent that something had happened to change the social climate in New York between the Civil War and 1893. Henry

Ward Beecher's "white frost" had, it would seem, turned into a hard freeze.

1. WHAT CAUSED THE FREEZE?

What Charles Beard has called "the second American Revolution" — the revolution that assured the triumph of the business enterprise — had been fought and largely won by 1877. "In 1865," writes Matthew Josephson, "three-quarters of the American people set to work instinctively, planlessly, to build a heavy industry where there had been almost nothing of the sort, and to produce twice as much goods, food, and wealth of all kinds, as they had produced in 1860." [4] In four great lines of endeavor — manufacturing, extractive industries, transportation, and finance — business marched from one swift triumph to another. In 1860 about a billion dollars was invested in manufacturing plants which employed 1,500,000 workers; but in less than fifty years the investment had risen to 12 billions and the number of workers to 5,500,000. The output of American iron and steel — true measures of industrial power — had been far below the tonnage of England and France in 1870; but within twenty years the United States had outdistanced both nations. Even in retrospect, it is difficult to measure the swiftness and the magnitude of the transformation which the second American Revolution worked in American life.

The year 1877 was of decisive importance in determining the fate of this revolution. A bloody and riotous year, violence was everywhere evident in the America of 1877. The great railroad strike of that year was the first significant industrial clash in American society. "Class hatred," writes Denis Tilden Lynch, "was a new note in American life where all men were equal before the law." [5] The South was in the turmoil of reconstruction; sand-lot rioters ruled in San Francisco; and 100,000 strikers and 4,000,000 unemployed surged in the streets of Northern cities. At a cabinet meeting on July 22, 1877, the suggestion was advanced that a number of states should be placed under martial law. For a moment, the issue seemed to hang in the balance; but after 1877 it became quite clear that the industrial bourgeoisie had triumphed. With society being transformed by processes which the people did not understand and by forces which they could scarcely identify, American public opinion seemed aloof, vague, indecisive, suffering from war weariness and exhaustion.

Once triumphant, the industrial tycoons discovered that they could not function within the framework of the social and political ideals of the early Republic. To insure their triumph, a new social order had to be established; a new set of institutions had to be created of which the modern corporation was, perhaps, the most important; and a new ordering of social relationships had to be effected. "In the swift transformation of the whole economic order," writes Beard, "the very texture of American society had been recast." A new hierarchy of social, economic, and political command was imposed on American society, and with this hierarchy came a new set of status relationships. "The locomotive," wrote E. L. Godkin, "is coming in contact with the framework of our institutions." With the industrial machine came the political machine. Dating from 1870, the "boss system" had become so thoroughly entrenched

in American politics by 1877 that public life was everywhere discredited by the conduct of high officials.[6] Men
began to question the value of democracy as they saw the
robber barons ride roughshod over the rights of the people
and as they witnessed an almost universal corruption of the
ballot. This questioning led, in many cases, to an eventual
repudiation of the earlier American ideals and traditions.

As the revolution swept forward, it uprooted the earlier
democratic cultural pattern with the ruthlessness of a tor-
nado. The simplicity of taste which had characterized the
"classic" years of the early Republic gave way to a wild,
garish, and irresponsible eclecticism. "The emergence of
the millionaire," writes Talbot Hamlin, "was as fatal to the
artistic ideals of the Greek Revival as were the speed, the
speculation and the exploitation that produced him." In one
field after another, the wealth of the new millionaires was
used to corrupt the tastes, the standards, and the traditions
of the American people.

"It was in the seventies," wrote Parrington, "that good
taste reached its lowest ebb. . . . A veritable *débâcle* of
the arts was in process . . . and that *débâcle* was an expression of profound changes taking place at the bases of
society." Godkin applied the term "chromo civilization" to
the works of a generation dwelling between two worlds,
the one dead, the other seeming powerless to be born. "The
dignified culture of the eighteenth century, that hitherto
had been a conserving and creative influence throughout
the Jeffersonian revolution, was at last breaking up. Disrup-
tive forces . . . were destroying that earlier culture and
providing no adequate substitute . . . and until another
culture could impose its standards upon society and re-
establish an inner spiritual unity, there would be only the

welter of an unlovely transition."[7] To many Americans it
may have seemed as though this *débâcle* were being brought
about by changes in the population through immigration;
but the real dynamic — the transforming process — was to
be found in the industrial revolution itself. In this sense
both the breakup of the earlier culture *and* the rise of anti-
Semitism were symptoms of the profound transformation
taking place at the bases of society.

In the two decades prior to the Civil War, Emerson,
Whitman, Hawthorne, Thoreau, Melville, and Lincoln —
to mention only the giants — had richly fulfilled the promise
of the earlier democratic culture and its traditions. But their
spirit did not carry over into the years of the second American Revolution when Big Business occupied the country
like an alien armed force. While a new culture started to
grow in these years, its promise was never realized. Peirce,
Shaler, Marsh, Gibbs, Ryder, Roebling, Eakins, Richard-
son, Sullivan, Adams, and LaFarge, as Lewis Mumford has
written, are names that any age might proudly exhibit;
but "the procession of American civilization divided and
walked around these men," much as it divided or walked
around the earlier tradition and culture upon which their
work was based. The tragedy of the artist in these years
consisted in his deep-rooted hostility to the society ushered
into being by the rise of the industrial bourgeoisie who had
succeeded in vulgarizing and intimidating American culture. Something of the "drought and famine" of which
most of the artists of the period complained must have
been sensed and experienced by wide elements in the population. For the new industrial culture was neither satisfying
nor meaningful; it lacked sustenance.

The nature of the cultural transformation that accompanied the second American Revolution has never been more graphically described than in a passage from Thorstein Veblen's *The Theory of the Leisure Class* (emphasis added). "The wave of revulsion," he wrote, "seems to have received its initial impulse in the psychologically disintegrating effects of the Civil War. Habituation to war entails a body of predatory habits of thought, *whereby clannishness* in some measure *replaces the sense of solidarity,* and a sense of invidious distinction supplants the impulse to equitable, everyday serviceability. As an outcome of the cumulative action of these factors, the generation which follows a season of war is apt to witness *a rehabilitation* of elements *of status* both in its social life and in its scheme of devout observances and other symbolic and ceremonial forms. Throughout the eighties, and less plainly traceable in the seventies, also, there was perceptible a gradually advancing wave of sentiment favoring quasi-predatory business habits, *insistence on status,* anthropomorphism, and conservatism generally."

One of the ways in which this new clannishness and insistence on status expressed itself at the expense of the older solidarity was in an effort to achieve unity, out of the chaos of the times, by the negative device of opposing something — the Negroes, the Chinese, the Indians, the foreigners. For these outsiders furnished a counterconception upon which, as Oscar Handlin has noted, "all the qualities the community feared and disliked could be ascribed and around opposition to which it could unite."

In 1879 about 177,000 immigrants had arrived in America; but by 1882 the annual influx had risen to 788,000. Faced with a growing competition for place and power, their security threatened by the forces of a rampant industrialism, the groups identifying themselves with the dominant cultural pattern sought to maintain that pattern at all costs. For it was in part through such dominance that they hoped to retain their status. After the Civil War, status lines were drawn more sharply than ever before and the struggle for status became one of the major motivations in American culture. There is, therefore, much meaning in the opening sentence of Booth Tarkington's *The Magnificent Ambersons:* "Major Amberson had 'made a fortune' in 1873, when other people were losing fortunes, and the magnificence of the Ambersons began then." Feeling the pinch of the new economic dispensation, the native Americans and the older immigrant groups sought to exclude first one group and then another from identification with the dominant cultural symbols. A remarkable correlation developed between nationality and status; between race and status; and, to a lesser degree, between religion and status. In an increasingly insecure world, the maintenance of status distinctions created the illusion of security and group differences of all kinds suddenly acquired a new meaning. "In spite of the magnificent dimensions of our continent," wrote Hjalmar H. Boyesen in 1887, "we are beginning to feel crowded." In view of these tendencies — all too briefly sketched here — it is not surprising that the first overt manifestation of anti-Semitism should have occurred in the summer of 1877.

2. THE WEDGE IS DRIVEN

For the first time in the history of the nation, the minorities question became important in this same period. To be sure, the issue had previously arisen with the Irish and Roman Catholicism; but the Know-Nothingism of this earlier period came into much sharper focus after the Civil War. There is a sense, for example, in which it can be said that an Indian problem had not existed prior to 1876. Until the last Indian tribes had been pacified, an Indian problem could not arise. Our prior relations with Indians had been those of one belligerent to another; but once pacification had been effected we were confronted with the problem of what to do with the Indian. The moment we adopted a reservation policy (and the reservation policy dates from the seventies) and failed to invest the Indian with citizenship, a deep wedge had been driven into the fabric of American democracy.

Similarly a Negro problem hardly existed prior to the Emancipation Proclamation. Until the Negro had become a nominal citizen, a Negro minority problem could not arise. No problem occasioned more doubt and uncertainty in the post-Civil-War period than the question of what to do with the freedmen. In one sense, the situation was quite unique, for as Beard has written there had suddenly been created "a large and anomalous class in the American social order — a mass of emancipated slaves long destined to wander in a hazy realm between bondage and freedom." Nothing just like this, adds Beard, had ever happened in history, at least on such a scale. And in the confusion of the period — to which the Negro problem contributed — the issue was fatefully compromised after first being correctly resolved.

In adopting the Fourteenth Amendment, the American people had set forth a broad and daring policy toward minorities. Not only did the amendment greatly extend the frontiers of American democracy, but it was adopted for the specific purpose of making it clear that the federal government could, and by inference should, affirmatively safeguard the civil rights of all citizens against the unlawful actions of the states and private groups. To carry this policy into effect, Congress then adopted the Civil Rights Act, which was aimed at eliminating such practices as the exclusion of Joseph Seligman from the Grand Union Hotel.

But the Supreme Court held the act unconstitutional — in defiance of the purpose, meaning, and intention of the Fourteenth Amendment. In an equally perverse decision, the court then proceeded to give to corporations the protection that the amendment had intended for human beings. Having thus opened the door to discrimination, the court later placed the stamp of its positive approval upon the practice of segregation in *Plessy* v. *Ferguson* (1896). In a vigorous dissenting opinion, Justice Harlan prophetically warned that the effect of this decision was "to permit the seeds of race hate to be planted under the sanctions of law." The emasculation of the amendment by the courts had the effect, of course, of creating a second-class citizenship for Negroes.

Oriental immigration confronted the American people, in the post-Civil-War period, with still another challenge to the democratic concept. Professing its inability to cope with anti-Chinese agitation in California, the federal government paid a series of heavy indemnities to China for acts of violence against the persons and property of Chinese nationals. For the Supreme Court decisions which had made it impossible to protect the rights of the Negro had also made it impossible to protect the rights of the Oriental. In an effort to escape from this humiliating position, the federal government was then forced to adopt the Chinese Exclusion Act of 1882. Representing a radical departure from traditional American policy, this act laid the foundation for a series of subsequent exclusion measures finally culminating in the Immigration Act of 1924 which was in part aimed at excluding further Jewish immigration. While Congress had extended the privilege of citizenship to "aliens of African nativity and persons of African descent," it refused to extend this privilege to Oriental immigrants. It then only remained for the courts to rule, as they did for the first time in 1878, that Chinese were "ineligible to citizenship." Thus the wedge was driven still deeper.

Strange as it may seem, the Chinese Exclusion Act is related to the problem of anti-Semitism. When the act was passed in 1882, an active anti-Semitic movement had just been organized in Germany. "The German anti-semites lost no time," writes Gustav Karpeles, "in pointing to the exclusion of Chinese from the United States and using it in all seriousness as an example which would gradually prepare the way in public opinion for sentiment in favor of the exclusion of the Jew." [8] Other writers have commented on the parallel and called attention to the fact that alien Orientals were denied the privilege of farm ownership on the West Coast much as Jews had been denied this right in Europe. [9]

When anti-Japanese agitation developed on the West Coast, the government found itself powerless to protect the treaty rights of Japanese nationals or the rights of American citizens of Japanese descent. In attempting to prevent the San Francisco School Board from segregating Japanese students, President Roosevelt quickly discovered that the

Supreme Court had robbed him of any legal basis for intervention. Informal exclusion of further Japanese immigration, which Roosevelt was then compelled to negotiate, was followed by formal exclusion in 1924 and by the denial of citizenship to the first-generation Japanese.

While similar measures were not enacted against European immigrants, it is nevertheless apparent that they were also being singled out as scapegoats. On March 14, 1891, a mob stormed the jail in New Orleans and lynched eleven Italian immigrants. The Italian government withdrew its ambassador when the federal government confessed its inability to cope with situations of this kind. One could, in fact, document literally hundreds of similar riotous actions in the seventies, eighties, and nineties which involved attacks on minorities.

Surveying this record in retrospect, one notes the growth after 1876 of a dualism in federal policy toward minority groups. By its failure to protect civil rights, the federal government indirectly sanctioned discrimination against minorities. Placing Indians on reservations, stripping Negroes of effective protection, excluding further Oriental immigration, drawing the color bar in naturalization proceedings, holding the Mexican-American population of New Mexico and Arizona at arm's length for a sixty-four-year period, pursuing a similar policy in Hawaii and Puerto Rico, tolerating violence against the foreign-born, adopting a "national origins" quota system — all these acts indicate the growth of a tradition of bigotry and intolerance dating from the triumph of the industrial revolution. Hence the pertinence of Ralph Ellison's observation that "since 1876 the race issue has been like a stave driven into the Ameri-

can scheme of values, a stave so deeply imbedded in the
America ethos as to render America a nation of schizophrenics."

3. THE TECHNIQUE OF DOMINANCE

The tycoons that rose to power with the triumph of the
second American Revolution were, as Charles Beard has
pointed out, largely of North European stock, mainly English and Scotch Irish, and of Protestant background, as a
rollcall will readily confirm: Gould, Vanderbilt, Huntington, Hill, Harriman, Rockefeller, Carnegie, Cooke, Mor-
gan, Armour. Only Gould, in the characteristic phrase of
Henry Adams, "showed a trace of Jewish origin." The
first threat to the unchallenged dominance of these industrial tycoons came from German-Jewish immigrants in the
United States.

At the time of the first census in 1790, there were only
about 2000 Jews in the United States in a population of
approximately 2,000,000. From this figure the number increased to about 250,000 in 1880. This increase was largely
made up of German Jews who, like the Seligmans, had
been discouraged by the wave of reaction which had en-
gulfed Europe in the wake of the Napoleonic Wars. Swept
immediately into the current of westward expansion, the
German Jews were carried far from the ports of entry. In
the rapidly growing communities of the Middle West, the
Far West, and the South, many of these immigrants made
the transition from peddler to prosperous merchant with
extraordinary swiftness. In such cities as Cincinnati, Chicago, Louisville, St. Paul, Dallas, San Francisco, and Los

Angeles, German Jews were accorded a high status based
upon priority of settlement — they were among the "first
families" — and the wealth and distinction which they had
achieved. The mention of such names as Straus, Rosenwald, Seligman, Warburg, Schiff, Morgenthau, Sloss, Sutro,
and Lubin is alone sufficient to indicate this amazing upward mobility.

That the first overt manifestation of anti-Semitism in
the United States took place in 1877 is to be explained in
terms of the corrosion which the industrial revolution had
brought about in the American scheme of values and the
revolutionary democratic culture and its traditions. But
that this initial act should have taken place in the upper
reaches of society, and that it should have assumed the form
of social discrimination is to be explained by the rapid
rise of German Jews in the new social and economic hierarchy. As prosperous and successful merchants, bankers,
and traders, the German Jews could not be altogether excluded from the civic and social life of the communities
in which they had settled; but they could be made to feel
a subtle sense of rejection, and limitations could be imposed
against their further encroachment on the citadels of power.
The erection of these invisible barriers at the top levels
of society was largely prompted by the feeling that, at
this level, they were to be regarded as serious competitors
for place and power. While the non-Jewish tycoons were
prone to war among themselves, they were quick to protect their social power and dominant position in American
industry by the exclusion of these agile newcomers. In
the period from 1840 to 1880, when the bulk of the
German Jews arrived, some 10,189,429 immigrants en-

tered the United States. Lost in this avalanche of peoples, the German Jews were numerically insignificant and aroused almost nothing in the way of popular antagonism or hostility. It was only in the upper reaches of society that their remarkable success excited feelings of envy and disdain.

Social discrimination always lays the foundation for subsequent discriminations of a more significant character, first, in the sense that it has a tendency to check the process of assimilation and to emphasize differences; and second, in the sense that it forces the minority to develop its own social institutions. Once the latter development has taken place, the minority feels that it has insulated itself against discrimination and regards the uneasy equilibrium thus established as a permanent and satisfactory adjustment, which is never the case. Had the German Jews not met with systematic social discrimination, integration for all Jews in America would have been much easier. Once having acquiesced in the pattern of social discrimination, the spokesmen for American Jewry were thereafter blinded to those aspects of Jewish experience in America that did not square with their thesis that the battle against anti-Semitism had been won in the United States.

It was precisely the capacity of the German Jews for assimilation that most distressed their upper-class rivals. Hoffman Nickerson in his book on *The American Rich* (1930) points out, with evident approval, that the upper classes in this country had forced the Jew to renounce "his hope of concealing his separateness in order to rise to power within non-Jewish societies, half unseen by those among whom he moves." It was the American rich who checked this tendency. "Had the American rich accepted social relations and intermarriage with the Jews to the same extent as the French or the British rich, the comparative looseness and fluidity of our social structure might well have bogged us down badly in the hopeless blind alley of assimilationism"! Fortunately, from Nickerson's point of view, we had "no classes of poor nobles or gentlefolk open to the temptation of marriage with rich Jews and able on their side to obtain a measure of social recognition for their Jewish partners." The American rich had raised the social bars just in time so that "the larger organism might continue its life without harmful disturbances." This was much the same view as that expressed by Hilaire Belloc.[10] There had been no trace of anti-Semitism in the United States, according to Belloc, through the early and middle nineteenth century. When it did arise, it took the form of "a certain social prejudice among the wealthier classes in the East." [11]

Thus when the doors of the Grand Union were slammed in the face of Joseph Seligman, an important precedent had been established. And it is not without significance that this precedent was established along with other precedents of a similar nature involving Indians, Negroes, and Orientals, all as part of a new status system which arose in America in the latter part of the last century. The Chinese Exclusion Act of 1882 led directly to the passage of the Immigration Act of 1924 which was largely aimed at the exclusion of further Jewish immigration. When correlated with other phases of the minority problem which began to loom large after 1876, it is, indeed, apparent that the Saratoga Springs incident was not a slight breath, a white frost, a momentary flash of insult. For once the pattern of social discrimination and exclusion had been established against Jews, the way was cleared for later anti-Semitic manifestations of a far more serious character.

CHAPTER II

From Little Acorns

IN THE ANNALS of the *American Jewish Yearbook*, the years from 1910 to 1916 seem to mark a noticeable upsurge in anti-Semitism. Articles in the press by Jewish writers commented upon a "deep-seated and widespread antipathy" against Jews and pointed to the existence "under an apparently calm surface of a general antagonism." In 1909 Ray Stannard Baker reported that the Christian churches in America had "awakened as never before to the so-called Jewish problem" and had intensified their proselytizing activities. Social discrimination was the subject of numerous reports and much comment.[1] In a series of articles, Norman Hapgood pointed out that a sharp line separated Jews from Gentiles in America and concluded that anti-Semitic prejudice was becoming more distinct. "Americans do not deprive Jews of any rights," he wrote, "but they do not on the whole like them."[2] In fact, Hapgood concluded that the situation in America in 1915 was approximately the same as in Germany. For in Germany, too, the cruder forms of discrimination were then unknown: "There is no pale of settlement, no denial of ordinary education. The discrimination is in the *upper walks of life*, in general exclusion from participation in university, political, and military life." Dr. Richard Gottheil reported that "social ostracism" was increasing in America and John Foster

Fraser, in one of the first anti-Semitic books published in this country, observed in 1916 that "the white-skinned American has a feeling of repulsion from the Jew. . . . The antipathy for the Jew is only surpassed by the general recognition that the Negro should be kept in a state of perpetual inferiority." [8]

The formation of the Anti-Defamation League in 1913 and the enactment in that year of a civil-rights statute in New York (passed at the request of Jewish organizations) indicate that American Jews had come to sense a distinct change in the social atmosphere. "Of late years," reads the *American Jewish Yearbook*, "various hotel-keepers have advertised extensively in the newspapers and through circulars, and by means of other publications, that Jews or Hebrews are not accepted as guests; that Hebrew patronage is not solicited or desired. Railroad companies and steamboat companies have issued folders in which appear similar advertisements." That anti-Semitic prejudices were becoming more pronounced is shown also in the calling of a conference in 1915 on "racial prejudice against Jews" and by continued "incidents" of social discrimination. For example, J. McKeen Cattell of Columbia University resigned, about this time, from the Century Club in protest against the rejection of the application of the distinguished scientist Dr. Jacques Loeb of the Rockefeller Institute. What significance can be found in this upsurge of anti-Semitism?

1. *A DELAYED REACTION*

In the period following 1880 rapid industrialization had created in the United States an enormous demand for workers at a time when the flow of immigrants from Great Britain, France, and Germany had begun to abate in response to a similar industrial expansion in these countries. Since so many of the native-born Americans were constantly drawn westward by the promise of new economic opportunities, a vacuum was created in the industrial centers which was filled by shifting the point of recruitment to the south, east, and southeastern portions of Europe where the great bulk of the European Jews resided. In these areas, industrialism was either retarded or was being developed on so narrow an economic base as to bring about a determination to expel rather than to attract workers. For example, Russian industry was operated on far too narrow a base to absorb a large addition to her urban classes, while a rising non-Jewish middle class in Poland had begun to clamor for the jobs and functions that had been filled for many years by Jews.[4]

The assassination of Czar Alexander II on March 13, 1881, provided the Russian government with an excuse for launching a movement deliberately aimed at forcing the Jews within the Pale of Settlement to emigrate. Over 165 pogroms were reported in Southern Russia alone and these pogroms were followed by the enactment of the May Laws of May 3, 1882. Anti-Semitism became, in the phrase of Solomon F. Bloom, "a settled policy of the state, a policy implemented by 'spontaneous' outbursts of suborned mobs." Much the same motivation prompted the enactment of severe anti-Semitic measures in Rumania and Austria in the latter part of the nineteenth century.

Terrified by the prospect of their own countries being flooded with Jewish immigrants, the well-placed Jews of

Western Europe hit upon the idea of directing this stream of immigration to America. At a time when Great Britain was receiving only 2500 Jewish immigrants a year (New York City alone was then receiving about 11,000 a month), Parliament adopted the Aliens Act of 1906 aimed at excluding further Jewish immigration. The effect of this measure, and of similar measures enacted on the Continent, was to shunt the refugees across the Atlantic. Sharing the alarm of their well-placed brothers in Europe, the German Jews in America brought great pressure to bear upon the government to remonstrate against anti-Semitic measures in Russia. Thus President Harrison, in a message to Congress of December 9, 1891, said that "a decree to leave one country is in the nature of things an order to enter another — some other. *This consideration, as well as the suggestion of humanity*, furnishes ample ground for the remonstrances which we have presented to Russia" (emphasis added). That the remonstrances were unavailing, however, is shown by the arrival of 1,467,266 Jews from Russia, Rumania, and Austria between 1880 and 1910, an average for the period of 48,908 a year.

When the East European Jews landed in Boston and New York, no tide of westward expansion carried them beyond the ports of entry. A definite pattern of urban immigrant settlement had been established by 1880 and into this slum complex the Jews were inexorably drawn. Moving into already established "foreign" sections, crowding the tenements to overflowing, they took the places in industry previously filled by earlier immigrants. Since most of them were incredibly poor (40 per cent arrived with less than thirty dollars) and had families to support, they took what-

ever jobs were available. In the eighties the garment industry, in which many of them had worked, was at about the
same level of technological development in the United States
as in Europe. This factor, as well as the lack of training in
other crafts, the absence of strict apprenticeship requirements, and the circumstance that the industry was largely
controlled by German Jews, brought large numbers into
the needle trades.

While the Orthodox East European Jews were culturally more sharply set apart from the native-born population than the German Jews, what really distinguished the
two groups was the fact that the German Jews had settled
here fifty years earlier, under far more favorable circumstances, and were already "Americanized." Actually many
of the German Jews were from Posen, Moravia, and other
provinces right on the frontier of Eastern Europe and
might well have been regarded as Eastern Jews themselves.
Fearful of their hard-won and already threatened status,
the German Jews at first looked down upon their eastern
brothers "as a grotesque species of ill-bred savages," although at a later date external pressures forced them to
come to the aid of their "unprepossessing co-religion-
ists."

If one may judge public opinion by the periodical press,
then the first great waves of Jewish immigration provoked
little adverse comment. In fact, the East European Jews
seem to have aroused a mixture of contempt and pity rather
than a feeling of competitive hostility. Since so many of
them were concentrated in the needle trades in New York,
they were removed to some extent from direct competition
with other groups. Furthermore, the sympathies of the

American people had been aroused by the repressive measures enacted in Russia and by the pogroms. That the demagogic American Protective Association — the A.P.A. —
movement of the late eighties and nineties ignored the
Jews is, perhaps, the best confirmation of this fact. In
general, the public reaction justifies Oscar Handlin's conclusion that "there was no correlation at all between the
arrival of foreigners and the intensity of the hostility to
them." [5] Just as the German Jews had not aroused much
in the way of enmity until they came to be sensed as
competitors, so the East European Jews were largely ignored until the second generation began to impinge on the
native middle class. While heavy Jewish immigration had
something to do with the rise of a strong antialien movement after 1900, the correlation is neither direct nor causal.
The reaction to Jewish immigration was a delayed reaction,
as shown by the fact that the antialien movement reached
its maximum strength fifty years after the commencement
of large-scale Jewish immigration and at a time when Jewish immigration had already begun to decline.

The explanation for this "delayed reaction" has been
pointed out by Dr. A. L. Severson. Studying discriminatory
want ads in the Chicago press, Dr. Severson concluded that
the basic factor underlying opposition to the employment
of Jews and Catholics was "the flow into the clerical market of second-generation East Europeans." This movement
did not reach significant proportions until about 1910. For
example, Severson found no discrimination against Jews
reflected in the want-ad columns from 1872 to 1911. Beginning in the latter year, however, ads requesting "Christians only" or "Gentiles only" appeared at the rate of 0.3
per cent per 1000, rose to 4 per cent in 1921, to 8.8 per cent

in 1923, to 13.3 per cent in 1926; averaged 11 per cent from 1927 to 1931; dropped to 4.8 per cent in 1931; and then rose to 9.4 per cent in 1937. Most of the discriminatory ads were for female office employees, indicating that the second-generation girls were beginning to seek white-collar employment. The first discriminatory resort ad, incidentally, appeared in 1913.

If Dr. Severson's thesis is accepted, then one can say that it was not East European Jewish immigration, per se, that touched off latent prejudices; nor was it any "cultural conflict" between Jews and non-Jews. The decisive factor was the appearance, on the clerical labor market, of a new group of competitors who could be identified for purposes of discrimination.[6] The moment this happened, the doors to clerical and white-collar jobs began to be slammed in the face of Jewish applicants much in the same manner that the doors of the Grand Union Hotel had been slammed in the face of Joseph Seligman.

Prior to 1880, the immigrant's chief task had been the relatively easy one of "Americanizing" himself in a rural environment or frontier community. But with the rise of industrialism the position of the immigrant was rapidly transformed. As more immigrants became workingmen, their problems were easily confused with issues which were beginning to generate conflict between capital and labor. As a consequence, all immigrants suffered a loss of prestige in the eyes of those who were determined to maintain the traditional American pattern of an open society. It was this change in the status of immigrants, not the change in the character of immigration after 1880, that accounts for the new attitudes toward the "alien" and "the foreigner." Thus, as Stow Persons has pointed out, "the most striking aspect of the immigrant problem in industrial America has been the tendency on the part of native Americans to transform the economic and social conflicts of industrialism into culture conflicts wherever the immigrant has been concerned." [7]

While avoiding the use of the word "Jewish" as far as possible, a myth was evolved about the East European Jews based upon a point-by-point comparison with the "desirable" German Jew. This distinction made it possible for people to be anti-Semitic while professing great admiration for certain successful Jews. The presence of a large mass of "unassimilated" East European Jews had the effect, also, of inducing the German Jews to acquiesce in the Maginot line of discrimination that was being erected against them in the upper walks of society. Since they were being politely excepted from the "undesirable" category, they failed to challenge the validity of the distinction. At the same time, the stiffening of opposition to "undesirable" Jews gave an added impetus to social discrimination which the German Jews consistently rationalized as trivial and sought to evade by parallel social institutions which served in turn to emphasize differences.

2. RITUAL MURDER IN AMERICA

In 1911 America, along with the rest of the civilized world, had been deeply shocked by the Beilis "ritual murder" trial in Europe. Even in pogrom-ridden Europe, ritual murder prosecutions seemed utterly anachronistic in 1911, a grisly survival of medieval superstition. But that a ritual murder trial, bedecked with fancy nativistic trimmings, could take place in the United States was a possibility that never occurred to the writers of indignant American editorials devoted to the Beilis case.

On April 27, 1913, the dead body of Mary Phagan, fourteen years of age, was found in a pencil factory in Marietta, Georgia. Leo Frank, a young Jew, twenty-nine years of age, a graduate of Cornell University, was part owner and manager of the factory. In a note written before her death, Mary Phagan had charged an unnamed Negro with having assaulted her in the factory. At the time of the crime, Frank and a Negro, Jim Conley, were the only persons in the building. Yet the law enforcement officials lost no time in convicting Frank on the uncorroborated testimony of the Negro. For the word of a Negro to be given this weight in a murder prosecution against a white man in Georgia was, in itself, a rather remarkable manifestation of anti-Semitic prejudice.

Prior to 1913, Tom Watson, the Georgia demagogue, had been violently anti-Catholic; but apparently he had never realized, before the Frank case, that Jews could be made the target of a vicious demagogic attack. But no pogrom organizer in Czarist Russia ever leveled a more savage, ruthless, and unprincipled attack against Jews than Watson did in this case. "Every student of sociology knows," he wrote, "that the black man's lust after the white woman is not much fiercer than the lust of the licentious Jew for the Gentile." Parenthetically, it is interesting to note that, in this campaign, Watson used certain conclusions of the distinguished American sociologist, Dr. Edward A. Ross, to bolster his demagoguery.

When the Governor of Georgia commuted Frank's sentence, Watson denounced him as "King of the Jews." While *Watson's Magazine* was screaming for his blood, in a long series of inflammatory articles and editorials, poor Frank was beaten to a pulp and knifed by white and Negro prisoners. Later, on August 16, 1915, he was taken from the prison hospital by a mob and hanged on the outskirts of Marietta. Following the lynching, Watson continued to repeat the old charge of ritual murder against the Jews and denounced the world-wide campaign to save Mendel Beilis as the same type of "conspiracy" that had won freedom for Dreyfus.

Looked at coldly, what was there to distinguish the Leo Frank case from the Beilis case? Mendel Beilis managed to escape death in Kiev, Russia, under the Czar in 1911; but Leo Frank was lynched in Georgia, U.S.A., in 1915. The innocence of Frank, established by careful investigations, is today universally admitted. In light of the Frank case, how could it any longer be said that there was some special elixir about the American environment that made it immune to the virus of anti-Semitism? Yet precisely this contention continued to be voiced, by Jew and Gentile, long afterwards.

Born in Georgia in 1856, the son of a Georgia squire, Tom Watson had been an outstanding progressive, a leader of the Populist Party, and "the first native white Southern leader of importance to treat the Negro's aspirations with the seriousness that human strivings deserve." [8] Robbed of two elections to Congress by fraud and violence, Watson had become embittered and had turned against his old Negro allies in Georgia. The champion of Negro rights in the nineties, he led the fight to disenfran-

chise Negroes in 1906 with its tragic sequel in the Atlanta
race riot of that year. Old friends and supporters began to
ask, "What is the matter with Tom Watson?" and one ob-
server said, "He is like a hydrophobic animal . . . he is
snapping and biting at nearly everything nowadays." One
cannot recite these bare facts of the Watson story without realizing that the culture that produced these two Tom
Watsons was, in some sense, a schizoid culture, a culture
in which two traditions were in sharp conflict.

3. BOLT FROM THE BLUE

In its report on the war years, the *American Jewish
Yearbook* concludes on the optimistic note that "the termination of hostilities has brought to an end the abnormal
conditions which . . . resulted in a number of instances of
anti-Jewish discrimination." And then, like a thunderclap,
Henry Ford's *Dearborn Independent* in the issue of May 20,
1920, suddenly discovered "the Jewish problem." There
had been, of course, some premonitory rumblings from
the Sage of Dearborn. During the war years, he had vaguely
intimated that "a small clique" was pushing President Wilson toward war. Later Ford said that it was not until about
1916, "on the peace ship," that "the full importance of the
subject came into view."

The son of an Irish immigrant, born on a farm near
Dearborn in 1863, Ford had become by 1920 a world-
famous figure, an oracle whose views were eagerly solicited
on every domestic and international question. Nothing
reflects the terrible swiftness with which America had
made the transition from the Frontier to the Big Money

quite as vividly as Ford's career. Incorporated in 1903, the Ford Motor Company had assets of $536,000,000 in 1923 and its revenues averaged $8,000,000 a month. The genesis of Ford's anti-Semitism is to be found, therefore, not in the influence of sinister forces close to the throne, but in the circumstances by which this country boy with a talent for tinkering with machines had become overnight a multi-millionaire and an elder statesman.

It would be difficult to overestimate the damage which Ford's vicious, persistent, and heavily financed anti-Semitic campaign caused the Jews of the world. From 1920 to 1927, the *Dearborn Independent* conducted a relentless anti-Semitic campaign. With a circulation of 700,000 copies, the paper had a powerful grass-roots following, particularly in the Middle West. From the pages of the *Independent*, anti-Semitic diatribes were collected, edited, and published in book form: *The International Jew, Jewish Activities in the United States, Jewish Influences in American Life*, and *Aspects of Jewish Power in the United States*. No figures are available to indicate how many copies of these four volumes were published, but they came off the presses in a seemingly unending stream and circulated throughout the world. What made these volumes doubly poisonous was the circumstance that they carried the imprint, not of some crackpot publisher in an alleyway of Chicago, but of one of the most famous industrialists in the world. It is one of the cruel ironies of history that the savage anti-Semitism which developed in Germany after the First World War should have been stimulated in part by an American industrialist who, in a number of respects, was so typical a product of American culture. If one correlates the period of Ford's active anti-Semitism with developments in Germany for the same period, it becomes apparent that, in one sense, Hitler began where Ford left off.[9]

Nowadays it has been charitably forgotten that, as part of this campaign, the *Dearborn Independent* tried to manufacture an American Dreyfus case. For three years, the paper sought to pin a murder charge on Captain Rosenbluth in connection with the accidental death of another officer at an army post near Tacoma. Although a military court of inquiry had found that the death was accidental, the *Independent* went to incredible lengths to make it appear that this finding had been brought about by sinister influences working "behind the scenes." It has been estimated that over $200,000 was spent in the successful effort to extricate Captain Rosenbluth from these unfounded and utterly malicious charges. Dragged through the state and federal courts, the Rosenbluth case might easily have become an American Dreyfus case had it not been for the vigilance of the leaders of American Jewry, notably Felix M. Warburg and Herbert H. Lehman.

By a curious lapse of memory, most Americans have also forgotten that Ford's campaign was not an isolated adventure. In fact, it was part of a loosely organized nationwide anti-Semitic campaign, the first in American history.[10] Revived in 1916, the Ku Klux Klan first began to attract a large mass following in 1920 when Ford launched his campaign against the Jews. Both campaigns were part of a larger antialien movement which culminated with the passage of the Immigration Act of 1924. Coming when the need for a liberal immigration policy was never more obvious, the passage of this act profoundly shocked the leaders of American Jewry. As Louis Marshall pointed out in a memorandum to Congress: "For the first time in the history of American legislation there has been an attempt to discriminate in regard to European immigration between those who come from different parts of the continent. It is not only a differentiation as to countries of origin, but also of racial status and of religious beliefs." That the debate on the measure took the form of a discussion of "quotas" and "restriction" cannot disguise the fact that it was, in large part, aimed at the exclusion of further Jewish immigration. Proponents of the measure said that it was aimed at the Jews and suggested that "we might just as well be frank about it."

Passage of this act marks a turning point in modern Jewish history. For the act had the effect of barring the principal avenue of escape for the Jews of Eastern Europe and of riveting their attention more firmly than ever upon Palestine as an ultimate homeland. Cut off from further numerical reinforcements, the Jews in the United States were forced to depend upon themselves; to develop an American Judaism. The measure altered the physical basis of American Jewish life, shaped the structure of Jewish institutions, and profoundly influenced the social psychology of American Jews. For example, passage of the act accelerated the movement of the second generation into white-collar occupations. In the period from 1900 to 1925, about 50 per cent of Jewish immigration had been absorbed in industry and in the handicraft trades; but after 1924 the Jewish population tended to become predominantly middle class.[11]

Seen in this perspective, it is apparent that the anti-Semitic movement after the First World War was not a crazy flash-in-the-pan affair, but a reflection of forces long maturing in American life. The movement collapsed, in fact, largely because these forces had not yet reached full maturity, and also, of course, because the postwar boom robbed the movement of much of its popular appeal. Whoever it was that prepared *The International Jew* for Mr. Ford was clearly aware that organized anti-Semitism belonged more to the future than to the period from 1920 to 1927. On page 56, for example, one reads that "anti-semitism in almost every form *is* bound to come to the United States"; again, on page 64, "anti-semitism *will* come to America"; and, on page 66, "the whole problem *will* center here" (emphasis added). Actually Ford had been rebuked more for the violence with which he had expressed his views than for his anti-Semitism per se. Henry Adams Gibbons said, at the time, what other publicists were saying who also "deplored" Ford's anti-Semitism: "For the Jews it is either into the melting-pot or back to the Ghetto." [12] After 1920 the existence of anti-Semitism in the United States had become, as Mr. Gibbons said, "a demonstrated fact."

"Lately," wrote Louis Weitzenkorn in the *Nation* of May 4, 1921, "I have been made aware of my Jewishness." Certainly the pattern of anti-Semitic incidents after 1920, quite apart from Ford's campaign and the revival of the K.K.K., was in itself sufficient to reawaken a consciousness of Jewish identity in thousands of American Jews. In February 1922, the head of placement in a Chicago employment office reported that 67 per cent of the requests for employees specified that Jews were not wanted. A survey of teacher agencies in the Middle West in 1925 revealed that from 95 per cent to 98 per cent of the calls for teachers requested "Protestants only." In August 1922, the Sharon, Connecticut, Chamber of Commerce distributed a leaflet requesting property owners not to sell to Jews. A bulletin of the Philadelphia Chamber of Commerce advocated specific restrictions against "the Hebrew element." The board of directors of a Milwaukee golf club asked eight Jewish charter members to resign. Well-documented charges were filed that the American consular service was honeycombed with anti-Semites.[13] On June 21, 1927, three Jewish interns in Kings County Hospital in New York were dragged out of bed in the middle of the night, bound, gagged, and ducked in a bathtub of ice water. An official inquiry later confirmed charges of anti-Semitic practices and policies in this institution. When a four-year-old girl disappeared at Massena, New York, on September 22, 1928, the local rabbi was called to answer charges of "ritual murder" on the Day of Atonement. The secretary of the Chamber of Commerce in St. Petersburg, Florida, announced that the time had come to make St. Petersburg "a 100% American Gentile City." An official in Bryan County, Georgia, acknowledged that Jews were automatically excluded from jury polls in that area. A pamphlet distributed by several large real estate companies in New York complained of an increase in the number of Jewish realtors. Several large real estate concerns in New Jersey, New York, Georgia, and Florida were found to have restricted new subdivisions against Jewish occupancy. Excluded from a hotel in Lakewood, New Jersey, Nathan Straus proceeded to build Laurel-in-the-Pines.

Of more than passing interest, in this period, was President Lowell's graduation address at Harvard in June 1922, in which he advocated quotas against Jews. While the trustees of Harvard later rejected this suggestion, it was painfully apparent that the quota system was spreading. Two years after the First World War, Columbia University cut the number of Jewish admissions by 40 per cent. The whole question of quotas was frankly discussed at a meeting of the Association of Medical Colleges in November 1929. Actually the situation in the prep schools and colleges had first attracted attention at an earlier date.[14] Between 1914 and 1930, the quota system had become well-established in most Eastern colleges and universities. What the spread of the quota system signified, as Heywood Broun pointed out, "was nothing less than a silent cultural assent to the Klan crudity that 'this is a white man's country.'"

Despite these unmistakable symptoms of a universally recognized disease, the *American Jewish Yearbook* for 1929 concludes with the comment that "the past year witnessed a practical cessation of all anti-Jewish propaganda." While the election returns in Germany in September 1930 were disturbing, still they seem to have aroused no more serious apprehension than the continued pattern of anti-Semitic incidents in the United States. "While several Jewish organizations in the United States were deeply stirred by the results of the German elections," reads the *Yearbook*, "they took no action, knowing that the sister community in Central Europe is well able to deal with the situation."

Nor were Jews alone guilty of a failure to correlate the world-wide manifestations of anti-Semitism after the First World War. The proposal to establish a quota system at Harvard coincided with the demand of Aryan student organizations for the revival of a *numerus clausus* policy at the University of Berlin.[15] Still later, when ghetto benches had been ordered for Jewish students in Polish universities, two hundred non-Jewish American scholars protested the action but said not one word about the quota system in the United States.[16] I dare say that Paul Masserman and Max Baker accurately reflected the opinion of most Americans, Jews and Gentiles, on the possibility of anti-Semitism becoming a serious factor in America on the eve of Hitler's conquest of power. "Anti-semitism in America," they wrote, "is still a subtle, whispered thing; something sensed, felt under the skin, as it were. In all probability, it will never amount to more than that." [17]

4. THE EVER–WIDENING STAIN

By 1933 it was clearly apparent, however, that anti-Semitism had entered upon a new phase in America. "In the United States," wrote Johan J. Smertenko, "prejudice against the Jew has been markedly noticeable for twenty-five years. At first the manifestations of it were so trivial that it seemed absurd to take them seriously, much less to combat them. . . . But gradually the blot of discrimination spread into an ever-widening stain of ostracism — from society to the school, from schools and offices to shops and factories. And there followed, as a matter of course, exclusion from common privileges and communal enterprises. Today it is no secret that Jews have great difficulty in gaining admission to the institutions of higher learning and that their opportunities for legal and medical training are limited to a minimum. It is equally well-known that the professions of banking, engineering, and teaching are closed to all but a few, and the quasi-public service corporations vigorously exclude them. In the mechanical trades, the discrimination is almost as widespread as in the professions, and in clerical work, generally speaking, it is worst of all." [18]

This new phase was to be distinguished from earlier manifestations of anti-Semitism, first of all, by the increased evidences of economic discrimination. "Formerly," writes Morris S. Lazaron, "anti-Jewish discrimination here was almost exclusively social; today it is economic, which is much more serious." [19] While the depression affected all groups, it had special significance for the Jews. As the competition for jobs increased, special barriers against Jews multiplied. So striking was this development that a student of the Jewish employment problem concluded in 1930 that "the normal absorption of Jews within the American economic structure is now practically impossible." As the depression deepened, the struggle to enter the "free professions" became more intense than ever before. Prominent New York Jews even advocated quotas as "an economic necessity."

The new phase was also characterized by a sharp increase in *the number* of organized anti-Semitic groups. According to Dr. Donald S. Strong, 121 organizations were actively spreading anti-Semitic propaganda in the United States between 1933 and 1940. It should also be noted that this propaganda barrage concentrated on the Jew-Communist theme and soft-pedaled the Jew-Capitalist line. "There is no doubt," to quote from the *American Jewish Yearbook*, "that the fact that there are Jews who are communists is today perhaps the most widely used anti-Jewish propaganda material." [20] "There is no way of calculating the effect of anti-Jewish agitation during the past two years," the *Yearbook* for 1936 reported, "the first time in

American history that it has been carried on by so many agencies and on so wide a scale." As the crisis deepened, anti-Semitism began to take on the most unmistakable political overtones; nor was it long before certain reactionary politicians began to echo the anti-Semitic themes developed by the organized groups.

In a speech in Congress on May 29, 1933, Louis T. McFadden, for twenty years a Republican member of Congress from Pennsylvania, made a violent attack on the Jews of America. Rabbi Lee J. Levinger has characterized this speech, and I believe accurately, as "the first open evidence of political anti-semitism in the United States of America." [21] As the 1936 campaign approached, anti-Semitism became a favorite symbol of the native fascist groups. The fake Benjamin Franklin letter on the Jews first made its appearance on February 3, 1934; the first meeting of the Union for Social Justice was held in Detroit on April 24, 1935. In a speech in the fall of 1935, the manager of the Coughlin-Lemke third party charged that "the trouble with this country now is due to the money powers and Jewish politicians. . . . The American people must shake off their shoulders the Jewish politicians." During the 1936 campaign Alf Landon was forced, again and again, to disavow various anti-Semitic "angles" that some of his supporters kept injecting into the issues. A fake birth certificate, purporting to prove that Frances Perkins was of Jewish descent, was widely circulated in this campaign. For the first time in American political history, anti-Semitism was used as a deliberate propaganda device in a presidential election. By the end of 1936, even the historian of the *American Jewish Yearbook* was somewhat alarmed:

"Anti-Semitism is not far from the surface in American life . . . it would require comparatively little provocation to bring it to the surface"!

Underlying this new outcropping of anti-Semitism was a factor directly related to the earlier agitation. Throughout the nineteenth century, the lowest positions in the occupational system had been filled by the most recent immigrant groups. In the Chicago stockyards, for example, the labor force was originally of Irish descent; later predominantly Polish and Italian; and still later Mexican and Negro. "Thus every group," wrote Talcott Parsons, "except the most recent, has had someone to look down upon. In a sense our system of social stratification has been an incomplete one, in a state of parasitism with regard to the recent immigrants. It is clear that with the closing of the frontier and the consequent halt to economic expansion, *as well as with the virtual cessation of immigration*, this situation is rapidly disappearing" [22] (emphasis added). In other words, one consequence of the passage of the Immigration Act of 1924 had been to narrow the range of possible scapegoats.

After the election of 1936, there was a slight pause in the developing anti-Semitic agitation (the thumping Roosevelt victory was doubtless responsible for this recession); but by 1937 anti-Semitism was being used more brazenly in American politics than at any prior period in our history. By midsummer 1939 as many as sixty anti-Semitic street meetings were being held in New York each week, most of them organized by the Christian Front and the Christian Mobilizers. On December 22, 1940, LaGuardia announced that 238 arrests had been made in the preceding six months for inflammatory street speeches, disturbances, and the like. "The emergence of anti-semitism as a political platform," reported the *Yearbook*, "was probably the outstanding development of 1939."

The key figure in this developing political anti-Semitism was Father Charles Coughlin. While there had been certain overtones of anti-Semitism in his propaganda prior to 1936, it was only after the defeat of his third party in that year that he began to use anti-Semitism as a political weapon. In 1938 he announced that henceforth the Christian Front would "not fear to be called anti-semitic." As the owner of one of the largest libraries of anti-Semitic materials in this country, Coughlin quickly demonstrated that he could work artful variations on the stock themes. In reprinting the Protocols, he pointed out that the authenticity of the document was, in his opinion, an immaterial issue; what mattered was its "prophetic nature." On November 30, 1938, Coughlin made an anti-Semitic broadcast on a nationwide radio network. With an estimated radio listening audience of 3,500,000 people, no one could dismiss this sort of propaganda as insignificant. While mounting public pressure finally forced Coughlin off the air, the mystery of his finances has never been solved. This same question becomes of paramount interest in connection with the activities of William Dudley Pelley. In a period of nineteen months prior to July 31, 1938, Pelley mailed approximately three and a half tons of anti-Semitic propaganda from his headquarters. That large subsidies were involved, in both cases, can hardly be doubted.[23]

It is also important to note that, during the late thirties, some respectable newspapers began to dabble in a type of journalism which proved most embarrassing to the Jews.

On December 15, 1938, the *New York Daily News* reprinted a scurrilous pamphlet by William Dudley Pelley, devoting one half of its second page and pages 4 and 38 in their entirety to a digest of the pamphlet. When a young man named David Ginsburg was reported to have secured a commission in the army on being dropped by the OPA, the *Daily News*, ably seconded by the Hearst press, attempted to make a nationwide scandal of the incident and injected the most unmistakable anti-Semitic slant into the story by linking the name of Ginsburg with that of Justice Felix Frankfurter. During the 1944 campaign, the *Daily News* launched the attack on Sidney Hillman with a story calling attention to his "rabbinical education." In a series of columns, John O'Donnell kept needling the administration with charges, veiled and direct, of "Jewish influences," culminating in his false and malicious charge that General George S. Patton had been removed from his command because he had slapped "a Jewish soldier." Generally speaking, the entire nationalist press cultivated the theme that the Jews were driving America into the war. In a remarkable editorial of December 16, 1938, the *Daily News* said that the Bill of Rights means only "that our government shall not officially discriminate against any religion. It does *not* mean that Americans are forbidden to dislike other Americans or religions or any other group. Plenty of people just now are exercising their right to dislike the Jews."

Perhaps the real peak of the anti-Semitic campaign that began in the thirties was reached on September 11, 1941, when Charles Lindbergh, speaking in Des Moines to an audience of 7500 people, charged that the Jews were seeking to force America into the war, and, in a most sinister phrase, warned them of the consequences. Even prior to this speech, substantially the same charge had been made by Senator Burton Wheeler in a speech in the Senate on February 28, 1941, and by Congressman John Rankin, who told his colleagues that "Wall Street and a little group of our international Jewish brethren are still attempting to harass the President and Congress into plunging us into the European War." [24]

ை

Two recent surveys describe, with considerable accuracy, the present status of anti-Semitism in the United States. In general both surveys agree that anti-Semitic sentiment has not receded below the levels of 1944–1945. Discrimination in employment has increased; restrictions against Jews at resorts and in real estate developments have continued at a high level; heavy enrollment in colleges has "accentuated the degree of discrimination at colleges and universities"; and there is evidence that the practice of exclusion in some areas has appeared to spill "over into civic, business, and political circles, discoloring the pattern of American community life." Both reports agree that, while *organized* agitation has abated, prejudice *on an individual* basis has become more widespread and more intense. That the organized efforts have been less successful than might have been expected is attributed to the continued high level of employment and to "a greater resistance by potential recruits and positive counteraction by an informed public." In the South, one of the reports notes, "anti-semitism . . . continued unabated during 1946." Accurate as I believe these reports to be, it is apparent that the current situation is far from encouraging. The increase noted in what is termed "individual anti-Semitism" — that is, unorganized anti-Semitism — is perhaps the surest indication that, in a period of general unemployment, a resumption of organized anti-Semitism on a large scale is to be anticipated.[25]

The emergence of political anti-Semitism in American life is a matter of profound importance. Political anti-Semitism can never be projected in a social and cultural vacuum. It is a growth; not an invention. Political anti-Semitism must always be based on such pre-existing factors as social cleavage, a fairly well-developed anti-Semitic ideology, and a pattern of social and economic discrimination. When William Dudley Pelley issued his "New Emancipation Proclamation" on September 5, 1934, he promised "to impose racial quotas on the political and economic structure, observing rigorously in effect that no racial factions shall be allowed further occupancy of public or professional office in excess of the ratio of its blood-members to the remaining sum total of all races completing the composition of the body politic." Stripped of its verbiage, this statement reflected an existing social and economic reality. By 1934 racial and religious quotas were embedded in the structure of a large number of American institutions, educational, financial, social, and industrial.

It is, indeed, a long path that leads from the Grand Union Hotel incident of 1877 to the manifestations of organized political anti-Semitism that developed in the thirties; but for all its twists and turns, the path is clearly marked. Each phase of anti-Semitism has developed logically out of the phase or phases which preceded it and has paralleled changes in the economy. One can see the broad outline of a pattern in this progression: first social discrimination, then increasing economic discrimination, and, finally, overt organized political anti-Semitism. The mote in our eye has always consisted in the firm belief that anti-Semitism could not take root in the United States. But viewing the record in retrospect, one cannot escape the conclusion that anti-Semitism now has fairly deep roots in American life and that it has been assuming increasingly more significant forms of expression over a period of many years.

One reason why this emerging pattern has not been more widely noted is that anti-Semitism in America differs from the so-called "classical" European variety in this major respect: that here, as will be shown later, the main limitations imposed on Jews have been imposed by our "private governments" — industry and trade, banks and insurance companies, real estate boards and neighborhood associations, clubs and societies, colleges and universities. "In Czarist Russia," as the late Alexander H. Pekelis pointed out in an unpublished manuscript, "it was the Ministry of Education and the Ministry of Justice that put a ceiling on the number of Jews to be registered in schools of medicine. . . . In the United States these ceilings are imposed by our 'private' medical schools. . . . Anti-Semitism here is private or communal, not public or governmental in nature." It is precisely for this reason that anti-Semitism has now entered upon a critical phase in this country, for nongovernmental restraints by "private governments" have become of increasing importance as we have moved into the pattern and mold of a closed society. Looking for governmental anti-Semitism, in the European tradition, we have failed to observe the peculiarity of the American pattern.

CHAPTER III *The Snakes of Ireland*

ONE OF THE MOST puzzling aspects of the growth of anti-Semitism in the United States has always consisted in the difficulty of locating, or isolating, the tradition which has sanctioned its use. For, on first thought, it is precisely this tradition that seems to be lacking. Hugo Valentin was merely one of many investigators to emphasize the absence in America of "the anti-semitic tradition which in so many countries of Europe furnishes the most favourable antecedent for a revival of anti-semitism." On the other hand, Horace M. Kallen, who regards the Christian tradition as virtually synonymous with the tradition of anti-Semitism, has explained anti-Semitism in the United States by reference to Christian influences in the culture. But so little religious hostility, as such, has been shown toward Jews in America that it is difficult to believe that the Christian tradition has been a dominant or decisive factor. Still other observers, such as Lewis S. Gannett, have suggested that anti-Semitism in the United States is "essentially a part of a long Anglo-Saxon tradition of dislike of the newer arrival." [1] There is no evidence, however, that such a dislike, if it exists, can be correlated with the actual arrival of new immigrant groups. The fact is that we have two conflicting traditions in the United States, one sharply opposed to and the other sanctioning anti-Semitism; the one classical, the other modern; the one based on the Revolution of 1776, the other a rationalization of the undemocratic social order that came into being with the rise of industrial capitalism in the latter part of the last century.

1. THE CLASSIC TRADITION

America is the last country in the world where one would look for anti-semitism.

— RABBI LEE J. LEVINGER

"Free America," wrote Hugo Valentin, "was the first modern state which, relying on the idea of religious liberty, made no legal difference between Christian and Jew. To this extent, the Declaration of Independence marks the beginnings of Jewish Emancipation." It was in America, not in Europe, that the Jews were first emancipated. When emancipation finally came in Europe, it was more rhetorical than real: the old heritage could not be banished by a mere verbal declaration of the rights of man, for it existed in Europe not as a vague memory of things passed, but as an ever-living force in society. In the United States, emancipation was complete in the sense that, the medieval heritage never having existed, formal emancipation meant precisely what it was intended to mean in Europe: that theological differences would never be permitted to form the basis for secular sanctions and discriminations. When the men who wrote the Constitution provided that "Congress shall make no law respecting an establishment of religion or prohibiting the free exercise thereof," they merely declared an existing state of affairs. "It is only in the North American Free States," wrote Karl Marx in 1844, "that the Jewish question loses its theological significance and becomes a really secular question. In the United States there is neither a state religion nor a religion declared to be that of the majority, nor the predominance of one cult over another. The state is alien to all cults." While the United States has of late years departed from this rock-bottom separation of church and state — recently President Truman in a letter to the Pope stated that this was a Christian nation — the separation was real at the outset. "The government of the United States," wrote George Washington, "is in no sense founded on the Christian religion. The United States is not a Christian nation any more than it is a Jewish or a Mohammedan nation." Article XI of the treaty which the United States concluded with Tripoli in 1796 clearly stated that the United States "is not in any sense founded on the Christian religion."

The political institutions of the United States have always been free of the taint of anti-Semitism. "Upon this soil," writes Ludwig Lewisohn, "no Jewish blood has flowed; in these cities no ghettos have stood nor have their market-places known the crackle of faggots or the despairing cry of Israel. Here alone citizenship was won without humiliating delay and tedious struggle." Modify Lewisohn's rhetoric as you will, the fact remains that America provided the first fair test in history for the proposition that a Jewish minority could flourish in a non-Jewish society without humiliating governmental disabilities and discriminations.

To be sure a few miscellaneous disabilities existed in some of the colonies prior to 1776 and survived, in one form or another, for some years after the Revolution. But it would be misreading history to assume that these disabilities arose out of intergroup conflicts or that they were demanded by the majority. On the contrary, they were mimetic in character and found expression, as obsolete verbiage often finds expression in documents drafted by lawyers. Most of the colonial disabilities had been removed prior to the Revolution, not as a concession to a minority but as a matter of right. No amount of historical quibbling can impugn the great historic fact that the United States is the one nation in the Western World that, from its inception, has been without the heritage of the yellow badge. That a Dutch colonial governor once attempted to drive a few Jews from New Amsterdam does not, in any manner, alter the significance of this fact. A study of American political institutions, therefore, would lead one to the conclusion, once expressed by Bernard Drachman, that "anti-semitism in America should be like the snakes of Ireland: there shouldn't be any" — not, that is, if one looks at the official record.

A glance at the impressive evidence assembled by Cyrus Adler and Aaron M. Margalith in their study of American diplomatic action affecting Jews in the period from 1840 to 1945 (*With Firmness in the Right*) is sufficient to indicate that our official attitude toward anti-Semitism has always been a good one, notable for its consistency, firmness, and insistence on human rights. In fact, it is doubtful if any element in our tradition has done us greater credit as a people than has this policy toward Jewish persecution.

The first representation made by the United States to any foreign power relating to the Jews was embodied in a note of protest dispatched in connection with the Damascus ritual murder case of 1840. Throughout the nineteenth century, the United States repeatedly lodged protests against the persecution of the Jews in Russia, Rumania, Poland, Austria, Persia, Morocco, and Turkey. It was the persistent intervention of the American minister, in the years from 1853 to 1861, that finally won freedom from discrimination for the Swiss Jews. When Austria refused to accept the credentials of Anthony M. Keiley as ambassador, because his wife was Jewish and therefore "could not be accorded that reception by Vienna society which we judge desirable for the representative of the United States," President Cleveland refused to withdraw the appointment and left the post vacant for two years.

As early as March 5, 1891, a petition was presented to President Harrison, signed by a group of distinguished non-Jews, asking that an international conference be called "to consider the conditions of the Israelites and their claims to Palestine as their ancient home, and to promote, in all other just and proper ways, the alleviation of their suffering." In a famous note to our ambassador in Rumania in 1902, John Hay laid down a basic tenet of American foreign policy when he wrote:

This government can lose no opportunity to controvert such a distinction (between Jewish and non-Jewish American citizens), wherever it may appear. It can admit no such discrimination among its own citizens, and can never assent that a foreign state, of its own volition, can apply a religious test to debar any American citizens from the favor due to all.

Developed in the course of a long diplomatic controversy with Czarist Russia, extending from 1873 to 1911, our insistence upon this principle finally culminated in the termination of our commercial treaty with Russia.

Throughout the years, America's policy toward Jewish persecution has found warm support in American public opinion. "In the name of civilization," reads a resolution adopted at a great mass meeting held in Chickering Hall in New York on February 2, 1882, "we protest the spirit of medieval persecution. In this age of recognized equality of all men, irrespective of their religious confession, an essential element in American constitutions is a principle and practice which secure the loyal devotion of all classes, the principle of religious liberty." When a series of frightful pogroms was launched in Russia in 1903 — the fateful year of Kishineff — over seventy large protest meetings were held in the United States; in fact, the world-wide protest which these pogroms aroused centered in the United States and was initiated here. "A whole nation," in Lewisohn's phrase, "embraced the distress of Israel as though that distress were its own, and the chief magistrate of the Republic caused the record of that sympathy to be embodied in the archives of the nation."

America's loyal adherence to what Theodore Roosevelt once called "the diplomacy of humanity" not only encouraged European Jews to continue their fight for freedom and survival, but was an important factor in stimulating large-scale Jewish immigration. Every Jew that came to the United States from Poland, Russia, or Rumania strengthened the chances of Jewish survival and, at the same time, added to the security of American Jewry which in turn gave new hope to Jews throughout the world. Beyond all question, the favorable experiences of Jews in America exerted a profound influence on Jewish morale everywhere. Over a long period of years, the hope for an eventual Jewish homeland in Palestine received indispensable support from American Jews and official encouragement from the American government.

While the Jewish experiment in America has not been concluded, by any means, it has afforded the most satisfactory adjustment yet achieved in a long history of similar experiments. For here the circumstances have been and still remain unique. "Here," as James Parkes has written, "the old battle of assimilation and nationalism is being fought out within a new framework. European Jewry was asked in the Nineteenth Century to assimilate to an already existing non-Jewish culture and way of life, and the assimilation was primarily that of surrendering what was characteristically Jewish and accepting what was characteristically non-Jewish, even Christian. The position in America is different; for the whole continent is simultaneously assimilating the significance of its own existence, and the task to which Jews are called within that assimilation can be creation rather than renunciation; for one of the things to be assimilated in a new tolerance and equality is the variety of national traditions of which the continent is the repository and the expression." [2]

While our official record toward anti-Semitism at home and abroad has been a good one, and has created an exceptionally favorable environment for Jews, the unofficial record is another matter. Scrutinizing the official record one would dismiss, as most unlikely, the possibility of anti-

Semitism ever reaching alarming proportions in this country. Unfortunately, however, we have long tolerated the growth of a set of undemocratic practices in sharp conflict with our democratic tradition. To seek out the tradition that sanctions the "private and communal" variety of anti-Semitism in America, therefore, one must turn from the official record to the unofficial; from the real tradition to its mythical counterpart. How was the dualism in federal policy toward racial minorities, which came into such sharp focus after the Civil War, rationalized? What factors made this rationalization seem plausible? Who were the myth-makers?

2. THE MYTH-MAKERS

In the period after the Civil War, the American people began to be concerned, as Matthew Josephson has noted, over the difference between what men said and what they meant in politics; between the eternal principles which they voiced and the incidental objectives which these principles served to mask; with the contradiction, in short, between ideology and interest. To rationalize the glaring discrepancy between what was happening in American life and the traditional American ideals, a myth had to be created. In the creation of a myth, certain basic essentials are required. A myth cannot be spun out of whole cloth; it must relate to an objective set of facts, a complex of events which has brought about the need for rationalization. Successful myth-making also requires a background that can be manipulated. The myth must have the appearance of reviving an older story and must appeal to some antecedent set of values.

To create a myth, various types of verbal skills are required. At the grass-roots level, there must be certain vulgarians who can hammer away at the agreed-upon themes. These are the active Klansmen — the window smashers, the lynchers, the authors and circulators of scurrilous tracts and anonymous pamphlets, the unskilled craftsmen. But a myth can never be traced to its source or understood by studying the ideological antics of these elements. For they lack the learning and intelligence, the prestige and position, to launch a myth. The real myth-makers are always of a different stripe. They come from different backgrounds — occupy different positions in society, speak a different language, and have a different status. Hitler was preceded in Germany by a number of these refined upper-class racial theorists and myth-makers, just as Gerald L. K. Smith did not invent the ideology that he manipulates today.

Three names figure prominently in the architecture of the Great Myth in America: Madison Grant, Burton J. Hendrick, and Lothrop Stoddard. Grant was born in New York in 1865; Hendrick in Connecticut in 1871; Stoddard in Massachusetts in 1883 — all native born of native born parents. From the meager data in *Who's Who*, one can identify their backgrounds as old-stock New England, Anglo-Saxon, Protestant, Upper Class. Grant was a graduate of Yale and Columbia; Hendrick of Yale; Stoddard of Harvard. Long ardent students of eugenics, Grant and Stoddard were both trained in the law. It would also appear that the three men, at different times, were members of the same clubs. Judging by the extraordinary number of his club affiliations and the circumstance that he was a bachelor, Grant must have been a very lonely man. An active member of the Society of Colonial Wars and the Loyal Legion, he was also a member of the Tuxedo, Union, Knickerbocker, University, Century, Down Town, Turf and Field, Boone and Crockett, Half Moon, Ends of the Earth, and Shikar clubs.

Madison Grant — explorer, adventurer, amateur scientist, lawyer, and publicist — was Houston Stewart Chamberlain's most influential disciple in this country. In 1916 Grant published *The Passing of the Great Race or The Racial Basis of European History*, which was largely based on Chamberlain's romantic notions. Although the intellectual parentage is clearly apparent, Grant did not cite Chamberlain nor did he list *The Foundations of the Nineteenth Century* in the pretentious bibliography to be found in the fourth revised edition of his book issued in 1921. Chamberlain's racist primer, first issued in 1899, had sold 100,000 copies by 1914 and had gone through printing after printing. The Grant book was hardly less successful: it was reprinted twice in 1916; a second edition was reprinted in 1918 and in 1919; a third revised edition was reprinted in 1921; and the fourth, and final, edition was issued in 1924, with an introduction by Henry Fairfield Osborn. The bible of the Nordics, the book had an enormous influence. Grant contended, and not without reason, that its publication was largely responsible for the passage of the Immigration Act of 1924.

The Passing of the Great Race contains the frankest and the most clear-cut statement of the racist ideology ever published in this country. Premised upon the assumption that race is the prime determinant of history, it proceeds to "demonstrate" that racial lines correspond with class and social cleavages. Since racial lines obviously cut across nationality and linguistic groups and never correspond exactly with class cleavages, it is apparent that Grant was using the racial theory to rationalize an antidemocratic position. This is apparent, also, in the hatred that he spewed upon the democratic ideal "and its illegitimate offspring socialism." Throughout the book one finds "races" and "classes" being used interchangeably, there being superior and inferior classes just as there are superior and inferior races. It was Grant's hatred of democracy that explained his hatred of "inferior peoples"; nor could he be accused of mincing words. Either we abandoned, he wrote, the boast that America recognizes no distinctions in "race, creed, or color," or we were doomed as a nation.

Later Grant applied the racial interpretation of history to the American scene in *The Conquest of a Continent or the Expansion of Races in America* (1923). The book is a clever piece of myth-making, for it did investigate, as I will show later, a real situation. Up to the Civil War, Grant wrote, the United States had succeeded in preserving its religious, racial, and political unity. But the Civil War had destroyed this unity. As he viewed the war, it had been fought on both sides "almost entirely by unalloyed native Americans." It was our native aristocracy, the flower of American manhood, that had been slaughtered on the battlefields of the Civil War. To fill the void created by this slaughter, millions of immigrants had been brought to our shores. Together with the emancipated slaves, these immigrants were in process of destroying our racial, linguistic, cultural, religious, and national unity. Unrestricted immigration had resulted in a lowering of the birth rate among the native stock and in a rapid deterioration of their eco-

nomic position, for the natives were "too proud" to mingle
with the motley immigrant hordes.

Among the various immigrant types, Grant had a special
disdain for "the Polish Jew . . . with his dwarf stature,
peculiar mentality and ruthless concentration on self-
interest." As for the Negroes, they had to be rigidly
segregated from the mass of the population and denied full
citizenship. Unfortunately the "farming and artisan classes
of America" had not awakened to the changes taking place
in this country until it was too late; and now they were
threatened with extermination. That "inferior people" could
successfully compete with "superior people" was an inconsistency that did not bother Grant. One would think that
a racist like Grant would favor intermarriage between
"superior" and "inferior" types in the hope of improving
the stock. But it seems that "a law" precluded this possibility: the law that the mongrel offspring of such marriages reverted to the inferior caste. Thus Grant wrote that
"a cross between any of the three European races and a
Jew is a Jew." Slavery had preserved the white man's vigor,
but now this lord of the earth was being compelled to work
and his powers were waning. America had reached the
zenith of its powers in 1860 and the future for Grant was
enshrouded in a deep Spenglerian gloom. It should not be
forgotten that the spread of industrial civilization in Germany produced similar rationalizations there.

3. THE MYTH OF UNDESIRABILITY

One can trace this same myth-making process in an extremely influential book by Burton J. Hendrick published

in 1923 — *The Jews in America*. Although the jacket carried such provocative questions as "Do Jews Make Good Americans?" and "Is There a Menace in the Polish Jew?" the tone of the book is polite, scholarly, and well-mannered. Anti-Semitic violence is consistently deplored and it appears to be fair throughout.

Hendrick has kind words for "the first Jews" who came to America. The Sephardic Jews had a delicacy which was "decidedly non-Jewish." Not theirs "the thick lips, the curly hair, the swarthy complexion, the hooked nose, or the round heads" which are "generally regarded as Jewish characteristics." The Sephardic Jews were "superior to other representatives of Israel" — a polite concession to Benjamin Cardozo and Bernard Baruch. Toward the German Jews, the tone is still polite but one detects a certain edge. It seems that the German Jews included too many of those "characteristically Jewish figures — the rag picker, the petty tradesman, the pawnbroker." But, since it would never do to say that Oscar S. Straus, Solomon Loeb, and Benjamin Altman were "undesirable," the German Jews were also excepted from the category. Now and then a few German Jews were even elected "to one of the most exclusive city clubs, — although here, it must be admitted, progress is more difficult." The Sephardic Jews had a large admixture of Spanish blood and there was much good German blood in the German Jews; but with the appearance of the Polish Jews with "long, unkempt beards, the trailing hair, and the little curls about the ears," the whole situation had changed most deplorably.

After this introductory flourish, the distinction so carefully preserved between Sephardic and German Jews, on the one hand, and Polish Jews on the other suddenly vanishes and the author describes Jews in general. The trading instinct with Jews "is inherent in the very germ-plasm of the race." While Jews are talented, their talents are essentially imitative. "They can develop the ideas and principles of others; but the mighty gift of creation they possess only in a moderate degree." Not superior to Gentiles in any sense, they are "quick, nimble, and talented." Far from dominating American finance and industry, Hendrick concluded that Jews were biologically incapable of creating or of operating large enterprises. For the nature of the control of American business and finance compelled him to take notice of the fact that "the racial stocks which founded the United States . . . still control its wealth." Having made these observations, Hendrick then drew the conclusion that further Russian-Jewish and Polish-Jewish immigration should be barred. One year after the book was published, his wish was granted. Contrary to his predictions, however, anti-Semitism did not abate but reached new depths of intensity and rancor fifteen years after the great wall was erected!

Today it is quite apparent that this picture of the Polish Jew merely reflected the general tendency to rationalize economic and social conflicts as cultural or racial conflicts. For had the myth-makers been guided by objective criteria, they could hardly have imagined a more desirable immigrant than the Russian Jew. Haunted by memories of pogroms in Europe, he came to this country with the fixed intention of permanent residence and with the minimum in the way of nationalistic European loyalties. With the possible exception of the Irish, the East European Jews showed the least inclination of all immigrant groups to return to Europe. They brought their families with them; they were slightly more literate than the average immigrants of the period; and they were an urbanized people possessed of many important skills and talents. Nevertheless, a clever rationalization placed them in the "undesirable" category from which the German Jews, who had already achieved status, were neatly excepted.

4. 1000 HARVARD GRADUATES

The career of Dr. Lothrop Stoddard presents an interesting case history of the how and why of racial mythmaking. His book *The Revolt against Civilization* (subtitled *The Menace of the Under Man*) went through six editions after publication in 1922, while an earlier volume, *The Rising Tide of Color* (1920), went through fourteen editions and created, according to Dr. Louis L. Snyder, "an international sensation." Stoddard starts, like Grant, with the assumption that the rise and fall of civilization is to be explained in terms of changes in the human stock. For a civilization to arise at all, a superior human stock must first have been evolved. The barbarian stocks are a menace to civilization since they upset living standards, socially sterilize the higher stocks, and mongrelize the population through interbreeding. In fact, these inferior elements, "including many of the peoples of Asia, the American Indians, and the African Negroes," are the conscious enemies of mankind: they are the Under Men.

From his adventures in the field of eugenics, Dr. Stoddard had discovered four elements in the American stock:

the old Native American stock — the best; the earlier immigrant stock — "somewhat less superior"; the new immigrants — "decidedly inferior"; and the Negroes — "inferior to all other elements." In America, as elsewhere, civilization was threatened not by social causes, but by the encroachment of the Under Men. Thus the crisis of our time is racial, not social, in character. Starting from a theoretical discussion of the ebb and flow of civilization, one notices that the argument has now become emphatically antidemocratic in tone and content. This becomes quite apparent in Stoddard's characterization of the Russian Revolution as "a savage upsurge of revolutionary atavism," essentially racial in origin.

Dr. Stoddard was acutely distressed by a study which had been made by the biologist Davenport. This study concluded that, at existing rates of reproduction, 1000 Harvard graduates of 1923 would have only 50 descendants two centuries hence; while 1000 Rumanians in Boston, at their rate of reproduction, would have 100,000 descendants in the same space of time. One can naturally appreciate the consternation that this equation must have caused a devoted Harvard man. But only the existence of an acute xenophobia can explain the remarkable fact that Dr. Stoddard was apparently willing to assume that none of the 100,000 descendants of the 1000 Rumanian immigrants would ever graduate from Harvard College and thus add to the number of Harvard men. Since he had already consigned the Rumanian immigrants to the category of the Under Men who could never meet the educational standards of Harvard, Dr. Stoddard was, in effect, compelled to make this assumption. Merely as an aside, one notes the appearance in the line-up of the 1946 Harvard football team of players with such names as Drvaric, Fiorentino, Feinberg, Gudaitis, Moravec, and Lazzaro.

What also acutely distressed Dr. Stoddard was his conclusion that the middle class was being made to assume a disproportionate social burden: the burden of being taxed for the relief of the poor; of having to do all the brainwork for the Under Men; and of having to educate their own children as well as the children of the less fortunate. It seems, also, that Jews are part of the burden that the middle class must carry. Jews were not a menace until about 1848. But once released from the ghetto, the Jew had joined the vanguard of the revolutionary movement. The Jew is a dangerous leader of the Under Men since he has few national loyalties and possesses "a quick, clever intelligence."

Having defined "the cause of the world unrest" in racial terms, it only remained for Dr. Stoddard to prescribe the remedy: eugenics or the science of race betterment. The eugenics doctrine, as developed by Stoddard, is certainly not a socially neutral doctrine. Not only does it shift the scrutiny of causes from the social to the racial, but it leads to such notions as that poor relief should carry with it the obligation of sterilization. Race building is coupled with "race cleansing" and race cleansing implies the planned elimination of the unfit. If social unrest is caused by "tainted geniuses" and "degenerates," the elimination of these types will eliminate the sources of unrest. The goal of such a program is the evolution of a "neo-aristocracy," for democracy "as a fetich has no more virtues than Mumbo-Jumbo or a West African ju-ju."

In 1939 Dr. Stoddard visited Nazi Germany as a correspondent and wrote a book about his visit — *Into the Dark-ness*, 1940. On this visit, he had the good fortune to study eugenics in application; in fact, he was invited to sit with a three-man Nazi court for a day, listening to the appeals of individuals whom the Nazis had ordered sterilized. Despite all that had been written between 1922 and 1939 to clarify the racial issue, Stoddard describes the eugenics court with admiration.

In a number of respects, the myth-making of Grant and Stoddard carries the same burden of argument. What is of special significance is the manner in which Grant and Stoddard equate the colonial issue with the unrest among the Under Men in America. Nothing illustrates the danger of racism more clearly than the manner in which, once assumptions of racial superiority are granted, a psychosis of fear immediately arises. To Grant and Stoddard the appearance of Oriental immigrants on the West Coast was alarming in the same sense, and for the same reason, that social unrest in China and India was alarming. Although insisting that the cause of social unrest is racial, the writings of Grant and Stoddard fairly quiver with hatred of social change. What was it that they really feared — the encroachment of "inferior" races or a threatened loss in social status? While Grant and Stoddard showed a consistent preoccupation with racial theory, Hendrick falls in a quite different category. In view of his fine historical writings and the generous spirit they reflect, it is apparent that the book he wrote about the Jews was a journalistic undertaking which he would almost certainly repudiate today. I have mentioned the work of these myth-makers, not for the purpose of exploding their racial theories (the theories were exploded years ago), but to trace the development of an ideology and to show how this ideology rationalized the socio-economic conflicts of the period and served as a mask for privilege.

5. THE BUFFALO AND THE ANGLO-SAXON

The great myth was not, however, the creation of three men. Contributions to its creation came, in fact, from many diverse sources. In a brilliant article in the *Political Science Quarterly*,[3] Dr. Edward Norman Saveth has traced the process by which an authoritarian bias colored the teaching of American history in the period between the Civil War and the turn of the century. A generation of American historians and political scientists, many of whom were trained in German universities, made a point of teaching that our political institutions had their origin, not in the Revolution of 1776, but in the dark huts of Teutonic villages. Herbert Baxter Adams, John W. Burgess, Hermann von Holst, James Schouler, and James Ford Rhodes were all impressed, in varying degrees, with the difference in political capacity between races.[4] The notion that the native American stock was being pressed to the wall by hordes of European immigrants was a favorite theme of Dr. Edward A. Ross and other American sociologists of the period. "Is it any wonder," asked Dr. William Z. Ripley, "that serious students contemplate the racial future of Anglo-Saxon America with some concern? They have seen the passing of the American Indian and the Buffalo; and now they query as to how long the Anglo-Saxon may be able to survive." [5]

John E. Edgerton, at one time president of the National

Association of Manufacturers, joined the chorus with a solo
part in which he insisted that most manufacturers were of
"native American stock" and that they were "a native, loyal,
and God-fearing" lot. He was particularly annoyed with
the Jews for their arrogant refusal to observe the Christian
Sabbath. Dr. Charles Conant Josey, formerly of Dartmouth
College, was sure that the white race "possessed certain innate superiorities"; that the belief in white supremacy made
for "new supplies of psychic force"; and that "the maximum
good of the world lies in the continued prosperity of the
white race." [6] Dr. David Starr Jordan, who had given utterance on more than one occasion to thinly veiled anti-
Semitic sentiments,[7] told a Congressional committee that
"it is a plain fact that our population has been diluted to
an alarming extent by the incoming of peoples which are
biologically incapable of rising either now or through their
descendants above the mentality of a 12-year-old child.
Education and Americanization may help the individual a
little, but never the stock." This from a liberal educator,
the president of Leland Stanford University.[8]

༄

While this great myth was shot through and through
with transparent fallacies and was essentially a rationalization of the socio-economic conflicts that came with an
industrial society, it did square in a superficial way with
certain social realities. The post-Civil-War years were
unquestionably chaotic and corrupt, violent and riotous.
Evil did sit in high places; foreigners were inundating the
American landscape; the fabric of the older democratic
culture was being ripped apart. To trick a freedom-loving

people into accepting industrial regimentation in the name of democracy, the tycoons of the period needed a diversionary issue. Hence the alien, the foreigner, the Jew, the Negro, and the yellow peril. In a sense the stratification of the American people into functional groups based upon ethnic status had been consciously planned. James J. Hill brought over the Irish to build the railroad lines; the Germans and Scandinavians to run the shops and to operate the farms; the Croatians, the Slavs, the Lithuanians, and the Finns to work the mines on the Mesabi. Of Protestant background but married to a Catholic, he shrewdly appraised the importance of religious backgrounds in the selection of immigrants. "Look at the millions of foreigners pouring into this country," he once said. "The Catholic Church represents the only power that they either fear or respect. What will be their social views, their political action, if that single force should be removed?"

On the face of things, the Anglo-Saxons were the most successful group (hence, by implication, a superior group). Humorless scholars examined *Who's Who* gathering statistics to prove that a correlation existed between men of eminence and Anglo-Saxon, white, Protestant backgrounds and, of course, they found what they were looking for. This apotheosis of the Anglo-Saxon was naturally gratifying to those of Anglo-Saxon background, particularly those who were being sorely pressed economically by Big Business (which was controlled by other Anglo-Saxons). The great myth also appealed to a strain of old-fashioned Roman Republicanism in our tradition. "The Republic was being threatened." Taste was being debauched. Morals were being undermined. Standards were being destroyed. Many Americans of the period began to be nostalgic, to look back upon the first years of the Republic with misty eyes. Their great emotional attachment to the traditional values upon which American culture had been predicated was itself a powerful dynamic to be manipulated. These various tendencies should be correlated, also, with similar tendencies in Europe, after 1848, to explain social phenomena in terms of race. Had not the great Ernest Renan written that "divers races lead downward to a common estate of moral putrefaction"?

Under the impact of the new forces which the second American Revolution had released, the contradiction between ideology and interest was finally resolved, for many elements, by the substitution of a new ideology, or countertradition. Essentially this is what Henry Adams meant when he said that the society of *post bellum* America had swept into the ash heap the cinders of his misdirected education. Although he regarded the new dispensation as inevitable, he could not accept it because he was too deeply immersed in the older democratic culture. He was, indeed, "landed, lost, and forgotten," as were many of his contemporaries.

When a Westbrook Pegler, therefore, refers to "that vicious and hateful word democracy"; when he charges that under certain circumstances bigotry and intolerance are not un-American; when he states that no correlation can be made between fascism and the K.K.K. (because the Klan is a good old-fashioned American institution); and when he defends lynching, as he did at the time of the San Jose lynching in California, he is doing so in terms of this bogus countertradition in American life.

6. "PATHETIC PILGRIMS TO FORGOTTEN SHRINES"

Growing up in the Old South in the 1890's, the German-born son of German-Jewish parents, it seemed that the "Americanization" of Ludwig Lewisohn was complete and final. Apart from appearance there was nothing Jewish about him: he was a Southerner, a Methodist, and a member in good standing of the Epworth League. Unaware of the existence of anti-Semitism, he was profoundly shocked when, upon his graduation from Columbia University in 1902, he was refused a teaching position. When a "kindly" instructor informed him that an academic career was most unlikely, in view of his being a Jew, he suddenly realized that "only faint remnants of the ideals of the early Republic still lingered in American life."

For a time it seemed to Lewisohn as though "the evil unveracity of early influences" had crippled his soul. He had grown to maturity in a society in which it was generally agreed that "there was no anti-Semitism in America"; in fact, it was un-American to assert the contrary. Wherever he went in search of a teaching position, however, Lewisohn found the same strange "duality of conscience." The men who refused him positions were "Anglo-Americans, pillars of democracy, proclaimers of its mission to set the bond free and equalize life's opportunities for mankind." Firmly believing that they lived in a democratic society that provided equal opportunities for all, they were not even aware of an inconsistency between traditional values and contemporary practices; between the older scheme of values and the new realities. It was Lewisohn's discovery that the America of the turn of the century was a "nation of schizophrenics" that drove him to revive his forgotten "Jewishness" and its traditional values. "Who was he," writes his biographer, Adolph Gillis, "to defy the unwritten law to which professors like Brander Matthews and Carpenter, the secretary of the department, gave their allegiance, that Americans should learn the literature of their mother tongue from Saxons like themselves?" With understandable bitterness Lewisohn concluded that "the notion of liberty on which the Republic was founded, the spirit of America that animated Emerson and Whitman, is vividly alive today only in the unassimilated foreigner, in that pathetic pilgrim to a forgotten shrine." [9]

The disillusionment of Ludwig Lewisohn, however, was not complete at this point. Another rude shock awaited him when, on returning to Germany, he discovered that "the country bore no resemblance to the one in which Lessing and Schiller and Heine had lived." Germany, like America, appeared to have repudiated its classic tradition. Although Lewisohn was painfully aware of the trauma which had occurred in the traditions of both nations, he never succeeded in identifying its cause. "When new means of productions are introduced in any country," writes Franz Hoellering, " 'classical traditions' are for the time being pushed into the background. . . . Where is the happy nation which is able simultaneously to absorb modern technology and to stress the values achieved during more reflective periods?"

7. *CHRISTMAS EVE IN LITCHFIELD*

Wherever one looks in these "dark and little understood years" after the Civil War, the same schizophrenic tendencies come to light. Consider, for example, one phase of the remarkable career of John Jay Chapman (born March 2, 1862). On August 14, 1911, a Negro named Ezekiel Walker killed an employee of a steel company in Coatesville, Pennsylvania. While pursued by a lynch mob, Walker shot himself in the mouth and was taken to a hospital. Screaming "Don't give me a crooked death because I'm not white," he was later taken from the hospital, roped to his cot, and dumped on a pile of rubbish to which a match was touched. When the flames burned the ropes, Walker rose from the cot and attempted to escape, only to be hurled back into the flames.

Terribly moved by this grisly lynching, Chapman rented a hall in Coatesville one year to the day after the incident occurred. On this anniversary occasion, he proceeded to deliver, to an empty hall, his magnificent Coatesville Address, as moving, in its own way, as Lincoln's Gettysburg Address. In the course of this short address, he said:

As I read the newspaper accounts of the scene enacted here in Coatesville a year ago, I seemed to get a glimpse into the unconscious soul of this country. I saw a seldom revealed picture of the American heart and of the American nature. I seemed to be looking into the heart of the criminal, — a cold thing, an awful thing.

I said to myself: "I shall forget this, we shall all forget it; but it will be there. What I have seen is not an illusion. It is the truth. I have seen death in the heart of this people." For to look at the agony of a fellow-being and remain aloof means death in the heart of the onlooker. Religious fanaticism has sometimes lifted men to the frenzy of such cruelty, political passion has sometimes done it, personal hatred might do it, the excitement of the amphitheater in the degenerate days of Roman luxury could do it. But here an audience chosen by chance in America has stood spellbound through an improvised *auto-da-fe*, irregular, illegal, having no religious significance, not sanctioned by custom, having no immediate provocation, the audience standing by merely in cold dislike.

I saw during one moment something beyond all argument in the depth of its significance. You might call it the paralysis of the nerves about the heart in a people habitually and unconsciously given over to selfish aims, an ignorant people who knew not what spectacle they were providing, or what part they were playing in a judgment-play which history was exhibiting on that day.

No theories about the race problem, no statistics, legislation, or more educational endeavor, can quite meet the lack which that day revealed in the American people. For what we saw was death. The people stood like blighted things, like ghosts about Acheron, waiting for someone or something to determine their destiny for them.

Yet despite these eloquent words, and the courage which the occasion demanded, Chapman actually shared some of the phobias of Tom Watson. Early in his career, he had been associated with a number of Jews and had often expressed warm admiration for the Jewish people. One of his colleagues in the reform movement in New York politics, which he helped to initiate, had been Isaac H. Klein; but by 1918 Chapman had ceased to be interested in reform politics. In the middle twenties, he suddenly discovered the Catholic "menace" and, at about the same time, the

"Jewish menace." It is simply incredible that this man should have written a sonnet entitled "Cape Cod, Rome, and Jerusalem" and that it should have been published, as it was, in the *Ku Klux Kourier*.

And yet it is not so incredible when one reflects that Chapman's old friend, Henry Adams, shared somewhat the same views. Writing to Charles Milnes Gaskell from Washington on February 19, 1914, Adams said: "The winter is nearly over, I am seventy-six years old, and nearly over too. . . . It is quite astonishing how the circle narrows. I think that in reality as many people pass by, and I hear as much as I ever did, but it is no longer a part of me. I am inclined to think it is not wholly my fault. The atmosphere has become a Jew atmosphere. . . . We are still in power, after a fashion. Our sway over what we call society is undisputed. We keep the Jews far away, and the anti-Jew feeling is quite rabid. We are anti-everything and we are wild up-lifters; yet we somehow seem to be more Jewish every day."

Had Chapman and Adams acquired this prejudice from actual association with Jews? In the case of Chapman, it can be demonstrated that the contrary was true; he had formed warm and lasting friendships with a number of Jews. Yet Chapman, in a letter dated January 20, 1924, writes a friend that he has just finished "a lecture on the Jews — but put it aside because its agitation and agitation makes me sick." Another letter, dated December 23, 1925, reads, "I am dining tonight in a palace of gold plate and shall talk Jew-baiting with a very able American woman, wife of an English peer." In still another letter, written from Atlantic City on December 29, 1919, he writes:

Judea — Israel — the Lost Tribes — lost no more! Found —
very much found, increased — multiplied — as the sands of the
sea — upon the sands of the sea — in the city of the sea —
Atlantic City — with cliff dwellings of 10,000 each, — and re-
gurgitating with Hebrews — only Hebrews. Families of tens
and dozens — grave old plodders, gay young friskers — angel
Jews, siren Jewesses, — puppy Jews — mastiff Jews — bulging
matrons — spectacled backfish — golden-haired Jewish Dianas
— sable-eyed Jewish Pucks, Jewish Mirandas — Romeos and
Juliets, Jew Caesars — only no Shylock. It is a heathen me-
nagerie of Israel.

Both Chapman and Adams, in fact, are prime examples of
how it is possible to be anti-Semitic without being an anti-
Semite.

The key to an understanding of the anti-Semitism of
such men is to be found in the fact that America had not
turned out to their liking or in accordance with their ex-
pectations. Adams had written that, "fit or unfit," his education had ceased in 1871. The balance of profit or loss for the
twenty years that followed was "exceedingly obscure in
1892." He had lost twenty years and what had he gained?
"Landed, lost, and forgotten, in the centre of this vast plain
of self-content, Adams could see but one active interest,
to which all others were subservient, and which absorbed
the energies of some sixty million people to the exclusion
of every other force, real or imagined." This active interest
consisted in getting ahead in the world, in making money,
in widening the distance between "you" and the fellow
next below.

For years Adams had "hugged his antiquated dislike of
bankers and capitalistic society until he had become little
better than a crank. He had known for years that he must

accept the regime, but he had known a great many other disagreeable certainties — like age, senility, and death — against which one made what little resistance one could. The matter was settled at last by the people. For a hundred years, between 1793 and 1893, the American people had hesitated, vacillated, swayed forward and back, between two forces, one simply industrial, the other capitalistic, centralizing, mechanical. . . . A capitalistic system had been adopted, and if it were to be run at all, it must be run by capital and capitalistic methods. . . . There, education in domestic politics stopped. The rest was question of gear: of running machinery; of economy; and involved no disputed principles. Once admitted that the machine must be efficient, society might dispute in what social interest it should be run, but in any case it must work concentration. . . . Society rested, after sweeping into the ash-heap these cinders of a misdirected education. After this vigorous impulse, nothing remained for a historian but to ask — how long and how far!" [10]

Discrepancy between ideal and act is a trait, as Waldo Frank has observed, of our schizoid culture. To quote Emerson to the tycoons of the post-Civil-War period was about as futile as hiring a hall in Coatesville, Pennsylvania, to denounce a lynching. Today the split in our cultural tradition, occasioned by the rise of industrial capitalism, has become so wide that one can, by a number of simple tests, measure the extent of the rift. "Measure," writes Frank, "what we revere in this man of simple humbleness [Lincoln], this sharer in the guilt of his brothers on both sides of the battle line — measure this man of sorrow, this *conscious* man, with what we cultivate and admire in the actualities of life. Measure his total strangeness from the ways of a folk — complacent, ignorant, and greedy — which daily adores him." Such is one measurement of the gulf that now yawns between ideal and practice in American life. Memories of the older tradition have not expired, but they have become extremely faint. In revering Lincoln as we still do, we acknowledge, as Frank says, "what is most real in ourselves, however our present life deny it." [11]

Recently the chapter of the National Association for Advancement of Colored People in Springfield, Illinois, released a report on the status of Negroes in Springfield. Included in the report is an account of how six police officers broke into the coal shed in which a Mrs. Willie Bradley, a Negro woman, sixty-four years of age, lived with her daughter. Although they were not armed with a search warrant, the officers broke into the coal shed, arrested both women, and held them in jail in default of $5000 bail on a vagrancy charge! While in the jail, Mrs. Bradley was beaten into a state of unconsciousness by the turnkey and was left lying on the floor without medical attention. When she was taken to the hospital the next day, it was found that she had two broken ribs. This incident occurred on the eighty-third anniversary of the issuance of the Emancipation Proclamation by Abraham Lincoln of Springfield, Illinois. The same report concludes with a note to the effect that Lincoln's tomb in Springfield has recently been permitted to fall into a state of disrepair. . . .

It is this rift in our cultural tradition that accounts for the omnipresent ironies in contemporary American life. A year or so ago, Willson Whitman described a visit to Litchfield, Connecticut, on Christmas Eve. Candles shone behind fanlights; wreaths had been placed on the doors of the lovely old white houses; wineglass elms curved above the quiet streets; and pendants of snow hung from the handsome carved gateposts. Harriet Beecher Stowe was born in Litchfield. A tablet on the village green marks the place where Lyman Beecher's church once stood. Out in the hills, not far away, John Brown was born. It was a son of Litchfield, Henry Ward Beecher, who preached a great sermon against anti-Semitism on June 22, 1877. And yet Willson Whitman discovered that Jews are not permitted nowadays to live or to own property in Litchfield, Connecticut. "Just a sort of agreement," one Litchfield resident explained: "you might call it a Christian unity among Litchfield people on that point."

CHAPTER IV *A Most Peculiar*

Disease

THAT a countertradition sanctioning the use of anti-Semitism now exists in the United States is a matter of the utmost importance. Today we know, on the basis of scientific evidence, that frustration breeds aggression. We know also that aggressive impulses are often displaced or misdirected; that frustrations are frequently projected — that is, attitudes and behaviors which cannot be accepted in the self are attributed to others; and that frustrations are often rationalized, which is another way of saying that consciously acceptable motives are substituted for the true motives which are not consciously acceptable. But the selection of a target against which an aggressive impulse is directed is largely determined by tradition rather than by personal experience. "With each frustration," as Dr. Ellis Freeman has written, "the choice of target will tend to be determined not so much by actual responsibility of the target as by *commonly shared habits of assigning blame.*" [1] The bulk of the conditioning influences that produce prejudice, racial, religious, political, and nationalistic, find their source, as Julius Drachsler once pointed out, in the tradition that the group carries down, and not in personal experiences of the individual. If the personal experiences are of an irritating sort, then the individual finds his rationalization by going back to tradition.[2]

The countertradition in America has always assigned the role of target to the minority groups, including the Negro; but a chain of circumstances has now advanced the Jew to the front rank in the target category. When demagogic movements have arisen in times of crisis in the past, a confused and perplexed America has vented its wrath on diverse and miscellaneous groups: Jews, Catholics, foreigners, Negroes, Orientals (as witness the A.P.A. and the K.K.K. movements). But today there is reason to believe that such a movement would concentrate its energies on the Jew. With the passage of the 1924 Immigration Act, the decline in numerical importance of the first-generation immigrant groups, and the successful assimilation of most of the second-generation immigrants, the generalized prejudice has become more specific than in the past. As circumstances have eliminated one after another of the possible scapegoat categories, the Jew has been steadily advanced to a more prominent and a more isolated position. That the crackpot native fascist groups have concentrated their attack on the Jew is a striking confirmation of this trend. In the depression years, organizations were formed not to spread hatred of the Irish or the Poles or the Italians; they were formed to attack Jews. But there are other, and more compelling, reasons to support the belief that the Jew is now the residual legatee of the countertradition.

1. THE BEST OF SCAPEGOATS

For a variety of historical, psychological, and sociological reasons, which have been repeated *ad nauseam*, the Jew has always been the best, that is, the most vulnerable, of all possible scapegoats. The Jews are a unique minority, the minority of minorities. A people without a country, their religion, and the culture which grew out of it, came to take the place of territory. Thus they are not merely a religious sect or minority, but a people in exile. As Talcott Parsons points out, instead of being a people who *had* a religion, they came to be identified *with* their religion. It is as though all the Quakers in America were descendants of Basque refugees. While they are not a racial minority, long isolation and continued discrimination — one should say "universal" discrimination — have been responsible for certain social traits and characteristics which have, to some degree, marked the Jews as a distinctive people. For all practical purposes, therefore, they might be called a religious, ethnic, cultural, and racial minority, a compounding of all the disabilities under which minorities have long suffered. A conspicuous international minority, Jews can be baited everywhere. Furthermore their numerical weakness has generally frustrated their capacity for successful physical resistance. Occupying a peculiar historical position in relation to the Christian religion, most so-called "Christian" cultures contain a deep anti-Semitic bias.

Pages would be required merely to list the psychological reasons why the Jews have always made an ideal scapegoat group. Perhaps all of these reasons might be subsumed in the maxim of La Rochefoucauld that there is something in human nature that makes us hate those whom we have harmed. Whatever the motivation, there can be no doubt that a variety of psychological factors have created a predisposition to select the Jew for a target. The very fact that the Jew has been traditionally used as a scapegoat leads to his being constantly recast in this role. In short, anti-Semitism has long been a socially sanctioned and culturally conditioned mode of expressing aggressive impulses. Most of these factors have a general application in the United States as well as in Europe.

But there are more specific reasons why, from the point of view of the demagogue, the Jew is an ideal scapegoat. Paradoxically, the Jew is more vulnerable to attack than the Negro, for example, because he is more highly placed in our society. "Those whom we consider below us," writes Dr. J. F. Brown, "we may despise or pity, but we neither love nor hate them as we do our equals." The fact that Jews have risen rapidly on the status ladder lends a specious plausibility to some of the oldest and boldest lies of the anti-Semite. "No one can make political capital today," writes David Riesman, "out of an attack on witches. No one can unite a nation riven by caste and economic cleavages by presenting it with an enemy that is obviously trivial." [8] Related to this consideration is the fact that American Jews, by and large, lack social prestige with which to protect their economic position. Their economic position, furthermore, is such that it excites the envy of elements in the lower and the middle classes. Many of the businesses in which Jews have been successful — and into which they have been driven by discrimination — fall within the nonsensical "nonproduc-tive," as distinguished from "productive," category that the fascists invariably emphasize. Furthermore, Jew-baiting has a wide group appeal: to a section of Protestant Funda-mentalism; to the Coughlinite Catholics; and to many of the foreign-born groups. While they have made mistakes —

many mistakes — the native American fascists know what they are doing, and, as said above, their concentration on the Jew indicates that they have discovered both his vulnerability and his popularity as a scapegoat.

That the Jew is likely to be the residual legatee of the countertradition is a conclusion that also finds confirmation in the fact that he is a *special* kind of immigrant. Most European immigrant groups have been stereotyped in America but have managed, with the maturity of the second generation, to escape from the stereotype. The Jewish stereotype, on the other hand, has shown a remarkable persistence. A partial explanation for this phenomenon is suggested in a question once raised by Ralph Philip Boas, namely, "Why should it be treason for a Jew to abandon his religion and forget his birth any more than for a Frenchman or a Swede to do so?" That discrimination against Jews has been more pronounced than against other immigrant groups does not provide a complete answer to this question. When a Yugoslav immigrant "assimilates," in the traditional manner, by changing his name from Martinovitch to Martin, discarding his native customs, forgetting his native tongue, and joining Rotary, we applaud his agility and, somewhat reluctantly perhaps, make room for the New American. We certainly do not regard Martinovitch as either a traitor or a renegade. But the Jewish immigrant who changes his name, joins the Ethical Culture movement or the Christian Science Church, or marries a Gentile, is generally regarded, in both camps, as a social renegade. What is perhaps more important, he often comes to regard himself in much this same light. In some vague way, he is conscious of having betrayed an ennobling impulse of his own nature.

Suppose a Jewish immigrant has decided in favor of "total assimilation." He adopts an Anglo-Saxon name; marries a Gentile; cuts himself loose from Jewish communal life; and even manages to pass quite successfully for a non-Jew. How is this person going to feel, asks Maurice Samuel, when the conversation suddenly converges on "the Jewish problem" or takes on anti-Semitic overtones? When an advertisement specifies "No Jews Wanted" or "Gentiles Only," is this emancipated-assimilated Jew to apply anyway on the theory that he is no longer a Jew? In short, can he under all circumstances conceal his Jewish origin or forget it, without a twinge of conscience, a feeling of remorse, a sense of shame? Perhaps a few Jewish non-Jews can do so; but not many.

In the circle of my acquaintance, I have many Jewish friends who live outside the orbit of the Jewish world. They feel as out of place in a synagogue as I do in the Protestant Episcopal Church in which I was once confirmed. For the most part children of immigrant parents, they know only a few more words in Yiddish than I do in Gaelic. They do not live in predominantly Jewish districts; they belong to virtually no Jewish organizations; and they have only the slightest familiarity with Jewish culture. Yet not one of these individuals would deny, or think of denying, his Jewish origin. Although they have experienced only slight discrimination themselves, they remain extremely sensitive to the issue of anti-Jewish discrimination. I have asked many of these friends why they think they are "Jewish" and have yet to receive a plausible answer.

But there is, I believe, an answer. Until the Jewish people have a homeland, until their survival *as a people* is an assured fact, no person of Jewish origin is spiritually free to disclaim his Jewishness. He simply cannot make a free choice. For one thing, non-Jewish elements will not permit him to do so; but, more important, his own conscience will not sanction such a choice. For as long as Jews are scattered throughout the world, Jewish survival depends, to some extent, upon the loyalty of each individual Jew, more particularly upon the survival of Jewish communities. In this sense, therefore, each apostate is a renegade. The individual Polish immigrant may be the loser, as a person, when he forgets or abandons, disclaims or renounces, his Polish cultural inheritance. But he is not guilty of a betrayal, for Poland still exists and the continuity of Polish culture and tradition is assured. But the loss of every Jew through "assimilation" is a blow, at the present time, to Jewish survival. It is precisely this consideration, of course, that has worried Jewish leaders in America. How many times, for example, have the rabbis addressed themselves to the perennial topic: "Can Judaism Survive in America?" As Joseph Conrad demonstrated in *Lord Jim,* the natural history of the human conscience shows that the self-torture of the individual who abandons his companions on an imperiled ship is the most intolerable and exquisite of all tortures.

In the sense that he has not been morally free to make a choice, as to what he wanted to be, how he wanted to regard himself, and what faith, if any or none, he desired to affirm, the Jew has been a *special* immigrant. In an odd way, the Gentile has always taken this view of the Jew and has shown a lack of respect for the Jewish immigrant who has attempted to assimilate that he has not shown toward other immigrants. While the fact that the Jewish stereotype is widespread, ancient, pervasive, and firmly embedded in the culture — deeply etched in the consciousness of Gentiles — helps to explain this attitude, it does not explain the nature of the *special* problems which the Jewish immigrant has faced. That these problems are more acute today than ever before — what with the plight of European Jews and the aggravated Palestinian issue — merely means that we can expect a heightened, not a lessened Jewish consciousness in America.

It is not to be implied from the foregoing, however, that anti-Semitism is a disease of the Diaspora. Many Jews — Leo Pinsker is a case in point — have defined Judaeophobia as a psychosis which, transmitted from generation to generation for over two thousand years, has become essentially incurable. But this is to confuse "the Jewish Problem" with anti-Semitism. The Jewish minority problem is unquestionably related to the peculiar history of the Jewish people; but anti-Semitism is a specific social disease and, as such, is only indirectly related to the Diaspora. That Jews make an excellent scapegoat group is to be explained by their history and experience as a people; but one cannot explain the nature of anti-Semitism merely by calling attention to the factors — historical, psychological, sociological — which have made the Jew a favorite scapegoat.

2. THE NATURE OF THE WEAPON

Just as the Jew is the best of scapegoats, so anti-Semitism is a favorite weapon of proved efficiency in the socio-economic conflicts of a class-riven society. Whatever else anti-

Semitism is or may have been it is today a weapon of reaction — part of the mechanism of fascism — used for many
interrelated purposes: to confuse the people; to obscure the
basic causes of unrest; to divert attention from these causes;
to cloak the real purposes and objectives of reaction; to
arrest social progress; to fight democracy. Throughout its
long and devious history, through all its various and changing manifestations, the pertinent questions, in relation to
anti-Semitism, have always been: Who uses it? For what
purposes? Under what circumstances? Against whom? And
to these queries the answers are crystal-clear: anti-Semitism
has always been used by the enemies of the people; for the
purpose of arresting progress; in periods of social upheaval
and social stress; and against the interests of the people.

As an ideology, anti-Semitism is a figment of the imagination, a myth; but as a weapon used in social conflicts it has
long since proved its efficiency. As an ideology, modern
anti-Semitism has an interesting origin. In 1879 an obscure
Hamburg journalist, Wilhelm Marr, coined the expression
"anti-Semitism." The science of philology probably cannot
cite another instance where more fateful consequences have
attached to the coinage of a new word. Judaeophobia was a
centuries-old phenomenon in 1879; but, by a verbal trick,
Marr made it possible to invest this hatred with entirely
new implications. For the old hatred was now rationalized
as racial rather than religious in character; nor was it long
before the tendency to confuse racial with social conflicts
invested this hatred with a simply astonishing ambivalence.
A specific, historical phenomenon now became a shifting,
vague, indefinable, well-nigh invisible, many-sided weapon
of abuse. "The very term 'anti-semitism,'" writes S. W.

Baron, "became a source of strength to those who gathered under it. Without positive connotations, it could easily conceal the divergence among the different trends. There was, in fact, not one anti-semitic movement, but many. . . . Such an omnibus term could easily cover a multitude of motives and impulses."

In large part, the effectiveness of the new weapon of social conflict consisted in its elusive character: it could not be defined. The plain truth of the matter is that, today, there is no existing definition of anti-Semitism that is at all adequate to cover the various senses in which the term is used or the purposes to which it is put as a weapon of abuse. The definitions that do exist are confused, contradictory, and inconsistent, largely for the reason that people have been trying to define, in intellectually understandable terms, a myth, a vapor, a cloud of smoke. It is as though the doctors of the world were fighting a disease which they could not define but the symptoms of which they could easily identify. Even as a weapon, anti-Semitism is only to be understood by reference to the social context in which it is used; its use defines its character. To appreciate the efficiency of anti-Semitism as a weapon, it is necessary to explore, however inadequately, some aspects of this vast etymological confusion.

In the dictionaries, anti-Semitism is generally defined as hatred of or opposition to Semites, especially Jews. A moment's reflection is sufficient to indicate that this definition is both inadequate and misleading. Essentially this is the anti-Semite's definition of anti-Semitism. It is precisely the definition that, with malice aforethought, he seeks to propagate. It was by developing the rationalization, after 1879, that such a hatred existed and that it was based upon racial antipathy that the anti-Semites succeeded in investing anti-Semitism with a deadly dynamism, a self-generating, self-propelling fury. If the source of anti-Semitism is to be located in hatred of Jews as Jews, rather than in the social conditions that give rise to ambitious schemes for group dominance, then the weapon of anti-Semitism can be used like a dagger in the dark. By focusing attention upon the objects of hatred rather than the causes, such a definition actually fans the fires of hatred. The tendency then arises to confuse the myths advanced to justify the hatred with the objects of the hatred. Thus for more than fifty years, *Roget's Thesaurus* gave sanction for the use of the word "Jew" as a synonym for usurer, extortioner, cunning, heretic, lickpenny, harpy, schemer, craft, and shifty.

So deceptive is the nature of anti-Semitism as an ideological weapon that it has even deceived its victims. In many of the Jewish encyclopedias, for example, one will find anti-Semitism defined as "the dislike of the unlike." This definition is clearly misleading, for it fails to account, in any manner, for the rhythmic character of anti-Semitic movements, their rise and fall, their ebb and flow. As Dr. Otto Fenichel has written, "the instinctual structure of the average man in Germany was no different in 1935 from what it was in 1925. The psychological mass basis for anti-Semitism, whatever it may be, existed in 1925 too, but anti-Semitism was not a political force then." [4] The German Jew was no more "unlike" the German in 1935 than in 1925. It is quite obvious, therefore, that the ethnocentric resistance of in-groups to out-groups cannot possibly explain the rise of anti-Semitism in Germany after 1925.

Furthermore, it is simply not true that racial and cultural differences invariably give rise to feelings of prejudice and hostility between unlike groups. There have been long periods in the history of the Jews when they have lived among non-Jews under quite favorable conditions. They were no more "unlike" their neighbors in these periods than they were in the periods when these same neighbors carted them off to the stake. Where racial and cultural differences have existed apart from social contradictions, group differences have often been regarded in a comic light rather than as sources of annoyance and irritation. "The brown face of the Hindu mystic and the foreign accent of the Frenchman," writes Dr. Ellis Freeman, "are both social assets in those circles which are wealthy and secure enough to indulge their taste for the novel, strange, and even bizarre." Individuals who would be shocked to meet a Negro socially experience no psychological problems in employing Negroes as servants.

Then, again, anti-Semitism has been defined, as in the *Dictionary of Sociology* (1944), as "opposition by word and deed to equal participation of Jewish people in the social and legal rights which a nation affords to its people generally." Here the emphasis has shifted to the business, the activity, of opposing Jews. But the activities of anti-Semites do not constitute the sum total of anti-Semitism. A majority of the American people probably oppose anti-Semitism in the sense that they object to the activities of professional anti-Semites; but a large section of this same majority is anti-Semitic in the sense that it tolerates or practices discrimination against Jews. By drawing attention to their brutal anti-Jewish activities, the Nazis actually made it possible for many people to oppose anti-Semitism while remaining basically anti-Semitic. Any attempt, therefore, to define anti-Semitism in terms of the activities of anti-Semites only further confuses the issue. For such a definition diverts attention from a whole range of phenomena that can only be regarded as manifestations of anti-Semitism however well they may be masked by pretenses of one kind or another.

The effectiveness of anti-Semitism as a social weapon has always consisted in the fact that it has meant so many different things to so many different groups. This diversity in meaning has made it possible to use anti-Semitism as a cement to hold together groups otherwise quite divergent in outlook, position, and interest. To say, therefore, that an anti-Semite is inconsistent is to make a meaningless statement: it is his intention to be inconsistent. In fact, inconsistency is one of the conspicuous merits of anti-Semitism as an ideological weapon. No inconsistency in the anti-Semitic ideology has been more glaring than the charge that the Jews are the economic overlords, and, at the same time, the leaders of the revolutionary vanguard. But there is a touch of demagogic genius in this charge, for it permits an appeal to the dispossessed and a threat to the rich to be voiced in a single sentence. Furthermore, to charge that the Jew has the double and contradictory character of capitalist and communist can be psychologically acceptable to the middle-class individual because he feels that he is threatened simultaneously by both capitalism and communism!

An extremely versatile weapon, anti-Semitism has been used by different groups and social classes for a variety of purposes. Neither individuals nor groups can use anti-Semitism without becoming, to some extent, infected with the disease themselves. Therefore, since various social classes have used, or been tricked into using, anti-Semitism at one time or another in the disputes in which they have been involved, it has become possible to mobilize a powerful mass movement around an essentially negative — even a mythical — issue. For anti-Semitism extends throughout all reaches of society, in varying degrees, and is confined to no single region or nation or social class.

One moves a little closer to an understanding of the nature of anti-Semitism as an ideological weapon by examining the circumstances that gave rise to its invention. Classical anti-Semitism had always been premised upon the charge that the Jews insisted upon preserving a separate group identity. But modern anti-Semitism, the anti-Semitism that developed after 1879, owes its existence, as Rabbi Mordecai Kaplan has pointed out, "mainly to the circumstance that the Jew insisted upon taking the Emancipation seriously." What the anti-Semites objected to about the emancipation that followed in the wake of the French Revolution was that it enabled Jews to compete with non-Jews in a serious way. As long as the Jew was confined to the ghetto and denied equal status, he could not offer serious, general competition. But once these disabilities were removed, the basis of Jew-baiting shifted from the alleged "dislike of the unlike" to a dislike of the competitor, who was hated precisely because he was becoming so like the majority that he could not be readily identified for purposes of discrimination. This basic aspect of modern anti-Semitism has always been stressed by the professional anti-Semites.

"Where the Jew disregards and transgresses the boundaries that separate him from the non-Jew," said Wilhelm Stopel, "that is the point at which anti-semitism comes into being."

Thus the dictionary definition of anti-Semitism as hatred of or opposition to Jews might well be recast to read: "opposition to the tendency on the part of Jews after the Emancipation to become like non-Jews." It was this same aspect of modern anti-Semitism that Dr. Bruno Lasker had in mind when he once said that dislike of the Jew in America springs from the *too rapid* assimilation of Jewish immigrants in this country. When the reasons which prompted its invention are examined, therefore, it becomes apparent that anti-Semitism is essentially antidemocratic in character. First designed to arrest the revolution in Jewish attitudes after the emancipation, it later became antidemocratic in the broader sense of being used as a weapon to arrest social progress generally. "As a political ideology," writes Donald S. Strong, "anti-semitism without an anti-revolutionary aspect is so rare as to be almost unknown."

3. BISMARCK'S INSECT POWDER

One moves still closer to an understanding of the nature of anti-Semitism as a social weapon by observing how it has been used in the political and economic conflicts which came into being with the rise of industrial capitalism. Here the issue has been somewhat confused by the efforts of a coterie of economic historians to refute Werner Sombart's thesis that capitalism is an invention of the Jews. Many of these historians have become lost in the thickets of antiquity, from which they have not yet emerged. The origin of capitalism, however interesting, is irrelevant to the issue of modern anti-Semitism; what is of great importance, however, is the velocity and the magnitude of the social changes which came with the rise of modern industrial capitalism. How, when, and by whom capitalism was originated are debatable issues; but there can be no doubt that in the 1870's both Germany and the United States were in the throes of a period of profound social change. "The large scale use of machinery, the gigantic growth of cities, the rise of a proletariat," writes Marvin Lowenthal, "did not begin until the forties, and even in 1862 the industrial revolution was still more of a promise than a reality." But by 1880 the reality of the industrial revolution was unmistakable in Germany and it was in relation to the conflicts which this revolution brought into being that anti-Semitism began to take on an entirely new significance.

As leaders in the evolution of modern business and finance, Jews had played an important role in the bourgeois revolution which had cleared the way for the rise of modern industrial capitalism. In this earlier struggle between a rising merchant class and the landed aristocracy, Jews had been welcome allies of the former. In fact they had been summoned from the ghettos to aid in the transforming process. In the eyes of the non-Jewish bourgeoisie, however, "liberty, equality, and fraternity" meant, as Maurice Samuel has written, "liberty of capital from oppression, equality of capital in the hierarchy of rule, and the fraternity of businessmen." The emancipation of the Jews was essentially an accidental, unreal by-product of this initial collaboration. Once the bourgeois revolution was won, the ally of yesteryear was suddenly viewed as an undesirable competitor. Political emancipation was permitted to stand, as a *fait accompli,* but barriers were promptly erected, or, in some cases, were never lowered, against Jews in the social and economic fields. That the competition first occurred at the top levels of society is shown by the fact, properly emphasized by Samuel, "that the proportion of big Jewish traders and financiers dropped more rapidly than the proportion of small ones," and also by the fact that the first barriers erected against Jews after the emancipation were largely social in character.

Observing the conflict within the new bourgeois circles, Bernard Lazare defined anti-Semitism as "a mere struggle among the rich, a contest among the possessors of capital." It was the capitalist, the merchant, the manufacturer, the financier among the Christians, he wrote, and not the proletariat, that first made use of anti-Semitism as a weapon. "This will explain," he said, "why anti-semitism is essentially the sentiment of the middle classes." Many European socialists were so impressed with this, and similar interpretations, that they looked with mildly tolerant eyes upon organized anti-Semitism, often regarding it as a means of dividing their opposition. For example, Lazare thought that it was supremely ironic that anti-Semitism, "which everywhere is the creed of the conservative classes," should have developed into "an ally of the revolution." He actually believed that anti-Semitism was "working for the advantage of the revolutionary cause . . . it stirs up the middle class, the small tradesmen, and sometimes the peasant, against the Jewish capitalist, but, in doing so, it gently leads them toward socialism"! This is not to say, of course, that socialists encouraged anti-Semitism; but many of them did regard the "radical" anti-Semitism which began to develop after 1880 as a "pre-fruit" of Social Democracy which would eventually lead the lower middle class anti-Semites into their camp.

Having already used anti-Semitism as a means of placing limitations on Jewish emancipation, the beneficiaries of the new dispensation naturally resorted to the same weapon in an effort to divert the growing dissatisfaction of the lower classes. In the election of 1878, Bismarck, who had been in alliance with the liberals since 1867, suddenly decided to check the growth of the Social Democratic Party. As part of this strategy, he made use of the court chaplain, Adolf Stoecker, and the latter's Christian Socialist movement. The Stoeckerites were still close to the old social hierarchy, to the church, and to the monarchy. Their anti-Semitism was of the genteel, nonviolent, "Christian" variety, based on the assumption that baptism, undertaken in good faith, would solve "the Jewish Problem." When the Christian Socialists failed to make much of a showing in the elections, Bismarck lost interest in them. It was shortly before his death that he remarked, apropos the new "racial" anti-Semites, that "in fighting socialism with anti-semitism" the conservatives had got "hold of the wrong insect powder." [5]

By 1880 industrial capitalism was well advanced in Germany: the old social structure was crumbling; past forms of production and distribution were disintegrating; new cultural and political institutions were emerging; and, accompanying these changes, new political tensions and economic conflicts had developed. It was at this juncture that the new "racial" or "radical" anti-Semitism of Marr, Ahlwardt, and their colleagues began to assume the proportions of an organized movement. Born with the industrial revolution, this new anti-Semitism was of a quite different character from the old anti-Semitism of the *Junkers*, the big bourgeoisie, and the Christian Socialists. It attacked "the *Junkers and* the Jews"; described the Christian religion as "a child of Jewish religion and Platonism, born out of wedlock"; clamored for social reform; and was utterly irresponsible and intransigent in its attacks on the Jews. Being premised on racial considerations, it rejected assimilation *in toto* and called for the elimination of the Jews from all phases of German society. Existing outside the pale of respectability, it flouted the law, the church, and the *Junkers*. Obsessed with "racial purity" and "blood," it took over a racial ideology previously developed in France. This ideology quickly assumed dangerous forms in Germany, where the tensions born of the new industrial society were much greater than in France.

This new racial anti-Semitism was an urban phenomenon; its leaders were teachers, students, members of the free professions, shopkeepers, and minor government officials. Mixing their anti-Semitism with a wild variety of other ingredients — body-building, vegetarianism, soul-breathing, monetary reform, and so on — these elements represented the most unstable section of the middle class. These were the elements that had rushed headlong into the new occupations and vocations which had developed with the rise of modern industrial capitalism. Since these occupations, vocations, and professions had a definite absorptive capacity, and represented an area of economic life in which Jews were heavily concentrated, the issue could not be compromised from the point of view of the anti-Semites. Only the complete elimination of the Jews, so they reasoned, would open up the opportunities for which they clamored. It was precisely because the racial rationalization of anti-Semitism was uncompromising, totally exclusionist, and denied the possibility of assimilation that it made such an appeal to them. Unlike Stoecker these new anti-Semites showed a real ability to mobilize the lower middle class and by 1893 they dominated the movement which Stoecker had controlled in 1880. To a large extent, the new anti-Semitism divorced itself from conservatism; in fact it was this circumstance that prompted Bismarck's remark about the "wrong insect powder." By screaming against "the *Junkers* and the Jews," the new anti-Semites began to get a foothold in the rural areas. Essentially they were in rebellion against vestiges of the old social order as well as being against the new dispensation. "This radicalism," writes Dr. Paul Massing, "enabled racial anti-semitism to become the repository of a multitude of oppositional currents which, although incongruous and conflicting with one another, found in it a common denominator. The greater the social disorganization, the more numerous the elements of discontent which were attracted by the finality of the racial ideology, by its claim to total critique and guidance."

As elements of the lower and middle class became increasingly disaffected by a social transformation that threatened their security and status, they began to use anti-Semitism for political purposes. But it is important to note that their social betters had previously initiated them to the uses of anti-Semitism. "While the battle against capital as a whole seems hopeless at this point," wrote Karl Kautsky, "the conflict with Judaism, with Jewish capital, seems to afford better prospects of success." The assault upon Jewish or so-called "unproductive capital" is always attractive to the middle-class victims of the industrial revolution because it is never discouraged by their social betters and economic overlords. No one has ever been called a "communist" or a "revolutionist" for suggesting that the Jews have too much power or that restrictions should be imposed on "Jewish" capital. At this point, it is to the interests of the real beneficiaries (or so they believe) to encourage the process by which the rising animosity of the lower and middle classes is directed against the Jews. In fact it is their prior rejection of the Jew which has already provided the lightning rod or conductor by which this diversion is effected.

At the beginning of the industrial crisis, it will generally be found that anti-Semitic propaganda stresses the theme of the Jew as Capitalist, the Jew as the Rich Man. The social discrimination that the upper classes have long practiced against the Jew is then paralleled by an agitation for economic discrimination by the lower and middle classes. As the industrial system matures and the economic crisis deepens, anti-Semitic movements begin to acquire a velocity of their own. Once the diversion has become an organized political movement, once it has passed from literature to politics, from vague talk about nationalizing department stores to power issues, Jew and communist become interchangeable terms in anti-Semitic propaganda.

Despite Bismarck's warning, the conservatives in Germany continued to use anti-Semitism as an insect powder.

Disturbed by the "radicalism" and violence of the new racial anti-Semites, however, they used anti-Semitism only as it suited their purposes; not as a matter of consistent policy. The issue always seemed to turn on the relation of the reactionary upper classes to the government at any particular time. When they were in power, they took care to dissociate themselves from anti-Semitic rabble rousers; but when they were out of power or when they were opposed to the prevailing governmental policies, they never failed to make use of these same rabble rousers. In general their attitude toward anti-Semitism was completely cynical and opportunistic. "From its inception," writes Dr. Massing, "political anti-semitism had been for them an instrument of attack, intimidation and blackmail, first to resist the advancement of the liberal bourgeoisie and later to rally small property against socialist labor. Their relations to anti-semitism were governed by undiluted class interests." In connection with this point, it is interesting to note how the use of anti-Semitism as a political weapon momentarily subsided when reaction captured control of Congress in 1946.[6]

If the attitude of the conservatives in Germany toward anti-Semitism was cynical and opportunistic, that of the lower-class and middle-class anti-Semites toward the conservatives was essentially ambivalent. They both hated and envied, feared and respected, the conservative upper classes. But in the end they compromised with these elements and the two structures of power became identical. The basis of this compromise was, of course, the sacrifice of the Jews, their properties, and their lives. Always cynical about their ability to manipulate anti-Semites — a cynicism that found justification in practice — the conservatives saved their property but destroyed Germany.

Utterly absurd and irrational, the anti-Semitic myth has a powerful appeal to disaffected lower- and middle-class elements. If one examines the lengthy indictment of the Jews which Theodor Fritsch prepared in his anti-Semitic catechism — too lengthy to be quoted here — it will be noted that each count in the indictment reflected an objective reality in Germany: usury and sharp business practices existed; the handicrafts were being destroyed; the press was being monopolized; business frauds were prevalent; values of all kinds were being commercialized; vulgarity was rampant, and so on. The anti-Semitic myth rationalized all these consequences of the rise of industrial capitalism by fixing the blame on the Jews. Once its premises were granted, the myth represented a closed system, a logical scheme — false in all its conclusions, accurate in its reflection of existing social evils. Unable to enter the world of the rich, fearful of the socialist utopia, the anti-Semites created a world of their own, a world of fantasy, myth, and wishful daydreaming, but one which nonetheless reflected, however perversely, an unmistakable reality. "The total rejection of the Jews," writes Dr. Massing, "reflected total disaffection of the individuals and groups that took to the racial myth . . . they had no roots in any of the powerful social classes and no loyalties to any of the leading parties. The fury of their total assault was the fury of frustration and envy."

∾

Long used by the forces that rose to power with the industrial revolution, anti-Semitism has become part of the strategy and mechanism of reaction: a powerful instrument in a desperate and violent struggle for power. So thoroughly has it become part of the ideology of reaction that one may well doubt whether, at the present time, a fascist movement could avoid being anti-Semitic. Various public opinion polls have shown that antilabor and anti-Semitic attitudes are dynamically interrelated and interconnected parts of a single system of ideas. The *Fortune* poll of February 1946, for example, showed that anti-Semitic attitudes correlate with hostility to the Soviet Union and Great Britain; with disapproval of large-scale government work projects to help relieve unemployment; and with disapproval of labor unions.

This same poll showed that anti-Semites constituted 8.8 of the adult population in this country; but, as one might expect, that they constituted 13.5 of the rich. The following table, based on this poll, indicates clearly enough that the groups who most fear social change are the groups that are most anti-Semitic:

	All U. S. Adults		*Anti-Semites*	
Rich	6.8%	} 29.7%	10.4%	} 36.6%
Upper Middle Class ..	22.9%		26.2%	
Lower Middle Class ..	41.7%		45.3%	
Poor	21.0%		15.8%	
Negro	8.6%		2.3%	

Whatever significance one reads in these figures, it is apparent that only the upper-bracket socio-economic groups show an anti-Semitic score that is higher than the average for the nation. Upper-class anti-Semitism is admittedly a complex affair. As creatures of their culture, many upper class anti-Semites may honestly share the common belief in the guilt of the scapegoat; but more often, as the German experience indicates, they know better but remain quite willing to use the scapegoat when it serves their interests to do so.[7]

A number of recent studies in the social sciences confirm the distribution of anti-Semitic attitudes shown by the *Fortune* poll. For example, Frenkel-Brunswik and Sanford found that "high" anti-Semitic attitudes tend to score with social-political outlook (the high-score anti-Semites tend to support the *status quo*); and also that high extremes, in anti-Semitic attitudes, belong to the middle socio-economic class.[8] Still another study of anti-Semitic attitudes among university students has established that the anti-Semitism score increases directly with the amount of the father's income.[9]

Treitschke once defined anti-Semitism as "a natural re-action of the German national feeling against a foreign element which has usurped too large a place in our life." This type of definition belongs to the seedtime of an anti-Semitic movement. Then the stated goal is merely to keep the foreign element from usurping too large a place in the national life. Little is said of a specific character about economic sanctions or punitive measures. The literature of the movement, at this stage, is full of self-righteous, patri-otic, nationalistic sentiments. But if anti-Semitism merely expressed "a natural reaction" against a foreign element in the population, it is indeed strange that, at this same stage, such care should be taken to define those qualities of the foreign group that are supposed to constitute its "foreign-ness." Both in Germany and in the United States, "the Polish Jew" was used as a clotheshorse on which the anti-Semites draped whatever garments of "traits" and "characteristics" seemed best calculated to serve their purposes. If Jewish traits were so apparent as to provoke a natural reaction, it is also difficult to understand why, at this same period, specific questions should be included in club membership applications to determine whether applicants are Jewish.

This initial rationalization of the Jew as an "alien" who encysts in the body politic usually makes a strong appeal to certain elements. By uprooting the pre-existing cultural pattern, industrialism creates a feeling of alienage in large sections of the population. This feeling is then projected on the Jew. People brought up in the earlier culture feel that the nation is changing; that it is becoming "foreign" to them; and that they are somehow "aliens" in the land of their birth. They feel that they have been robbed of a sense of belonging, of social identification, of emotional security. They are readily disposed to believe that "something has gone wrong" — obviously something has; and that they are being "robbed of their birthright" — which, in a sense, is true. At this point they do not want to injure anyone: they merely want what they feel is rightly theirs. To individuals in this frame of mind, it seems plausible that it is the alien, the Jew, the newcomer who has disrupted the peace and tranquillity of society; who has turned the American Dream into the Industrial Nightmare.

4. THE ENEMY WITHIN

To suggest why the Jew is a favorite scapegoat and to demonstrate the uses of anti-Semitism as an ideological weapon, however, neither explains nor accounts for certain basic aspects of the phenomenon. How is one to account for the extraordinary savagery of latter-day manifestations of anti-Semitism? How is one to explain the undulant or rhythmic character of anti-Semitic outbreaks in history? How can sheer delusions drive an entire people to acts of madness? A key to these and many related questions is to be found, I believe, in the apparent *growth* of anti-Semitism in a particular society. This growth or progression is indicated in the various stages, however one may define them, through which an anti-Semitic movement passes. Walter Rathenau once defined anti-Semitism as "the vertical invasion of society by the barbarians," but do the barbarians have a fifth column? Is there an enemy within the gates?

Running through the literally hundreds of definitions of anti-Semitism that I have collected is the theme that anti-Semitism is a disease. It has been defined as "a pathological mental process," "a disease of the popular mind," "an instinctual rebellion directed against the authorities, and the cruel suppression and punishment of this instinctual rebellion, directed against oneself," "a sort of socio-pathology," "a manifestation of social disorganization," "a deep-rooted symptom of our culture," "a disease of Gentile peoples," "a cancer in the body politic," "a disease indigenous to our economic system," "a symptom of political, economic and institutional change," "a psychosis," and "a disturbance in the interaction of the relationships between the individual and civilization."

When definitions of this sort are compared with still another category of definitions, such as "an artificial product, a means for keeping reaction alive and leading it to victory," "a smoke-screen for confiscation," and "a wrench in the machinery of democracy," it is apparent that one group of definers or the other is confusing cause and effect, disease and symptom. Perhaps the answer is that anti-Semitism is a strange mixture of cause and effect. A symptom of unrest and disorganization, it is consciously used to spread unrest and disorganization. Used as a weapon in social conflicts, it is also profoundly symptomatic of social maladjustment. A product of social pathology, it is also an instrument in power politics. It is easy to demonstrate the *uses* to which anti-Semitism is put as an ideological weapon; it is not so easy to determine what it is, in our society, that seems *to produce* anti-Semitism or to induce its growth.

Assuming that anti-Semitism does have this dual aspect, that it is simultaneously a weapon and a growth or disease, the question then arises: What kind of disease? Obviously anti-Semitism is a social disease for it is only by this assumption that one can account for its rhythmic character. To regard anti-Semitism as a purely psychological phenomenon is surely as erroneous as to regard it, sociologically, as a mere manifestation of "the dislike of the unlike" or, in Hugo Valentin's definition, as "merely a special case of the hatred of the foreigner." Psychoanalytic techniques properly applied can give us a good account of the various anti-Semitic "types" and can provide valuable case histories of anti-Semites. If a sufficient number of such case histories could be accumulated and analyzed, much light would be thrown on the influences, cultural and otherwise, that produce the structure of the anti-Semitic personality and how this structure functions. But, as the psychoanalysts themselves concede, the question of the genesis of these influences would still remain unanswered. That the genesis is primarily social in character is shown by the incontestable fact that the great waves of anti-Semitism have always occurred during periods of sharp social conflict, or pronounced social change, of immense social upheaval. As Dr. Niles Carpenter has written: "The Jew has suffered when there were compelling economic and political reasons for making a victim of him." If there were an innate predisposition in human beings to devour "unlike" human beings, it can hardly be assumed that this appetite is so thoroughly satisfied at certain periods that it manifests itself only periodically. On the contrary, the history of anti-Semitism, in both its classical and its modern form, shows that it is profoundly symptomatic of political, economic, and institutional change.[10]

For purposes of clarification, one might say that anti-Semitism is a social disease having a number of peculiar characteristics. It is a kind of undulant social fever: a deep-rooted persistent disease; a disease that seems to remain dormant for long periods; a disease the manifestations of which are correlated with social disorganization. I am told that there are fevers known to science as specific diseases but which are also diagnostic of the general health of the patient. That is to say, the patient is ill with a fever but his fever chart accurately reflects, apart from the specific infection, the general state of his health. The fever is itself a disease: people can be inoculated with it; it can be communicated; it can cause death. But it is also diagnostic of conditions unrelated to the infection.

Anti-Semitism is a social disease that has permeated throughout the Western World and, to some extent, in Asia affecting, in various degrees, every class and element in society. Under certain conditions it is capable, such is its virulence, of destroying a society; of blighting a culture.

It is also an accurate symptom of the conditions which produce this blight or recession. Anti-Semitism is an excellent diagnostic device to use in studying the health and well-being of society. For it is a harbinger of war, a symptom of social sickness, a manifestation of social disorganization. The groups that spawn anti-Semitism are socially sick groups. The appearance of overt forms of anti-Semitism is always a warning sign. The society that produces the sweat or fever of anti-Semitism is a sick society — how sick, in fact, can be largely determined by the number of anti-Semites. When the fever chart shows a rise in anti-Semitism, one can rest assured that society, in some of its parts, in some of its relationships, has begun to show symptoms of deep-seated maladjustment and disorganization. The pathology of anti-Semitism leaves no room for doubt on this score.

The social function of anti-Semitism seems to be to provide people with an escape from a reality that has become intolerable. The panic stemming from an inability to master reality, writes Dr. Ernst Simmel, "has always been the underlying cause of their taking refuge in anti-semitic delusions and engaging in orgies of hate and destruction." In our time this feeling of panic arises in the individual, Dr. Simmel believes, because he has come to feel that "with the increasing industrialization of our civilization his ego is doomed to perish." While this feeling is real enough, it is not likely that it could result in group panic were it not for the fact that the same conditions that produced the panic also give rise to the temptation on the part of certain groups to use, manipulate, and organize this feeling for their particular ends and purposes. If Jews had all the traits and characteristics which anti-Semites assume that they possess, and if it be assumed that these traits universally give rise to feelings of antipathy in non-Jews, the phenomenon of anti-Semitism would remain as much of a mystery as ever. For these traits and characteristics, to the extent that they have any basis whatever in reality, are clearly the results, not the causes, of anti-Semitism. While all group antagonisms are socially conditioned, it is nevertheless clear that anti-Semitism has come to have a unique relation to the social crises of the Western World. The conditioning process has been so long, so pervasive, so thoroughgoing, that the Jew has come to be, so to speak, institutionalized as the lightning rod for aggressive impulses in periods of social crisis.

Since this manuscript was completed and delivered to the publisher, the *Fortune* public opinion poll (October 1947) has presented striking statistical proof of the contention urged in this chapter that the Jews have become the residual legatees of the countertradition in American life. Using a secret ballot — the best form of sampling to test prejudicial attitudes — *Fortune* conducted a poll on the question: "Do you think any of these groups are getting more economic power anywhere in the United States than is good for the country?" and secured the following results:

	New England and Middle Atlantic	East North Central	West North Central	South-east	South-west	Far West
	TOTAL PERCENTAGES					
Protestants	2	2	2	2	2	5	1
Catholics	12	12	11	14	10	14	12
Jews	36	34	40	41	30	32	46
Negroes	8	4	7	5	15	15	7
None of them	39	43	40	36	36	39	37
Returned blank ballot or refused	11	12	9	7	15	12	9

From a further question, "Do you think any of these groups are getting more political power anywhere in the United States than is good for the country?" the following answers were tabulated:

	New England and Middle Atlantic	East North Central	West North Central	South-east	South-west	Far West
	TOTAL PERCENTAGES					
Protestants	4	4	3	3	3	10	2
Catholics	15	17	14	15	14	16	17
Jews	21	20	21	26	16	18	31
None of them	49	50	53	49	44	49	45
Returned ballot or refused	12	12	9	7	16	13	10

Two striking conclusions can be drawn from this poll conducted by Elmo Roper, America's leading public opinion analyst: Jews are today the most popular scapegoat group in the United States (73 per cent of those who had any hostility to express along economic lines and 52 per cent of those who had any hostility to express along political lines selected the Jews as their target); and — most important — the poll shows that Jews appear to evoke the greatest hostility in those areas where they are least significant numerically. Only 16 per cent of the big-city dwellers expressed concern about their political power; but 22 per cent of the farm population and 28 per cent of the non-farm communities of 2500 and under think the Jews have too much to say in government. Agriculture in America, it might be noted, absorbs only 1 per cent of the gainfully employed Jews.

But here two important qualifications must be noted. Since Jews are heavily concentrated in large urban communities, one would have to deduct the Jewish from the non-Jewish total in order to interpret these figures with any accuracy. A general poll in New York City, for example, could be quite misleading. It is also important to keep in mind that while a high percentage of people in rural areas may give full credence to the anti-Semitic myth, it does not follow that discrimination is more pronounced in small towns than in large cities. On the contrary, it is probably less, if one may accept the testimony of Jews who have lived both in cities having a large Jewish element and in small towns where few Jews resided. What Roper was probably measuring, therefore, was the degree to which the Jewish stereotype is accepted; not the intensity of discrimination arising from group competition. The Jewish stereotype is to be found in the culture of Guatemalan Indians, few of whom have probably ever met a Jew. Hence the prevalence of the stereotype cannot be correlated with the number of Jews in a particular community; but discrimination against Jews is most rigorous in those areas in which they are sufficiently numerous to be regarded as serious group competitors.

The evidence of anti-Semitism, which this poll reveals, is as Mr. Roper rightly says "spectacular." The poll also shows, quite clearly, that Negroes are placed too low on the status ladder to make effective scapegoats in a time of crisis. Actually there is more "prejudice" against Negroes than Jews (as there is more systematic discrimination); but since the Negro is identified, as Mr. Roper points out, "as the nation's No. 1 underdog," he attracts the most sympathy and fails to incite the special form of social-economic envy which makes of anti-Semitism a most peculiar disease.

CHAPTER V

The System of

Exclusion

IN DEALING with racial minorities in the United States it is possible to measure the extent of discrimination in housing, employment, education, and related fields, by various statistical devices. The pattern of discrimination with these groups is blunt, overt, and utterly lacking in finesse or obscurity. Discrimination against Jews is no less real but it is enormously more complex. The basic explanation for this difference is to be found in the rather unique position that Jews occupy in the economy. Since this position is neither at the bottom nor at the top of the economic hierarchy, but rather in the marginal positions intermediate between these extremes, much discrimination against Jews finds expression in other than the usual forms.

Much of the discrimination against Jews is disguised as "mere competition." Discrimination against the Jew as businessman, as salesman, as doctor, as lawyer, is often hard to identify. For in an economy characterized by cutthroat competition, a specialized form of group discrimination can be readily passed off as merely another manifestation of the competitive impulse. The higher one ascends on the social and economic ladder, the less overt and the more urbane does the pattern become. And since prejudice against Jews is most intense at the middle or upper-class level, it is not

surprising that it should be difficult to trace. It is this peculiarity in the pattern of discrimination against Jews that has
always given special meaning to what is euphemistically
called "social discrimination."

1. THE POLITICS OF EXCLUSION

In a cheerful appraisal of the prospects of Jewish life in
America written in 1917, Ralph Philip Boas concluded that
"it is a happy chance for the American Jew that his age-
long persecution has either ended or has degenerated into
petty social discrimination in this country." With scarcely
a single exception, the leaders of American Jewry have
always written off "social discrimination" as petty or meaningless, an insignificant manifestation of anti-Semitism. In
large part this attitude is to be explained in terms of the
unwillingness of a proud and sensitive people to confess
that social discrimination had hurt, psychologically as well
as economically.

Not wanting to confess that social discrimination was
important, the upper-class leaders of American Jewry have
studiously discounted its significance and have attempted
to evade the pattern by establishing a set of separate and
parallel institutions. The very alacrity with which Jews,
once excluded from the upper sanctums of society, proceeded to build their own clubs, resorts, hotels, and recreational centers — and to establish their own fraternities and
sororities — is, however, the best proof that exclusion was a
real and not a fancied blow.

The failure on the part of both Jews and Gentiles to
admit the significance of social discrimination is also to be

explained in terms of the tendency in American culture to deny the existence of realities which conflict with our equalitarian ideals. "Democracy of feeling is expected of us," as Charles Horton Cooley once said, "and if we do not have it we usually simulate it." Thus social discrimination is frequently rationalized as "freedom of association" or as the tendency on the part of persons of similar backgrounds, tastes, interests, and culture to associate together. The trustees of the university club in the average American city would be grossly offended, for example, if it were suggested that the exclusion of Jews was a manifestation of anti-Semitism. "Haven't we a right," they would say, "to determine our own companions? Can't we be arbitrary in the choice of social associates? We have nothing against Jews. Some of our best friends are Jews. The point is that they would not be happy here." And so forth. Familiar in this, and many other versions, the argument seems quite plausible; but a moment's reflection is sufficient to demonstrate its specious character.

In most American cities it will be found that the reins of social control can be traced to a particular "prestige" club or similar institution. Not that the club, as such, holds the reins of power; but rather that the forces represented by its membership are the dominant forces in the community. The membership of such a club is a mirror which accurately reflects the identity and relationships of power groupings in the community. In fact, social institutions of this type are a favorite mechanism by which power relationships are established and maintained. It is precisely for this reason that membership is invested with a premium value and is regarded as important and desirable.

In *The Social Life of a Modern Community* (1941) Dr. Lloyd Warner and his associates have given a scientific demonstration of the functions of "prestige" organizations. They found, for example, that institutions of this sort help to maintain higher and lower ranking in the community; that they function as a mechanism for placing people in the class hierarchy; and that they serve to impede movement out of the middle class into the upper class. In short, they organize and regulate upward social mobility. The selective policies of such institutions have, of course, a dual effect: they impede upward social mobility for the groups excluded; but they smooth the way for those included. "If a man were accepted," they found, "by one of the upper class clubs, his position in society became higher and more secure. However, this same association, by refusing to admit certain individuals who wished to join it, might prevent their rise into a higher society than they at the time occupied." This consequence might, indeed, be regarded as a sociological commonplace. "The self-made man finds club life one of the best ways of entry into the ruling class." [1]

To say that such institutions are premised upon the mutual liking and affection of the individuals constituting the membership is sheer nonsense. Institutions of this character are not based on the innate congeniality of like-minded persons, but rather on the strategical consideration of consolidating a power relationship. Social power is organized by exclusion. The larger the number of groups that can be excluded, the less will power have to be shared. This is precisely what is implied by the term "exclusive." The function of an exclusive institution is to exclude. Therefore to characterize such institutions as "purely social" is to misconceive their reason for being.

Not only do such institutions serve to symbolize the exclusion of certain groups from decisively influential positions of power, but they consolidate and augment power in another way. Institutions of lesser social rank tend to imitate the pattern established at the top and thus the exception comes to be the rule. As an anonymous Jew wrote in the *Atlantic Monthly* for October 1924, "it is natural that men whose social life is spent together should also desire to be associated together in business. . . . This consideration cannot affect a business owned by an individual or a very small group. It will arise in concerns where the social life is well developed, as in banks, where officers are apt to belong to clubs of one kind or another."

Apart from considerations of this character, it is quite apparent, as Dr. Robert Lynd has observed, that "the overwhelmingly dominant criterion of significant likeness in our culture is likeness in wealth." Nearly all the subtleties of human likeness are played down. Our social system is one in which both "joining and the aims of organizations are not free and spontaneous but controlled by the need to muscle in on an apparatus of power which controls life chances in the culture." [2]

"Prestige" institutions show little concern for the "innate congeniality of like-minded persons." Existing to protect the positions of power and influence held by their members in the community, they concentrate on organizing social power by exclusion. In Los Angeles, where I live, everyone knows that the Athletic Club is less exclusive than the University Club and that the latter is less exclusive than the

California Club. Initiation fees, dues, and eligibility rules
neatly correlate with the measure of exclusiveness. "These
largely non-overlapping groups," wrote Dr. Lynd in *Mid-
dletown*, "carefully selected for prowess in business, highly
competitive, and constituting a hierarchy in the prestige
their membership bestows, exemplify more than do churches
or lodges the prepotent values of the dominant business men
of the city." The lodge of the small town is much less likely
to be exclusive than the city club, for the hierarchy of the
clubs reflects the hierarchy of the large, impersonal corporate enterprises — position in one is linked up with, and
makes easier the achievement of, position in the other. The
professional groups in particular are drawn to these aggre-
gates of social power, for they are well aware of the fact
that higher social position not only attracts clientele but
becomes an important measure of professional standing.

In a society verbally devoted to democratic ideals, invidious distinctions are often masked by the allegiance
which even the rich acknowledge to these ideals. In such
a society, as Lewis Browne has noted, what passes for society is wealth in its own right and is therefore "under no
duress to open its portals to Jews." [3] It was the absence of
a landed gentry and titles of nobility in America, coupled
with the existence of political democracy, that compelled
the moneyed classes to emphasize a rigid social exclusiveness as a means of consolidating their power. This pattern
of social exclusion, insofar as Jews are concerned, has been
more pronounced among the upper classes of America than
among their counterparts in Europe. Up to 1933 the exclusion of Jews from clubs, hotels, summer resorts, and residential districts was neither as obvious nor as deep-seated

in Germany as in the United States.[4] In fact, nearly every comparison of European and American anti-Semitism has stressed the fact that social discrimination has always been more flagrant here than in Europe. That social discrimination in this country reflects an underlying economic reality has merely tended to make its expression less offensive. "We do not commonly grudge a man superiority," as Cooley shrewdly observed, "if he consults our self-respect in the use of it." The folk-belief that any American can become a millionaire has, in effect, robbed social discrimination of its edge.

Where social power is based on the aristocratic concept, as in Great Britain, the Jew is more likely to find his place by achievement, as witness the careers of Disraeli, Sir Herbert Samuels, and Viscount Reading, and his social position tends to reinforce his economic power. But here the situation is quite different. "In the United States," writes David Riesman, "the locus of social power is not personified in a hereditary aristocracy. There is no feudal hierarchy, no established church, little military tradition, save in the South. Social prestige in the sense of dominating the American scene is attached to the big industrialists whose names or companies are household words: the Fords, the du Ponts, the Eugene Graces. A satellite glow attaches to the navy, the bishopric, the plantation owners, and the diplomatic service. These, and the 'old families,' have social prestige in the society-page sense. Every one of these rosters is conspicuously clear of Jews. The intellectual professions, in which Jews share: doctors, lawyers, professors, the civil service as a whole, have no accepted social place, even as compared with Europe." [5]

Social discrimination in a political democracy requires the elimination of groups since the elimination of individuals is often difficult to rationalize. From the point of view of the possession of wealth, social grace, and culture, individual Jews clearly meet the canons of social acceptability. And since they cannot be distinguished racially from the dominant groups, they must be excluded by name, as a matter of policy, as a social fiat. To be effective, such exclusion must be practiced in all institutions in which membership is the open sesame to social position. Hence the club — the social club, the university club, the country club, the town club — becomes an all-important symbol of social acceptability. Social discrimination naturally leads to economic and political discrimination since it isolates the excluded group from identification with the important symbols of power, and in the further sense that social power is an important means of protecting economic and political power. Political life issues from social life "like a somatic dream," as John Berryman has said in a brilliant short story, "The Imaginary Jew." [6]

Of the various "white" groups in our society, Jews can be most readily excluded from the category of the socially acceptable. In the first place, they are not Christians — an important count against them; and in the second place, they are mostly latecomers. Other groups would unquestionably have been excluded by name were it not for the curiously mixed character of the American population and the manner in which ethnic groups are bunched geographically. For example, where Scandinavian immigrants have settled in a community at an early date, it has been difficult to exclude them from social power as individual Scandinavians have prospered and acquired status. Once Scandinavians are admitted to social power in one community, the bar against them loses its snobbish effectiveness elsewhere. In other communities, Italians may occupy this secondary role or position. In fact, the Jews are the only secondary group not marked by racial difference that can be universally excluded.

It should also be noted that the exclusion of the Jew rests upon a pole opposite to the exclusion of the Negro. The Negro cannot be accepted because he is regarded as a member of an inferior race; but this charge is practically never raised against the Jews. When racial and cultural equality is admitted, the purpose of exclusion is much more sharply defined. By definition in the *Encyclopedia of the Social Sciences,* social discrimination involves the unequal treatment of equals and hence implies "an alteration in competitive power of those presumed to possess a freely competitive status." While it is true that certain nationality groups have not been permitted to share in social power to the extent that their numbers and success would warrant, and while it is also true that many nationality differences correlate with differences in religious affiliations, still it has been difficult to bar other white ethnic groups with the effectiveness that Jews have been barred.

The social exclusion of Jews is important, not merely in the sense that it exposes their economic position and leads to political discrimination, but also in the sense that it intensifies the prejudice against them. "It may of course be argued," writes Dr. Monroe E. Deutsch, "that as social institutions they [the clubs] have a right to choose their members as associates . . . but I firmly believe that the erection of such barriers tends to create or accentuate in the minds of some of our so-called first citizens a feeling that Jews *per se* are a separate and more or less segregated and undesirable group. If you decline to let a man eat beside you in a club, merely because he is a Jew, you are certainly helping to drive a nail into the wall of exclusion. In discussing the situation in Nazi Germany the point has often been made that those who, though not members of the party, nevertheless accepted the acts of the Nazis and helped perpetuate them in power cannot avoid sharing responsibility for the horrible deeds that were perpetrated by those whom they supported in office. I wonder whether the members of some of our exclusive clubs (*exclusive* in the proper use of the term) are not, unthinkingly (it may be), in spirit aligning themselves with Father Coughlin and Gerald L. K. Smith." [7]

The pattern of social discrimination against Jews in the United States is well-nigh universal. An examination of the membership list of the key prestige club in almost any American city will reveal that Jews have been excluded either by long-standing custom or by express provision. Even more significant, however, is the fact that this same examination will also reveal that, *at one time,* a few Jews were members of these clubs. Where German Jews were on the scene when the community started to grow, before the status lines were drawn with sharpness, they were quite frequently accepted as members. In fact, they were often taken into membership with a naïve unawareness of their Jewishness or a marked indifference to the fact. But in most cases it will be noted that, *at a later date,* further Jewish applications were not accepted, as a matter of policy, with an insulting exception being noted for "those now in good standing." Generally speaking, this change of policy has come about when status lines have begun to be drawn with sharpness in the particular community. This date has naturally varied from community to community. In some cities — Minneapolis is a case in point — the exclusionist policy first became pronounced immediately after the First World War; in other cities it developed at an earlier date; and in still other communities it did not emerge until the late thirties. Dr. Everett R. Clinchy has observed that social discrimination in general became more blatant in the 1920's.[8]

I will cite only one of many illustrations of this process. The Gipsy Club is the most important prestige organization in Huntington, West Virginia, a city of approximately 80,000 population with a small Jewish community of, perhaps, 800 people. The Jewish community in Huntington is approximately as old as the city itself. In the early history of the Gipsy Club, a few Jews were elected to membership. For the most part, they were professional men, of means, descendants of early Jewish immigrants. But the bylaws of the club were amended in 1939 to provide that membership was open only to "gentlemen of non-Jewish origin," with the usual exception noted for Jewish members then in good standing. When this amendment was first proposed, the Jewish members of the club requested that it be withdrawn and accompanied the request with two offers: first, they offered to resign from the club; and, second, they offered to secure formal written assurance from the Jewish community that the club would not be "embarrassed" by further Jewish applications. But this gesture of appeasement was flouted: the amendment was promptly adopted, in disregard of the request and its conditions.

The timing of exclusionist policies is important since it indicates that the bars are raised when social control promises to pass out of the hands of "the indigenous people." What the bars reflect, therefore, is not so much a prejudice against Jews as a desire to augment power by excluding the Jewish group. The rationalizations then offered to justify the change in policy are essentially *ex post facto* in character. The exclusion is not based upon any animus against Jews as Jews, nor is it based upon observation or experience. It expresses a social reality, not a personal eccentricity or prejudice.[9]

This brief analysis indicates that anti-Semitism in the United States, if it is to be understood, must be studied from the top down and not from the bottom up. Social exclusion, at the top, is repeated or imitated at the lower levels of the society. The business executive who has achieved the Nirvana of membership in the X club selects as his junior executives men who are ascending the socio-economic ladder on the same escalator. Seeing how the system works, these junior executives, in turn, apply exclusionist policies in the selection of their assistants. Clubs and social institutions are important mechanisms by which this self-generating, power-augmenting process is set in motion.

It is therefore absurd to regard social discrimination as an individual and unorganized phenomenon. It is, on the contrary, highly organized. A private prejudice is one thing; a policy of discrimination is another. Discrimination *against groups* necessarily implies organization. Group discrimination cannot be effective unless exclusion is adopted as a policy, and this implies a consensus or agreement which in turn implies organization. If it were simply a question of some individuals liking Jews and others not liking them, one would expect this diversity of sentiment to be reflected in a diversity of practice; but the practice, at certain levels of society, is uniform, consistent, and, one might say, universal. Even where Jews have separate clubs, these clubs are not recognized on a parity with non-Jewish clubs. For example, the Western Golf Association admits Jewish golf clubs to associate membership only.[10]

If the exclusion of Jews in the upper levels of society were unorganized, then one would expect this exclusion to cease at the point where public life begins. However, the exclusion of Jews from certain resort hotels, summer resorts, semipublic golf clubs, and certain residential districts, is part and parcel of the same organized discrimination to be found in the exclusive clubs. It represents, in fact, an extension of private policies to the outlying territories which the social elite are determined to pre-empt. In this semipublic, semiprivate area of social life, a pattern of discrimination against Jews has existed since the Grand Union Hotel incident of 1877. From the Eastern seaboard, it has gradually spread through the Middle West. In the resort areas around Lake Michigan "incidents" have been occurring for the last twenty years. For example, a colony of lake-shore cottages occupied by Jewish families near Milwaukee was burned in 1928 and again in 1929. The pattern is less pronounced on the West Coast but it exists even there.

This same upper-class snobbishness is reflected in what might be called "the concept of the gentleman." In the First World War, the manual used by medical advisory boards in selecting army personnel contained this extraordinary statement: "The foreign born, especially Jews, are more apt to malinger than the native born," while the manual used in training officers at Plattsburg defined the "ideal officer" as "a Christian gentleman." On February 6, 1932, the *Army and Navy Register* contained an article pointing out why more Jews were not to be found in the armed services: "The pay is poor, there is no profit in it, and, more, they might be called upon to die for the country of their adoption." The usual protest was filed, of course, and the usual disclaimer was noted in the *Register*. At about the same time, ads appeared in the Philadelphia press calling for "Gentile" recruits for the National Guard. Again the usual protests were entered and the usual retraction obtained. Minimizing the number of Jews in the professional officer class is, again, merely another device whereby social power is maximized for other groups. One may even infer that the pronounced anti-Semitism of men like Major General George Van Horn Moseley, U.S.A., Retired, stems from their identification with this class.[11]

2. THE OLD SCHOOL TIE

Social discrimination in American colleges and universities is one of the most important means by which group attitudes are conditioned in this country. To those who believe that social discrimination is a petty and insignificant issue, Heywood Broun gave the correct answer years ago, when he said that it was his impression that "social slights may be the most important of all" and observed that "the prejudice of the college fraternity and the college club can scar a youngster for his entire life." The freshman year in college is an extremely important year in the life of the average college student. Since so many students, particularly in the Middle West, come to college from small towns and rural areas where the word "Jew" has only metaphorical or possibly Biblical connotations, they receive their first basic instruction in the politics of prejudice in their freshman year. The experience is probably no less significant for Jewish than for Gentile students. Although he may be familiar with prejudice, the average Jewish student first encounters total and arbitrary exclusion in college.

In *Personal History*, Vincent Sheean gives a vivid and unforgettable account of how he happened by mistake to join a Jewish fraternity. "Incredible though it seemed afterwards," he writes, "I had never known a Jew in my life and had no idea that there were so many of them growing there under my eyes. I had only the romantic and provincial notions about Jews: thought of them as bearded old gentlemen with magic powers and vast stores of gold." John Berryman, in the short story to which I have referred, tells of how he "arrived at a metropolitan university without any clear idea of what in modern life a Jew was, — without even a clear consciousness of having seen one. . . . I had not escaped, of course, a sense that humans somewhat different from ourselves, called 'Jews,' existed as in the middle distance and were best kept there, but this sense was of the vaguest. From what it was derived I do not know; I do not recall feeling the least curiosity about it, or about Jews; I had, simply, from the atmosphere of an advanced heterogeneous democratic society, ingathered a gently negative attitude toward Jews." As with Sheean, his discovery of the

Jewish issue in college was "the beginning of my instruction in social life proper."

The exclusion of Jews from the leading American Greek-letter fraternities and sororities, like their exclusion from social clubs, is an almost universal pattern. It has existed — with an exception noted here and there — as long as these fraternities and sororities have existed. An examination of the dates on which most of the present-day Jewish fraternities and sororities were established indicates that they came into existence between 1906 and 1920. The years from 1906 to 1920 would correspond approximately with the period when the second-generation immigrant group was just beginning to reach college age. There can be no doubt that the Jewish fraternities and sororities came into existence as a reaction against the exclusionist policies of the non-Jewish organizations — as a defense mechanism.

The motivation for the exclusionist policies of American fraternities and sororities is essentially the same as that to be found in other social institutions. It is patently nonsensical to speak of college fraternities as though they were the end-product of some instinctive process by which like-minded individuals are sorted into special categories. If an instinctive aversion against Jews existed, how did Vincent Sheean, with no prior familiarity with Jews, manage to join a Jewish fraternity? It is a matter of common knowledge that freshmen are "rushed" for the most specific reasons: social standing, wealth, family connections, special talents, and athletic ability. Fraternities and sororities are power-building institutions, mechanisms by which social power is organized. The offensive-defensive alliances formed in college naturally tend to carry over into later life. Given four years in prep school and four years in college and the average non-Jewish student has been thoroughly instructed in the social uses of prejudice. This is not to say, however, that colleges originate the practice. "Every institution," wrote Charles Horton Cooley, "suffers from the sins of every other; and so our universities struggle as they can with deficiencies left by the family, the school, the economic system and the general trend of life, contributing, no doubt, a few errors of their own."

According to Horace M. Kallen, the cleavage between Greek-letter men and barbarians on American college campuses represents an embryonic form of class conflict which occurs on an intellectual and social level. When he writes that "undergraduate feelings, interest, and ambitions are *integrated*" by social institutions such as clubs and fraternities, he is, in effect, saying that prejudice is organized by these means.[12] It is this integration of sentiment that robs our educational institutions of much of their democratic significance. "For the necessary basis of democracy, particularly in the academic world, is social heterogeneity" — the social heterogeneity to be found in the larger world outside the campus.

In much the same curious way in which the exclusionist policies of clubs are often defended in terms of "democracy of association," so the college fraternity system has been praised as the epitomization of liberalism. Speaking at the thirty-eighth annual meeting of the National Inter-Fraternity Conference in New York on December 1, 1946, Dr. H. E. Stone, Dean of Students at the University of California, implied that only communists or fascists would think of challenging the right of fraternities to operate as secret societies with selected memberships. Branding all those who advocate the voluntary elimination of exclusionist bars or the abandonment of the fraternity system as "illiberal," Dr. Stone said:

It is no accident that specific demands have been made to break all racial bars to fraternity membership and that specific cases have arisen to force the issue.

The mass strikes, the effort for economic domination of the individual, the new race pressures and the opposition to secret selective associations are offsprings and outgrowths of a philosophy of "social action" deeply imbedded in a host of government agencies and taking its roots in Marxian concepts.

Here, by clear implication, a challenge to the exclusionist policies of the fraternities is correlated with an attack on the economic system; one can only assume, therefore, that Dean Stone considers secret selective associations a prop to economic privilege.

The exclusion practiced by fraternities and sororities is closely related to similar practices to be noted in the admission of students and the selection of faculty. Many university instructors and administrative officials are themselves members of fraternities which practice exclusion. Noting this fact, Heywood Broun suggested that "part of student prejudice might be traced to professorial or presidential policy." It cannot be denied that Jews have had a difficult time in securing appointments as college and university instructors; that particular departments in particular institutions have traditionally been closed to Jews; and that advancement for Jewish instructors has been retarded by anti-Semitic prejudices. For example, in the *American Jewish Yearbook* for 1937–1938 one finds the statement: "It is very difficult these days for Jews to become full professors in the leading universities." A detailed exposition of the difficulties which Jews have long encountered in the academic field may be found in Ludwig Lewisohn's famous autobiography. This difficulty, in turn, is closely related to the much larger question of the employment of Jews as teachers in secondary schools, both public and private, long a sore point with Jews, and the subject of numerous inquiries and investigations.[13] Discrimination in the secondary schools has, of course, made it difficult for Jews to advance to positions in the colleges and universities.

In appraising the significance of anti-Semitic practices of various kinds in American colleges and universities, it is well to keep in mind that in Europe colleges and universities were always seedbeds of prejudice. Furthermore, it is the totality of college experience, rather than any particular practice, that is important. It is a matter, as Broun said, "of slurring remarks, social aloofness, exclusion from honorary fraternities, glee clubs, managership of social organizations; difficulty of election to honorary fraternities, discrimination in campus politics, exclusions of Jewish fraternities from inter-fraternity boards; offensive jokes in student publications and student dramatics, and a general unfriendliness." While the general situation has probably improved since Broun wrote these comments in 1931, it is still bad. The anti-Semitism to be found in American colleges and universities is both a cause and an effect of middle-class prejudice. College and university students in this country are largely recruited from the middle class.[14] As such they reflect middle-class attitudes and, at the same time, these attitudes are re-enforced by college and university experiences. The trump card of anti-Semitism in higher education, however, consists in the quota system.

3. THE QUOTA SYSTEM

The only profession I know of that does not bar Jews is the rabbinical profession.

— DR. STEPHEN S. WISE

It is almost impossible to fix a date when American colleges and universities began to adhere to an official or unofficial quota system. The evidence would seem to indicate, however, that the exclusion of Jews from fraternities and sororities and from the teaching profession was a factor that antedated and contributed to the rise of the quota system. It is also apparent that the quota system first began to pinch, so far as Jews were concerned, in the period immediately after the First World War. In fact, it was President A. L. Lowell's commencement address in June 1922 — the celebrated "Harvard Incident" — that first brought the whole question into the open. President Lowell's address followed by two years the launching of Henry Ford's attack against the Jews. If the latter was given added significance by reason of the fact that it was launched by a leading American industrialist, so the formal proposal of a *numerus clausus* was given added emphasis when offered by a Lowell who was president of Harvard University.

With the apparently satisfactory resolution of the Harvard incident — the Board of Overseers repudiated the suggestion of quotas much as Henry Ford later retracted his charges against the Jews — the quota issue seemed to have been settled. But such was not the case. In *Christians*

Only, Heywood Broun and George Britt demonstrated that an ever-increasing number of Jewish medical students were being forced to study abroad, in Vienna, Glasgow, and other European centers. Starting in the Eastern universities, the quota system rapidly spread west and south. In 1931 the president of the University of Alabama stated that if the university accepted all the applications it was then receiving from Jewish students, the freshman class in the school of medicine would be filled twice over and native Alabamans would be altogether excluded.

The pressure of Jewish students to enter the "free professions," notably law and medicine, has always reflected the bias against them in those professions having a direct, functional relation to the key American industries. For example, the difficulty that Jews have experienced in securing employment as technicians and engineers has automatically deflected many of them into law and medicine. Jews have sought out the free professions for the simple reason that, once a diploma and certificate have been obtained, no one can prevent a Jew, or anyone else for that matter, from attempting to earn a living. Quotas have been more difficult to maintain in the law schools than in medicine, since medical training requires hospital facilities, internship, and so on. But there has been a great deal of prejudice, at one time or another, against Jews in law, and the bar associations of several American cities have in fairly recent times considered the advisability of a quota system. Since the free professions have always had a special attraction for students from the middle class, both Jewish and Gentile, it is not surprising that sharp conflicts have developed in the professions. It should be noted, in this connection, that several studies have shown that labor groups are more likely to be anti-Negro than white-collar groups; but that the latter are more likely to be anti-Semitic. The all-important factor here, of course, is group competition. Discrimination against Jews is likely to be most pronounced at the middle-class level because it is here that group competition is concentrated. Indeed, this is one of the peculiarities of anti-Semitism.

Two days after the atomic bomb story was released to the press, New York newspapers carried a small item to the effect that Dr. Ernest M. Hopkins, president of Dartmouth College, not only admitted but vigorously defended the existence of a quota system at Dartmouth. The admission came in the form of a letter written to Herman Shumlin under date of April 2, 1945, but not released to the press until August 7.[15] In this letter Dr. Hopkins took the position that a quota was necessary, first, to maintain Dartmouth's tradition of "racial tolerance," and, second, to protect the Jews from anti-Semitism. If Dartmouth did not have a quota system, Dr. Hopkins reasoned, it would soon be forced to exclude Jews altogether, which, in turn, would be adverse to Jewish interests generally. "Dartmouth College," said Dr. Hopkins, "is a Christian college founded for the Christianization of its students."[16] That Dr. John S. Dickey, the new president of Dartmouth, was a member of the President's Committee on Civil Rights would indicate that the Hopkins statement no longer represents official Dartmouth policy. I have heard, on excellent authority, that Dr. Dickey is making a strong effort to eliminate the quota policy.

Recently a great amount of evidence has been unearthed

which establishes beyond question that, pious commencement day disclaimers to the contrary, the quota system is deeply entrenched in American colleges and universities. One such study indicates that the enrollment of Jews in medical schools has been reduced by approximately 50 per cent in the last twenty years. In the medical schools included in this survey, the class of 1937 numbered 794 Jewish students; the class of 1940 only 477. In the class of 1920, 46 Jewish students were admitted to the College of Physicians and Surgeons of Columbia University, whereas only 12 were admitted in 1940, despite a constant and mounting list of Jewish applications. Jewish enrollment dropped in the medical school at Syracuse University from 19.44 per cent in 1936 to 6 per cent in 1942; from 40 per cent at Cornell University, twenty-five years ago, to 5 per cent at the present time. Practically every medical school in the country asks for a statement of race or religion or both and some of them request photographs and even inquire if the student has ever changed his name. A list of some of the medical schools which have a rigid quota system, denied in words but applied in fact, would include the following: Yale, Johns Hopkins, Harvard, Dartmouth, Cornell, Rochester, Duke, Virginia, Northwestern, Syracuse, Baylor, and Bowman Gray School of Medicine of Wake Forest College; while those having a mildly discriminatory policy would include the University of Chicago, University of Maryland, Boston University, Wayne University, Washington University, University of Cincinnati, University of California, Jefferson Medical College, Temple University, Columbia and the University of Pennsylvania.[17] Not only is this pattern fairly universal in American medical schools, but it has apparently become more rigid in the last twenty years.

That the quota system also exists in liberal arts colleges is well established. In a survey of the admission practices of 700 liberal arts colleges, Dan W. Dodson found that 99 per cent of the institutions that replied denied the existence of quotas against Catholics and Jews. Only 4 institutions of the 520 who answered his questionnaire admitted that they excluded Catholics; only 7 admitted that they excluded Jews; while 94 institutions, in the South, readily admitted, of course, that they excluded Negroes. "These figures," writes Mr. Dodson, "give a true measure of the pervasive hypocrisy on the issue. Virtually all college and university officials are aware that discrimination is the rule rather than the exception." Here, for example, are a few of Dodson's findings: Colgate regularly admits about 4 or 5 Jewish students a year although it receives from 200 to 300 Jewish applications; Dartmouth admits only 25 or 30 students a year out of 500 or more annual Jewish applications; while Princeton maintains a tight Jewish quota of less than 4 per cent of its enrollment. Mr. Dodson found that "flagrant discrimination" is practiced by the Big Seven women's colleges: Barnard, Wellesley, Smith, Bryn Mawr, Vassar, Mount Holyoke, and Radcliffe. While the existence of the quota system is usually denied, occasionally one finds a candid official. Thus Emerson College in Boston — and a slight irony may be noted here — rejected the application of a Jewish girl with the notation: "Due to the fact that our enrollments have become out of balance, we are obliged to refuse all Jewish applicants until a balance has been restored." [18] And, in the early thirties, Lasell

Seminary in Boston admitted the existence of a 3 per cent quota.

In a recent report, the Mayor's Committee on Unity in New York found: (1) that discrimination against Jews, Catholics, and Negroes is practiced in the private nonsectarian schools of higher learning; (2) that there is reason to believe that the situation has deteriorated rapidly in the last decade; (3) that almost without exception the nonsectarian private colleges and professional schools in New York City have established limitations on the percentage of students admitted from New York City in all or many of their divisions; and (4) that out-of-town institutions accept very few New Yorkers on the grounds that they give priority to their local populations.[19] That most of this discrimination is aimed against Jews cannot be denied. A similar pattern has been revealed in Boston.[20] It is, indeed, amazing to note that university officials have burned incriminating evidence in their files on the eve of official inquiries into their admission practices.[21]

The Decennial Census of Jewish College Students, issued on September 29, 1947, reveals that the proportion of Jewish students enrolled in professional courses fell from 8.8 per cent in 1935 to 7 per cent in 1946. "The fact that Jews go to college today in practically the same proportion as eleven years ago," the report states, "leads the vocational service to believe that the decline in professional courses is due, at least in part, to increased discrimination against Jews in professional schools and departments."

The discrimination against Jews as teachers and instructors has a significance which far transcends the individual frustrations to which it gives rise. "It is a pedagogic truism," writes Maxwell H. Goldberg, "that the teacher transmits attitudes, as well as facts and skills. . . . When, therefore, in building up and maintaining their teaching staffs, school executives and other authorities practice social discrimination or countenance its practice, the harm they do is many times compounded. Directly, and via intermediate officials, their biased policy and practice seep down into the body of the teaching staff itself. Here, other discriminatory attitudes are newly stimulated in teachers who may hitherto have been free of them; or such attitudes are strengthened in teachers who are already infected." [22] Then, of course, youngsters, taught by the example of their elders, carry the lessons learned into their lives as adult members of the community. "Education for democratic living is thereby doubly sabotaged at one of its main generators — the school."

The real significance of quotas in the professional schools consists in the fact that these quotas buttress the much more significant discrimination against Jews in our economy. While the evidence, here, is largely circumstantial, it is nevertheless quite persuasive. A year or so ago, Dr. Albert Sprague Coolidge of Harvard University testified before a Massachusetts legislative committee that "we know perfectly well that names ending in 'berg' or 'stein' have to be skipped by the board of selection of students for scholarships in chemistry." How did this curious practice arise at Harvard University? Because, as Dr. Coolidge explained, of "a gentlemen's agreement" between university officials and the chemical industry that sponsors the scholarships. The chemical industry in America happens to be rigidly exclusionist insofar as Jews are concerned. It is perfectly clear, therefore, that university practices in many cases have been brought into alignment with industrial practices.

While quotas have been more difficult to maintain in dentistry than in medicine, the dental profession and the schools in dentistry have been "alerted" to the danger of unrestricted admission policies. In the December 1944 issue of the *Journal of Dental Education* Dr. Harlan H. Horner, secretary of the Council on Dental Education, argued that "determined efforts should be made on a national scale to counteract the trend toward marked racial and geographical imbalance in the entire group of dental students." Originally prepared as a "confidential report" to an advisory body established by the House Committee on Education, this article aroused a storm of protest. The 1944 proceedings of the American Association of Dental Schools contains a passage deploring the tendency of students of foreign birth "or near-foreign parentage" to seek admission to dental schools. Still a third document, a report submitted to Columbia University by the Council on Dental Education, warns against "the excessive number of dental students from one or two racial strains . . . far in excess of the ratio of such groups to the total population." A similar report was submitted also to the officials of New York University.[23]

While the deans of the dental schools were later advised by the Council on Dental Education that the council was "unequivocally opposed to the use of quotas for admissions based on racial or religious lines," [24] this disclaimer came only as a result of the furore which the Horner report had aroused. Actually the report was published with the approval of the nine members of the Council on Dental Education, which is made up of three members from the

American Dental Association, three from the American Association of Dental Schools, and three from the American Association of Dental Examiners. It must have represented, therefore, something more significant than the personal opinion of Dr. Horner. One wonders if the dentists have ever suspected that a connection might exist between the number of Jews seeking admission to dental schools and the exclusion of Jews from a whole segment of American business, industry, and finance. If they were realistic, the dental associations should submit their protests, not to the dental schools, but to the leaders of heavy industry in America. Other professions are also being "alerted." In the January 1945 issue of the *Journal of Clinical Psychology*, the editor proposed that admissions "of a certain racial group," later identified as Jews, to professional training in psychiatry be restricted in order to prevent this group from "dominating" and "exploiting" the profession. Has anyone ever complained that the Welsh should not be permitted to "dominate" the coal mines of England or that Negroes should not monopolize domestic service in the United States?

The merits of the conventional arguments advanced to defend the quota system will be discussed later; but the facts presented in this section justify certain conclusions. First coming to general public attention in the early twenties, the quota system has now become a well-established institutional practice. More pronounced in the East than elsewhere, it has nevertheless tended to spread geographically and occupationally. Strikingly apparent in medicine, it has also been established in other professions and now exists in a fairly large number of liberal arts colleges. Where quotas have been established, limitations have tended to become increasingly severe. It is also clear that quotas have been established in the free professions largely because of the bar against the employment of Jews in the key industries, as shown by the fact that the engineering and technical schools have never bothered to establish quotas. In fact the real basis for the quota system, as for most forms of social discrimination, is to be found in the structure of the dominant American industries.

CHAPTER VI *In the Middle of the Middle Class*

THE FORMS of discrimination traced in the preceding chapter are essentially reflections of a basic reality — the anomalous position that Jews occupy in the American economy. In itself this position constitutes the best evidence of a strong underlying pattern of anti-Semitism in the United States. Similarly the best proof of the mythical character of the anti-Semitic ideology is to be found in an examination of the position which Jews occupy in our economy. For the notion that Jews dominate or control the American economy is one of the greatest myths of our time.

1. THE MARGINAL MAN

The quickest way to define the position that Jews occupy in the American economy is to mark off the fields in which Jewish participation is nonexistent or of negligible importance. This of course constitutes a reversal of the anti-Semite's technique, for he always starts by defining the areas in which Jews play a prominent part. A brief examination of the *Fortune* survey (*Jews in America*, 1936) will indicate, graphically enough, those sectors of the economy in which Jewish participation is of negligible importance.

Contrary to the ancient anti-Semitic myth, Jews are a minor influence in banking and finance. Of the 420 listed directors of the 19 members of the New York Clearing House in 1933, only 33 were Jews. "There are practically no Jewish employees of any kind," reads the *Fortune* survey, "in the largest commercial banks — and this in spite of the fact that many of their customers are Jews." While a few Jewish firms, such as Kuhn, Loeb & Company, J. & W. Seligman & Company, and Speyer & Company, have a well-established reputation in the investment banking field, Jewish influence in investment banking in the United States is wholly insignificant. Neither in commercial nor in investment banking are Jews an important factor. If the national rather than the New York scene were examined in detail, it could be demonstrated that Jewish influence in American banking is even less significant than the *Fortune* survey indicates. For the exclusion of Jews from the boards of local banks, outside New York, is a fact that can be readily verified by the most cursory investigation. In related fields of finance, such as insurance, the Jewish influence is virtually nonexistent. "The absence of Jews in the insurance business," to quote from the survey, "is noteworthy." Generally speaking, Jews participate in the insurance business almost exclusively as salesmen catering to a preponderantly Jewish clientele. Nor do Jews figure, in any significant manner, in the various stock exchanges across the country.

If the Jewish participation in banking and finance is negligible, it is virtually nonexistent in heavy industry. There is not a single sector of the heavy industry front in which their influence amounts to dominance or control or in which it can even be regarded as significant. A minor exception might be noted in the scrap-iron and steel business, an outgrowth of the junk business, which has been a direct contribution of Jewish immigrants to the American economy. The scrap-iron business, it should be emphasized, is wholly peripheral to heavy industry in general. Similarly the waste-products industry, including nonferrous scrap metal, paper, cotton rags, wool rag, and rubber, is largely Jewish controlled. But, here again, control of waste products is a symbol of exclusion rather than a badge of influence.

The following significant industries are all "equally non-Jewish," according to the *Fortune* survey, namely, coal, auto, rubber, chemical, shipping, transportation, shipbuilding, petroleum, aviation, and railroading. The important private utility field, including light and power, telephone and telegraph, is most emphatically non-Jewish; and the same can be said of lumber, agriculture, mining, dairy farming, food processing, and the manufacture of heavy machinery. So far as heavy industry is concerned, one can best summarize the findings of the *Fortune* survey by saying that Jews are the ragpickers of American industry, the collectors of waste, the processors of scrap iron.

Jewish participation in the "light industries" field is largely restricted to the distribution end. In the manufacture of wool, the Jewish influence is slight (from 5 to 10 per cent of production); somewhat higher in silk, it is only 5 per cent in cotton. In the distribution of wool, silk, and cotton products, however, Jews do play a significant role. Their participation in the important meat-packing industry is limited, as one might expect, to the production of the kosher meat pack. In a few industries, such as the manufacture of furniture, they are an important factor. But in most of the light industries, their numerical significance is often greater than the volume of production which they actually control. In the manufacture of boots and shoes, for example, they are a 40 per cent minority in numbers but control only 29 per cent of the volume of production. In the entire light industries field, the principal exception to the generally non-Jewish pattern of control is to be found in the clothing industry, which, like the scrap business, might properly be regarded as a Jewish contribution to American industry.

While Jews play an important role in the buying of tobacco and control some of the large cigar manufacturing concerns, their participation in the mass production of cigarettes, which is emphatically big business, is negligible. Controlling about half the large distilling concerns, Jews fall far short of outright control of the liquor industry. In the general merchandizing field, the important fact to be noted is that, with the exception of apparel goods, Jews have been rigidly excluded from the various chain-store enterprises. Jewish participation is virtually nonexistent both in the drugstore chains and in the food distributing chains. Woolworth and Kress, for example, are 95 per cent non-Jewish. In the mail-order business, Montgomery-Ward and Sears, Roebuck are both non-Jewish, although it was Julius Rosenwald who built the latter company into the great institution it is today. While some of the department stores in New York and in the East are controlled by Jews, their influence in this field diminishes as one moves west.

Again contrary to popular belief, Jewish participation

in publishing is not significant. In the magazine field, the *New Yorker*, the *American Mercury*, and *Esquire* are about the only magazines that are controlled by Jews. The measure of Jewish influence in this field might, therefore, be estimated by comparing the circulation of these publications with the circulation of such magazines as the *Saturday Evening Post, Collier's*, the *Woman's Home Companion, Good Housekeeping, Look*, and *Time, Life*, and *Fortune*. Jewish participation in the advertising field is about 1 to 3 per cent of the total. However, they are a fairly important factor in the book publishing business and in the job-and-trade printing industry in the larger cities; and, in two new industries, radio and motion pictures, their influence is significant. "The whole picture of industry, business, and amusements," concludes the *Fortune* survey, "may be summed up by repeating that while there are certain industries which Jews dominate and certain industries in which Jewish participation is considerable, there are also vast industrial fields, generally reckoned as the most typical of our civilization, in which they play a part so inconsiderable as not to count in the total picture."

Ironically enough, the negligible influence of Jews in American industry and finance is usually cited, as in the *Fortune* survey, as proof that they do not control the economy and therefore should not be regarded as a "menace" by non-Jews. So much is, indeed, eloquently self-evident. But what this same pattern also indicates is the far more significant fact that Jews have been excluded from participation in the basic industries of the country, the industries that exercise a decisive control over the entire economy. It is precisely this pattern of exclusion from industry and finance that one finds reflected in the pattern of social exclusion traced in the preceding chapter. Since Jews have been unable to penetrate entire segments of the American economy, it naturally follows that their concentration in certain fields is a result, not a cause, of discrimination. "What is remarkable about Jews in America," to quote from the *Fortune* survey, "is not their industrial power but their curious industrial distribution, their tendency to crowd together in particular squares of the checkerboard." But to explain this concentration, as the *Fortune* survey does, in terms of "psychological traits — their clannishness, their tribal inclination" — is certainly to ignore economic realities. One might with greater plausibility explain the crowding together on the checkerboard in terms of the tribal inclination of non-Jews. While certain cultural and sociological factors have been influential in bringing about the concentration of Jews in certain restricted fields of economic endeavor, and also help to explain their association together as Jews in these fields, the basic explanation must be found in the systematic exclusion of Jews from the dominant businesses and industries.

2. THE MARGINAL BUSINESS

Just what are the characteristics of these "particular squares on the checkerboard" in which Jews are concentrated? Generally speaking, the businesses in which Jews are concentrated are those in which a large risk-factor is involved; businesses peripheral to the economy; businesses originally regarded as unimportant; new industries and businesses; and businesses which have traditionally carried a certain element of social stigma, such, for example, as the amusement industry and the liquor industry. Not being able to penetrate the key control industries, Jews have been compelled to occupy the interstitial, the marginal, positions in the American economy. In short, it is the qualitative rather than the quantitative aspect of their participation in industry and finance that most graphically delineates their position.

The fact that Jewish businesses are essentially marginal in character has manifold collateral ramifications. It means, for example, that the Jewish lawyer occupies somewhat the same position in relation to the practice of the law that Jewish businessmen occupy in relation to American business. "The most important office law business in America," reads the *Fortune* survey, "such as the law business incidental to banking, insurance, trust-company operation, investment work, railroading, patents, admiralty, and large corporation matters in general is in the hands of non-Jewish firms many of which, even though they have numerous Jewish clients, have no Jewish partners." The success or failure of Jewish middle-class professional groups generally is related to the success or failure of those businesses in which Jews are a decisive or important influence. This circumstance gives the appearance of Jewish exclusiveness or clannishness to relationships which are primarily conditioned by non-Jewish exclusiveness and clannishness. Similarly, that Jews appear to wield more economic power than they do is the result of an illusion created by their concentration in businesses which make them conspicuous and which place them in a direct relation to the consuming public. Thus by and large the traditional European pattern of Jewish-Gentile economic relations has been repeated in America.

Today the marginal economic position of the Jew is more exposed in America than ever before. The structure of American capitalism has been profoundly altered since the first great waves of Jewish immigration in the eighties. Today heavy industry holds the reins of power in the United States, economically, politically, and socially. Our great industrial systems have long since achieved complete integration and the structure of power that they represent is an established and formidable reality. No longer directly dependent on finance capital, heavy industry nowadays finances its operations out of its vast reserves and accumulations. Generally speaking, Jewish businesses have been "nepotistic, speculative, and otherwise old-fashioned in comparison with the cartelized, impersonal industrial corporations." [1] Of 1939 sales in the United States, 87 per cent by value of mineral products, 60 per cent of agricultural products, and 42 per cent of manufactured products were cartelized. Opportunities for the small-scale type of enterprise, in which Jews have long specialized, diminish in direct relation to the growth of cartels and the rise of monopolies.

The types of business in which Jews are concentrated, by their very nature, fail to invest ownership with social power and prestige. Too often these businesses lack the artisan beginnings, the long identification with certain family names, and the intimate relationship to a particular community that have invested so many American industries and the families that control them with an extraordinary social power. Clothing stores and motion picture theaters are not nearly so impressive as mines and mills, factories and railroads. Some of the industries in which Jews have prospered, such as radio and motion pictures, have been exceptionally lucrative in their infancy precisely because they were on the fringe of modern capitalism. By reason of their lucky identification with these industries, originally regarded as quite unimportant, some Jews have risen more rapidly economically than they have socially or culturally. These are, in Mr. Riesman's phrase, "the flamboyant social pariahs" to whose activities the anti-Semites devote so much attention. But the economic "upstart," the *nouveau riche* type, has always been a product of similar conditions. "The Newport millionaires," writes Miriam Beard, "who entertained with 'monkey dinners' and 'bullfrog dinners' were not Jewish; neither were the Bradley-Martins and James Hazen Hyde, whose fetes so shocked American public opinion. Gentiles, not Jews, exhibited the most grotesque eccentricities in the Gilded Age." [2] As these new businesses have come to be recognized as a "good thing," they have been quickly stabilized by familiar economic processes and the upstarts have gradually been displaced by men "of sound judgment." Today, for example, Jewish influence in both radio and motion pictures is on the wane.

The steadily growing power which industrial groups have come to exercise in our society not only weakens such economic power as the Jews possess, but it also weakens the position of their allies, the liberal-minded elements of the non-Jewish middle class. Both in Germany and in the United States, the heavy industry groups have tended to be extremely reactionary in politics: protagonists of high tariffs, bitter opponents of organized labor, advocates of a blatantly nationalistic foreign policy. The nature of heavy

industry tends to insulate its owners and managers from
direct contact with, or dependence upon, public opinion.
As Mr. Riesman points out, the heavy industry groups have
everywhere shown a marked sympathy with the anti-
Semitic rationalization of "productive" versus "predatory"
capital. It is not by chance, therefore, that Henry Ford,
once the most influential American anti-Semite, should have
been smitten with this distinction or that he should have
inveighed so strenuously against "international finance,"
"Wall Street," and "the bankers." As the leaders of heavy
industry become increasingly preoccupied with the necessity of acquiring a direct control over government — a
tendency already most pronounced in the United States —
political power tends to merge with industrial power. This
tendency has universally marked, if not the end, the beginning of the end, of that happy period of bourgeois
liberalism in which the Jews have flourished and prospered.

3. THE MARGINAL CLASS

Measured in quantitative terms, Jews constitute a marginal class in American society; socio-economically speaking, they are in the middle of the middle class. "Of one
hundred Jews gainfully employed in the United States,"
writes Nathan Reich, "between thirty-five and forty draw
their sustenance from commercial occupations; between
fifteen and twenty from manufacturing industries; some
ten or twelve from the professions; and the remainder are
scattered among personal services, transportation, construction trades and other occupations." [3] For the general

population the corresponding figures are: trade, 13.8 per cent; manufacturing industries, 26.3 per cent; professional services, 6.8 per cent. The trading group, among Jews, is almost three times larger than the national average; the Jewish professional group is about twice the national average; while the number of Jews in manufacturing falls below the national figure. Claiming 17.5 per cent of all gainfully occupied Americans, agriculture absorbs only about 1 per cent of the gainfully occupied Jews. A large section of American Jewry is, therefore, concentrated in the lower, middle, and upper middle class. This concentration could be more strikingly indicated if the New York situation could be isolated from the national scene. For example, the "Yankee City" investigations of Dr. Lloyd Warner indicated that almost half of the Jewish families in Yankee City belonged to the middle class. It would be wide of the mark, however, to say that most Jews belong to the middle class, for the facts show that they constitute a special element within the middle class.

Sociologists have long called attention to a tendency on the part of ethnic groups to concentrate in particular occupational fields.[4] Related to the cultural backgrounds of the various groups, this tendency represents an aspect of cultural specialization and also, of course, of group discrimination. The Italian who was a bricklayer or stonemason in the Old World naturally gravitated to the same type of work in America. But the tendency is also, in some respects, an aspect of the interrelations that have existed between immigrant groups. Heavy Jewish immigration to the United States coincided with heavy non-Jewish immigration from the same or adjacent regions. Many of the Jewish immigrants were traders or the sons of traders, familiar by tradition with the ways of commerce and the techniques of trade. For generations Jews had filled the function of a middle class in relation to the peasants of Central and Southeastern Europe. Thus the mass immigration of peasants from these areas to the United States created a special opportunity for Jews to rise rapidly into the middle-class category by performing the same functions here that they had long performed in Europe for the same groups. The existence of this special opportunity vis-à-vis non-Jewish immigrants, coupled with their exclusion from other fields and the circumstance that they were late arrivals on the American scene, accounts for the striking economic concentration of American Jews in the middle-class category.

The conjunction of Jewish with non-Jewish immigration also accounts, in large measure, for the rapid rise of Jewish immigrants in social status. For example, Dr. Warner found that the Jews of Yankee City had climbed the status ladder faster than any other ethnic group, including groups that had been in the city for one or two generations longer than the Jews.[5] This remarkable upper mobility on the part of Jewish immigrants has tended to create toward them a dual hostility: on the part of the non-Jewish "native" middle class and on the part of those immigrant groups who have been slow in developing their own middle class. Furthermore this hostility is likely to increase as the pressure of monopoly undermines the security of the native-born middle class and as the other immigrant groups, such as the Poles, verge on middle-class status. The nub of the matter, as Jacob Lestchinsky has pointed out, consists in the fact that the Jews "have quite naturally taken, so to speak, a redundant position between the Anglo-Saxon and the other ethnic groups." It is this special or "in-between" position of the Jews that constitutes their particular peril in the United States. In the past, Jews have experienced comparatively little competition since, as Lestchinsky notes, "they largely occupied positions left over by the British-Americans and other dominant groups"; but today both prongs of a pincers movement can be seen encircling their exposed position.

Various economic factors, in the past, have tended to protect the Jews, as a group, against competition. The Jewish immigration from 1900 to 1925 included proportionately more workers than did the early waves of immigration in the period from 1880 to 1900. Since large numbers of these workers went directly into the needle trades in New York as other groups were leaving these trades for more profitable employment, direct group competition was kept at a minimum. But the decline of Jews in the needle trades, which began in 1919, has tended to eliminate the protected industrial position of Jewish workers. As S. M. Melamed has pointed out, "in the tailor shop the Jewish working man competed with no one else. But when he leaves the shop and invades the field of the retailer, the peddler, the promoter or the real estate man, he will tread upon somebody's corn." [6] It is perhaps not a mere coincidence, therefore, that the date on which Jewish employment began to decline in the pivotal needle trades should have also marked a sharp rise in anti-Semitism in the United States.

The "peculiarities" of the position occupied by Jews in the American economy has probably occasioned more concern and comment among Jews than any single aspect of their experience in this country. Literally hundreds of panel discussions and conferences have been devoted to the perennial topic of whether there is or is not a peculiar "Jewish economic crisis" in the United States. Quite often the discussion has turned on the related question of whether the Jewish economic position is really "abnormal." Those who have sought to read an optimistic meaning in events have naturally rationalized these "peculiarities" and "abnormalities" of the Jewish economic position. And there is of course a sense in which it is quite true that there is nothing peculiar or abnormal about the position that Jews occupy in the economy. For example, the fact that Jews occupy a peculiar position in the economy does not prove that Jews are essentially different from other people. But considerations of this order should not be permitted to conceal the obvious fact that there is something most peculiar and abnormal about the American economic structure — namely, its markedly anti-Semitic bias. More than any other single factor it is this bias which has brought about the peculiar distribution of Jews on the checkerboard of our economic system.

That this distribution *is* somewhat peculiar cannot be denied. If professional and white-collar workers are included in the middle-class category, then this class constitutes the overwhelming majority of American Jews. As Lestchinsky has written:

Even if we should classify the white collar workers among the proletariat, the wage earning element among Jews would still be only half as large as among the American population in general. Seventy per cent of the economically active population in the country are wage-earners; among Jews this group constitutes only about forty per cent. Furthermore, while seventy per cent of all wage workers among non-Jews are engaged in physical work and only about thirty per cent in clerical office work, this proportion is reversed among Jews. Since Jewish white collar workers are mostly connected with mercantile rather than with industrial enterprises, it is not surprising that they are actually and psychologically closer to the middle class. A large part of them eventually leave the proletarian status altogether, the women after marriage and the men through setting up in some business independently.[7]

Once the class position of American Jews is thus defined, the situation, as Lestchinsky notes, "is not likely to arouse optimistic thoughts."

In fact, the economic impasse which Jews now face in America is remarkably similar to that which they faced in Europe prior to the Second World War. The steady concentration of wealth and economic power in modern industrial nations has been, as Maurice Samuel has written, both the nemesis of capitalism and the nemesis of the Jew.[8] As this concentration progresses, the amount of the national income left for the middle class, after monopoly has extracted its share, becomes the prize of an ever-fiercer struggle. The exposed economic position of the Jew is then subject to increased pressure from three directions: from above (monopoly); from below (the working class); and from within the middle class itself. The peril of the Jew, as Waldo Frank has so well said, consists in the fact that he is allied with "an agonizing and desperate middle class. Whenever that class flourished, the Jews, functioning in it, were tolerated by it. Now that it droops and its spoils dwindle, it turns — like a threatened beast — against its weaker neighbor."

To gain a realistic understanding of the economic basis of anti-Semitism in the United States we badly need studies of the relationships between Jews and non-Jews engaged in similar lines of business in the same community. In the city of Los Angeles, for example, the credit end of the retail jewelry business is largely controlled by Jews, while the "cash" stores are just as exclusively non-Jewish. Since both risk and losses are greater in the credit stores, these stores must emphasize volume of sales and to increase volume they are driven to cut prices. On the other hand, the concentration of Jews in the credit end of the business operates to the indirect profit and advantage of the non-Jewish cash stores. In fact, some of these stores use anti-Semitism as a form of advertising. If a customer objects to the price of an article, they can always say, "Well, you can buy it cheaper, if that's what you want, at the kike store down the street." By emphasizing their non-Jewishness, these stores create a premium value for their merchandise. That the Jews are forced to operate the marginal stores, the stores that are compelled to offer credit in order to exist, also means that they are forced to fight harder to maintain their position and that, in doing so, they are often accused of sharp practices and high-pressure methods, accusations which are in turn used against them by their non-Jewish competitors. The non-Jewish stores are naturally delighted with an arrangement which enables them to monopolize the cream of the business and to escape, in effect, from the necessity of direct competition with their Jewish colleagues who have been relegated to the outer fringes of the trade. It is in relationships of this sort, seldom apparent on the face of things, that much of the economic reality of anti-Semitism is to be found.

Much of the job discrimination that Jews encounter in the United States today reflects a determination on the part of the majority to keep certain sectors of the economy in non-Jewish hands. The toughest resistance which Jewish job seekers encounter is precisely in those concerns which traditionally have been non-Jewish in ownership and management. For example, Jews have always experienced great difficulty in securing office or clerical employment in insurance companies [9] and in private utilities.[10] The effect of this "closed shop" attitude on the part of the industrial and financial giants is to intensify the pressure of Jewish applicants for jobs in those businesses which have always pursued a less systematic policy of exclusion, to become small enterprisers, or to enter the professions.

That discrimination against Jews in employment has been steadily increasing since V–J Day has been clearly established by a number of recent studies. In the period from February 20 to March 20, 1946, one study indicates that three Philadelphia newspapers carried over 3600 help-wanted ads containing discriminatory specifications. A study by the National Community Relations Advisory Council indicates that discriminatory help-wanted advertisements showed an increase of 195 per cent in the year following V–J Day; that 93 per cent more complaints of employment discrimination were filed with Jewish agencies in the six months following V–J Day than in the corresponding period for the previous year; that of 241 private employment agencies interviewed, 89 per cent required applicants to state their religion and lineage; and that 60 per cent of Jewish job seekers had been asked about their religion at the time they were interviewed for employment. It is significant that the situation in New York, where a state FEPC has been in force for some time, was noticeably better than in other cities. This study, incidentally, covered 15 large cities in which 80 per cent of the Jewish population resides.[11]

4. ECONOMIC PRESSURES AND GROUP DIFFERENCES

Economic pressures aggravate group differences in numerous ways. A minority that is subject to incessant economic pressure and to various forms of economic discrimination can hardly be said to enjoy freedom of religious worship despite the fact that there is no overt interference with this right. For pressures of this sort invest the profession of a particular faith with special disabilities, thereby placing it at a considerable disadvantage by comparison with other faiths. As the economic pressures mount, religious differences begin to take on a new significance and serious inroads are made on the concept of religious liberty.

That religious differences are being accentuated today despite an elaborate effort to keep up a pretense of inter-religious amity and brotherhood can hardly be denied. Worried by the growing strength of Catholicism, the Protestant churches have been stressing their Protestantism in a manner that serves to sharpen the differences not only between Catholics and Protestants but between Protestants and Jews. The recent decision of the Supreme Court approving the use of state funds to transport children to parochial schools is not likely to allay this heightened sense of group differences in matters of religious faith. Such recent developments as the "released time" religious education program in the public schools have also had a tendency to emphasize religious differences and, at the same time, to create subtle pressures against minority religious groups.[12] That these pressures are increasing today would seem to indicate that economic pressures against minorities are being intensified. For a group that is not permitted to develop its own religious institutions in its own way, free from pressures of the sort mentioned, is almost invariably a group that is being singled out for economic discrimination.

Merely to indicate how religious differences are being emphasized, I would refer to the bad-tempered and thoughtless polemic in which even that liberal Protestant journal the *Christian Century* engaged some years ago. In one of a series of editorials devoted to "the Jewish Problem," the *Century* charged that "fundamentally anti-semitism arises out of the Jew's unwillingness to submit himself to the democratic process" and proceeded to explain anti-Semitism in terms of "the Jew's immemorial and pertinacious obsession with an illusion," namely, his sense of difference based upon the character of his religion and its culture.[13] This is, of course, arrogant nonsense. There is nothing about the "democratic process" that requires the Jew to abandon his religion or that even requires him, as part of the ethics of religious sportsmanship, to listen to the missionaries of other faiths. If it is not to be utterly robbed of meaning, the concept of religious freedom must include the right to foster any type of faith which, in the words of Rabbi Mordecai Kaplan, "offers consolation or supports the human spirit" and to be free of economic penalties or disabilities arising from adherence to such a faith.

To urge the contrary is to negate the meaning of democracy as well as of religious freedom. "Can anything be more disgusting," wrote George Eliot, "than to hear people called 'educated' making small jokes about eating ham, and showing themselves empty of any real knowledge as to the relation of their own social and religious life to the history of the people they think themselves witty in insulting? They hardly know that Christ was a Jew. And I find men, educated, supposing that Christ spoke Greek. To my feeling, this deadness to world history which has prepared half of our world for us, this inability to find interest in any form of life that is not clad in the same coat-tails and flounces as our own, lies very close to the worst kind of irreligion. The best that can be said is that it is a sign of intellectual narrowness — in plain English, the stupidity, which is still the average mark of our culture."

Paradoxically, religious tensions are mounting at a time when secular influences were never more pronounced in our culture. It is the general crisis of the times, however, that is producing this heightening of religious tensions just as it is emphasizing group differences of all types. The fact that synagogues were desecrated in a dozen or more American cities in 1946, and that some thirty anti-Semitic acts of violence were reported in New York in the last half of 1945, merely indicates how group differences are being aggravated today.

CHAPTER VII *The Jewish Stereotype*

For MANY YEARS now, the social scientists have been debating whether anti-Semitism is a unique phenomenon or merely another manifestation of prejudice. In other words, is there something about the nature of anti-Semitism that warrants its inclusion in a separate and special category or is it to be regarded under the same head, for example, as prejudice against Negroes? The question is not one of purely academic interest for it bears directly upon the question of prognosis and therapy. While disavowing any intention of entering this debate on one side or the other, I do want to suggest that the clue to the riddle is to be found in the nature of the Jewish stereotype.

1. SOCIAL MYTHS

A stereotype has been defined, in the social sciences, as a judgment that does not coincide with the facts; it is in the nature of a social illusion or myth. Social structures that are marked by sharp class, caste, or status lines are fertile breeding grounds for stereotypes, since it is the function of stereotypes to rivet certain alleged traits and characteristics upon all members of a group or class. Thus, *all* Negroes are lazy and the exceptions acknowledged are merely used to prove the rule. When racial and ethnic stereotypes are studied on a comparative basis, one is immediately impressed with their extraordinary similarity. If these stereotypes were actually based upon personal observation and experience, then one would expect to find a wide range of variation in the characteristics attributed to certain groups. But such is not the case. When the stereotype of the Irish first arose in Boston, it was essentially similar to the present-day stereotype of the Negro. If the labels are omitted, it is almost impossible to identify the groups involved without reference to the social context in which the particular stereotype appears. This telltale similarity in stereotypes should be a sufficient warning that they are essentially illusions and that their origin is to be found in social rather than individual experience.

All stereotypes, however, are not the same. A basic distinction is to be noted, for example, between the Negro stereotype and the Jewish stereotype. The Negro stereotype runs somewhat as follows: the group is lazy, shiftless, irresponsible, dirty, can't learn and won't work, competes unfairly, lowers living standards and property values, has excessively large families, and is "incapable of assimilation." This is the basic stereotype of subordinated groups. It has been applied with amusing uniformity to literally dozens of different racial, cultural, and ethnic groups. For example, one could not distinguish the stereotype of the Polish worker which developed in Germany in the latter part of the last century from the stereotype of the Negro which exists in the United States today. This same basic stereotype was developed in California, in the years from

1933 to 1938, in reference to the so-called Okies and Arkies, who were uniformly white, painfully Protestant, and overwhelmingly Anglo-Saxon in ancestry. The very groups and individuals in California who had supported Madison Grant in the fight to enact the Immigration Act of 1924 were the first groups and individuals to apply the "non-Nordic" stereotype to the Nordic Okies and Arkies.

The Jewish stereotype is to be sharply distinguished from the Negro stereotype in two respects. In the first place, the Jew is universally damned, not because he is lazy, but because he is *too* industrious; not because he is incapable of learning, but because he is *too* intelligent — that is, too knowing and cunning. It should be noted, however, that the Jewish stereotype has been applied to such non-Jewish groups as Japanese Americans, Greeks, Syrians, and Armenians. In the Philippine Islands much the same stereotype has developed about the Chinese, who are the retail merchants of the islands. From the difference in the two stereotypes it is readily apparent, therefore, that different social situations are being rationalized and that, insofar as Jews are concerned, a different relationship must prevail between majority and minority than in the case of Negroes.

The rise of industrialism has everywhere stimulated migration. Since factories were initially located near sources of power and power was not easily transmitted, industry tended to be concentrated in particular areas. The rapid expansion of industry quickly exhausted the local labor market and created a powerful magnet by which new groups were attracted to the centers of industrial employment. In seeking out the social origins of stereotypes, it will generally be found that migration has been a factor.

Usually the stereotyped groups have moved from a backward to a more advanced area; from an area of lower to an area of higher economic organization; from a technologically retarded to a more advanced region. This has meant, in most cases, that the last group to arrive on the industrial scene has usually suffered from certain cultural handicaps, notably from a deficit in industrial skills. As a consequence, the last group to arrive has usually been fitted into the industrial hierarchy at the lowest rung, in the least skilled and lowest paid categories.

In areas where a rapid industrial expansion has occurred, the "native" groups, those on the scene when the expansion began, have usually enjoyed marked advantages in competition with later arrivals: the advantage of priority in settlement, of early training in industrial processes, of "being in on the ground floor" so as to capitalize upon the myriad subsidiary economic opportunities which an expanding industry creates. It was not by reason of any biological superiority, therefore, that the founders of the basic American industries in the post-Civil-War period should have been largely white, Anglo-Saxon, and Protestant. Their pre-eminence in industry and finance simply cannot be explained in terms of their racial origin, nor, Max Weber to the contrary, can it be correlated with the Protestant ethic. This correlation between social status and ethnic background, however, can be related to the rapid westward expansion of the United States. Madison Grant was to some extent right when he pointed out that it was largely the native stock that pushed through the Cumberland Gap, overran the prairie states, swept into Texas and westward to the Pacific. For the dynamics of expansion at-

tracted large numbers of the native-born westward at a time
when industry was ravenously seeking new employees in
the industrial centers of the East. It was this attraction of
western opportunities, rather than, as Grant supposed, the
innate reluctance of the native-born to accept certain types
of work, that created the vacuum in industrial employment
filled by the foreign-born.

New migrant groups attracted to industrial centers usually suffer from specific competitive disabilities in addition
to their lack of industrial experience. Differences in nationality and language, culture and religion, are often factors
marking off the new group from those already on the scene.
In the expansion of American industry, these differences
became more important as the center of recruitment shifted
from Northern and Western to Central and Southeastern
Europe. And this shift in origin happened to coincide with
the increased stratification of the industrial population that
came with the development of combines, trusts, and monopolies. Thus the most dissimilar cultural groups began
to arrive in the largest numbers precisely when the industrial system had begun to mature and when the new status
system which it created had become well established.

Once the new migrant group has been fitted into the
lower-bracket employments, every group on the industrial
ladder above these levels begins to feel that it has a vested
interest in maintaining the new relationship. This feeling
extends to the top management and ownership groups, who
frequently lend the prestige of their names and the power of
their positions to the circulation of the stereotype which
promptly develops about "the last group in." In other
words, the stereotype rationalizes the new group relation-

ship, not as temporary and fortuitous, but as permanent and inherent. In fact it is frequently contended that God, in His celestial ordering of the universe, decreed that the new group should forever be the servants of their masters. The new group is "only fit for" certain types of work. It cannot be trained for better jobs because it is inherently inferior; nor can its members be promoted because they are, as a group, shiftless, lazy, and irresponsible. Since industry constantly recruited new groups, the older groups naturally came to look upon each new group as a threat to their position and status and developed a marked hostility to immigration in general. Hence the moment relationships of this order began to develop in industry, the most powerful economic factors immediately re-enforced the initial stereotype and in effect perpetuated it.

The conditions of industrial employment, moreover, create powerful psychological re-enforcements for group stereotypes. Stratification in employment brings about a strong in-group feeling among the workers in particular categories. Cliques are formed in industry which tend to carry over into the world outside the plant. Feeling that the newest groups are the most likely competitors for their jobs, the groups who have already developed a vested interest in the industrial hierarchy tend to look with suspicion and hostility on all groups occupying positions subordinate to theirs. If the groups above the lowest rung on the ladder really believed that the newest groups were "incapable of assimilation," they would not fear them as competitors. But the rationalization invariably takes this form, since it serves to maintain the relationship by assigning a permanent and biological inferiority to potential competitors.

Once relationships of this sort have been established, they become institutionalized in the social structure of the plant and the community and of the larger society of which both are a part. The stereotype about the new group becomes imbedded in company policy and is perpetuated through personnel practices. The very nature of the relationships out of which the stereotype arises tends to create a vicious circle which perpetuates the stereotype. Since the new groups lack training for superior positions, for which they are regarded as inherently unfitted, it naturally follows that they are "unqualified" when openings in these categories arise. Furthermore, if members of the newest groups are promoted, their advancement is likely to disturb all the relationships which gave rise to the stereotype. Persons living in an atmosphere conditioned by such relationships come to accept the stereotype as part of the natural order of the universe. It never occurs to them that the stereotype might be a social illusion, for it seems to square with an unmistakable reality. They *know* that older women can't learn; that Negroes are lazy; and that Mexicans can't handle machines. For, in most cases, they have never seen a Mexican given the chance to operate a machine nor have they seen Negroes employed under circumstances which would give them some reason to hope that diligence might lead to advancement.

It goes without saying that relationships of this sort are often looked upon with high favor by the ownership and management groups, since invidious social arrangements of this order create a dog-eat-dog atmosphere and a strenuous competition for place and position. When a trade-union movement emerges from such an atmosphere, its policies will often reflect these same relationships and stereotypes. Thus the American Federation of Labor was lined up with Madison Grant in the fight to pass the Immigration Act of 1924.

If maintained over a sufficiently long period, a set of relationships of this sort and the stereotypes to which they give rise can become deeply imbedded in the culture. The stereotypes appear in story, novel, verse, song, and play. They become part of the vocabulary of the culture. Children are familiarized with the stereotypes in doggerel verses, epithets, offhand remarks, and in the attitudes, expressions, and mannerisms of their elders. Cultural reenforcements are of the greatest importance in maintaining the stereotype, since they operate continuously and uniformly in every section of the society. Thus even the groups subordinated come to accept, to some extent, the stereotype which is used to keep them in place. Furthermore, these same relationships have far-reaching implications in the world outside the plant. They determine, to a large degree, the type of residential district in which the worker lives, the type of school which his children attend and the social atmosphere in which they live, and so on through layer after layer of interacting influences.

And here sociology and psychology move hand in hand, for the monotony of many types of industrial work breeds frustrations which the hierarchical character of the relationships in an industrial society direct toward predetermined scapegoats. "As long as this type of group education and group life is tied to an extremely hierarchical form of society," writes Dr. Max Horkheimer, "the prevalent repressive features of our society make these groups (those subordinated) more irrational than they would be even in a society without social and economic injustices." [1] Hence the folly of talking about group differences as though these differences were *per se* a primary cause of group tensions.

It should be pointed out, however, that while migration stimulated by industrial expansion has been an important factor in the growth of stereotyped group judgments, it is not an indispensable factor. Nor is it essential that the group stereotyped should be a numerical minority. Where a minority has taken possession of a territory by superior force and has imposed a new economic and industrial order upon the native majority, the same relationships have often developed and the same stereotypes have frequently flourished. A case in point is that of the French Canadians in Quebec, numerically a majority in the Province but suffering from every disability usually associated with minority status. In fact, the forms and the techniques of group dominance are many and varied but they are alike in the sense that one group or combination of groups is always seeking dominance over other groups. Migration has been, however, an important factor in this process even prior to the rise of industrialism.

2. *THE JEW AS MIGRANT*

Jews have always been among the most mobile of peoples. Their mobility has been a product of numerous well-known factors: the lack of nationality status and citizenship; a high degree of urbanization; a lack of ties to rural areas; the lack of a homeland; the possession of certain traditional skills in trading and mercantile enterprises; and the discrimination which they have encountered wherever they have resided. Members of minority groups tend to emigrate more readily than members of dominant majorities and Jews have everywhere been a minority. Unlike most migrant groups, however, the Jews have usually brought a higher cultural endowment to the areas in which they have settled than that possessed by the resident groups. It would be more accurate, perhaps, to state that while their cultural endowment has not necessarily been "higher" it has been characterized by the possession of certain specific skills and experience. Also unlike some migrant groups, Jews have often brought considerable capital to the areas in which they have settled. On more than one occasion, Jews have been invited to settle in a particular community or nation precisely because they have possessed the capital or the skills, or both, which have enabled them to discharge the function of a middle class.[2]

Even in those cases where the Jews have been among the "last groups in" — as in the United States — they have lost little time in moving out of the lower bracket employments. Schooled in facing prejudice, they have learned to seek out the crevices, the marginal businesses, in which it has been possible to secure an economic foothold. I have already commented upon the quickness with which, by comparison with other immigrant groups, Jewish immigrants have moved up the status ladder in the United States. The positions which they eventually come to occupy, however, are neither at the bottom nor at the top of the ladder but are intermediate between both extremes and usually marginal to the economy itself. Hence the determination to subordinate them, to keep them in their corner, cannot take the usual form of rationalization. Obviously it would never do to say that Jews are lazy or that they are ignorant, for their skill at escaping subordination belies the judgment. The same consideration underlies the fact, noted by many observers, that the Jews, unlike most minority groups, are generally regarded as equals; in fact, they are regarded as dangerous precisely because they are viewed as equals. Thus, a special stereotype is evolved which condemns the Jew, not because he is lazy but because he is too industrious; not because he is ignorant or incapable of learning, but because he is too cunning, too successful in escaping subordination.

There is nothing miraculous or uncanny about the social traits or skills which have enabled Jews to rise so quickly from the positions of extreme subordination. Born of discrimination, these skills are socially, not biologically, conditioned, and cannot be regarded as inborn "traits" or "characteristics." In an essay on "The Intellectual Pre-eminence of Jews in Modern Europe," published in 1919, Thorstein Veblen advanced one of the most persuasive hypotheses to account for the existence of these social skills among Jews. As an alien, he reasoned, the Jew is born into a community with traditions different from those to be found in the Gentile community. From the day of his birth, he has the advantage (or disadvantage, however it be regarded) of occupying a detached position in relation to the culture of the Gentile world. The extent of this detachment, of course, has been a variable factor, depending upon the social distance between the two communities at any particular time or place. When the Jew discovers that his own traditions do not square with the world into which he has been born, he also discovers that the Gentile's traditions are

neither better nor more pertinent. Once free from the pre-
conceptions of both cultures, he often becomes a creative
leader in the world's intellectual enterprises. Thus of 38
Germans who won Nobel Prizes prior to 1933, 11 were
German Jews. According to the Veblen hypothesis, the
intellectually gifted Jew, like other men in a similar position, secures immunity from intellectual quietism "at the
cost of losing his secure place in the scheme of conventions
into which he has been born." At the same time, he is "in a
peculiar degree exposed to the unmediated facts of the current situation" and "takes his orientation from the run of
the facts as he finds them, rather than from the traditional
interpretation of analogous facts." [3]

While Veblen may have overstated this theory, it does
help to explain an acknowledged social reality. Long continued social ostracism has two closely interrelated consequences for the groups ostracized: it makes for the development of strong family and group solidarity (often an
advantage in a competitive society); and it also forces the
group to seek out new and often hazardous or socially stig-
matized avenues for advancement. The term "marginal
trading peoples" has been coined to describe such groups.
Other religious minorities, such as the Quakers and the
Huguenots, have shown much the same success in escaping
subordination that the Jews have shown and for much the
same reasons. "The exile," writes Miriam Beard, "thinks
of the future, not the past. He is shaken out of the common
and old habits; forced to seek new lands, to live on the outskirts of society, pioneering in young trades or transplanting
old ones. . . . Quakers pioneered in England in chem-
icals, chocolate manufacture, scientific brewing, and rail-

roading, all branches not pre-empted by good Anglicans; the amalgamation of Quaker dynasties formed London's first great banking combine. One might pursue the theme in America, showing how Quakers ran Salem and Providence — centers of the young rum-molasses-and-slave trade. Huguenots, experimenting with textiles or false teeth (like Paul Revere), overran New England; Huguenot money-lenders ruled Charleston. . . . Wherever possible, all these exiles avoided duplicating the efforts of natives among whom they settled." [4] While such exiles have "avoided" trespassing on pre-empted fields, they have also been systematically excluded from these fields. That the opposition to Quakers and Huguenots was often as violent as the most extreme manifestations of anti-Semitism is a fact eloquently attested by the history of both groups. Generally speaking, however, the resistance to Jews has been much higher since it has been conditioned by a much more complex set of factors and by a much longer history.

Real light is thrown on the origin of specialized group skills by a concept which Toynbee has developed, namely, "the impact of penalization." Consider, for example, the following characterization of a group, from Paul H. Emden's *Money Powers of Europe:*

Exposed to long persecution for their religion's sake and accustomed to look upon harsh treatment as a tribulation without offering — or indeed being able to offer — any great resistance, they went through a hard school for many generations and learnt calm and prudence. Prejudice on the part of others excluded them from the liberal professions, even from sport, and their own objections to taking an oath which was in conflict with their convictions rendered them incapable of holding even

the most unimportant office. . . . In view of their pariah position, the inherited gifts and the education of their children
were concentrated solely on religion and business; nothing
could keep them from the practices of their faith, and no pros-
pective profit, however high, could influence them when hour
of the Sabbath called to worship. The same high standard which
ruled their private and intimate family life governed their
business transactions, and their principles precluded expensive
tastes. They were intelligent, diligent, and above all — for this
is the inheritance of a persecuted sect — cautious. The habit of
having always to be prepared for anything compelled them to
exercise the greatest possible prudence, and consequently to be
constantly solvent, a quality indispensable in a manager of
other people's money. Inculcated self-restraint and discretion
turned them into reliable advisers on financial secrets and good
merchants. In constant activity they were ever on the lookout
for new possibilities of extending their business; they did not
wait for the customer to come to them; they sought him out
or sent to him, and in this way, by stages, the fraternity of
commercial travellers came into being. Trade, commerce, industry and traffic received new ideas from them, and they
found large sums for the purpose of carrying them into practice. . . . For children to marry outside the faith was not a
very frequent occurrence; any one so doing deliberately excluded himself from close communion and inter-marriage pre-
vented the dissolution of great wealth. In this way vast fortunes were made solely by accumulation.

This description of the origin of certain skills so neatly
fits the Jews that one would assume that Emden was writing
about them. Actually he is writing about the Quakers and
how it was that they became an important element in the
financial life of Great Britain. There is a wealth of similar
evidence to show that the possession of group skills of this
kind is a by-product of penalization. This historical evi-

dence merely fortifies a basic conclusion of modern social science that character is rooted in social structure. "Instincts and racially (i.e. genetically) determined properties," writes Harold Orlansky, "do not explain why groups of men differ in their character and behavior. . . . On the other hand, the social conditions under which men live do tend to explain differences in behavior."

As a matter of fact it has been the possession of these socially conditioned skills which accounts for the circumstance that, at one point, the Jews may have been actually solicited to settle in a country from which they have later been excluded. Louis Boudin has pointed out in a brilliant article in *ORT Economic Review* for September 1947 that the qualities of a minority which are regarded as "useful" by the majority tend to vary with time and place, more particularly with economic development. For example, Boudin demonstrates very clearly that Jews were regarded as most useful and valuable citizens in Portugal, Holland, and England when there was need for their special skills. In general, he shows that the curiously fluctuating nationalist policies toward Jews were related to the triangular struggle between Portugal, Holland, and Great Britain for pre-eminence in world trade.

Possession of a set of socially conditioned skills, such as those described by Mr. Emden, has made possible the financial successes which "penalized" groups have often achieved. But ironically it is precisely this success, for which the bigotry of the majority is historically responsible, that once again stimulates the envy of the majority. Individuals who would recoil in horror from the mere thought of becoming peddlers or ragpickers are enraged when the peddler becomes a prosperous merchant and the ragpicker ends up in control of an important and profitable waste-products plant. There is, of course, an element of poetic justice in this process by which the penalized group is often compensated economically for its exclusion; but one's satisfaction over the manner in which the process operates is chilled by the realization that it tends to be self-generating.

That Jews persist in the possession of such skills is to be accounted for by the fact that it is precisely their economic assimilation that has always been most emphatically discouraged by the dominant groups. "For what point is there," inquires Maurice Samuel, "in absorbing the Jews and adding to the number of undifferentiated competitors? As they stand now, the Jews are recognizable as a group which can be pushed out in the struggle and relegated to a lower position. Their racial or religious or psychological differential acts as a cement for both sides. Standing out from the rest of the world, the Jews form an excellent target to be shot at. *They help organize the struggle for bread. . . .* Suppose that, tomorrow, all Jewish merchants were to become unrecognizable as such. What advantage would that bring the ranks of the non-Jewish merchant class as a whole? None at all. On the contrary, the ranks of the non-Jewish merchant class would be greatly increased, and an important and 'helpful' feature of the economic struggle, *a certain channeling of competitive opposition*, would be removed. Roughly, it would be as though the Democrats were to wake up one morning as Republicans, and were to flock to Republican headquarters for their share of political spoils. The Republican Party certainly wants to be in a majority; but it does not want all Americans to be Republican because it *disorganizes the whole struggle-system.*" [5]

Almost every immigrant group in America has been compelled to struggle hard in order to escape from the particular position of subordination in the status system to which it has been assigned. Members of some groups have escaped by changing their names; others by intermarriage with the dominant group; still others by the lucky or deserved good fortune of financial success. The Italian American who makes a fortune becomes an artichoke king or a flower king and ceases, for most practical purposes, to be a "wop." Then, too, with the appearance of the second generation, the American born, raised, and educated generation, these groups have usually been able to evade or to escape the restricting limitations of the stereotype, for the badges of identification have by then begun to lose their distinctiveness.

For a stereotype to be effective, it is always essential that the group stereotyped should possess some badge of identification. Theoretically speaking, the nature of the badge is immaterial. It could consist of red hair or cleft palates, so long as it outwardly identifies the individual as a member of a particular group. But, practically speaking, some badges are much better than others. For example, racial badges, for obvious reasons, are the best badges. The effectiveness of the badge, however, varies in relation to many factors: its persistence in the culture; its universality; the extent to which it is felt to be necessary to channel competitive opposition; and, above all, in relation to the position which the differentiated group occupies in the economy. That Jews are singled out in preference to redheads is, as Dr. Otto Fenichel has said, to be explained by many factors: they are more defenseless; they are more vulnerable to attack; and the position they occupy in the economy makes them appear to be the cause of the misery suffered by the victims of social and economic injustice.

While there is nothing peculiar about the mechanism of scapegoating as applied to Jews or in the techniques by which their subordination is attempted, still the particulars in which the Jewish stereotype differs from the basic stereotype do indicate that Jew-baiting serves a special function. Again, the difference in function is related to the difference in social position. While concentrated in the intermediate socio-economic positions, Jews function to some extent in all levels of society. In a time of *general* crisis, therefore, when social unrest has begun to permeate the middle as well as the lower classes, Jews usually make a more vulnerable and a more plausible target than other minority groups. If a minority is confined to the lower levels of society, it can be baited for a variety of purposes; but it cannot serve as a general target against which the hatreds of all disaffected groups can be directed. While social cleavages of all kinds are emphasized in periods of economic crisis, anti-Semitism seems to bear an intimate and special relation to major crises, to periods of profound social maladjustment.

This special function of anti-Semitism may be illustrated by a passage from *The Sound and the Fury* by William Faulkner. Employed in a general store in a small Southern town, Jason Compson has been losing money, which he can ill afford to lose, through speculations on the cotton market. There is no evidence in the novel that Jason has ever had unfavorable personal experiences with Jews or that his disastrous speculations on the cotton market were made through Jewish brokers. From the following passage, however, one can see the function that anti-Semitism plays in the psychic economy of Jason Compson:

Along toward ten o'clock I went up front. There was a drummer there. It was a couple of minutes to ten, and I invited him up the street to get a coca-cola. We got to talking about crops.

"There's nothing to it," I says, "cotton is a speculator's crop. They fill the farmer full of hot air and get him to raise a big crop for them to whipsaw on the market, to trim the suckers with. Do you think the farmer gets anything out of it except a red neck and a hump in his back? You think the man that sweats to put it into the ground gets a red cent more than a bare living," I says. "Let him make a big crop and it won't be worth picking; let him make a small crop and he won't have enough to gin. And what for? so a bunch of damn eastern jews, I'm not talking about men of the Jewish religion," I says, "I've known some jews that were fine citizens. You might be one yourself," I says.

"No," he says, "I'm an American."

"No offense," I says. "I give every man his due, regardless of religion or anything else. I have nothing against jews as an individual," I says. "It's just the race. You'll admit that they produce nothing. They follow the pioneers into a new country and sell them clothes."

"You're thinking of Armenians," he says, "aren't you. A pioneer wouldn't have any use for new clothes."

"No offense," I says. "I don't hold a man's religion against him."

"Sure," he says, "I'm an American. My folks have some French blood, why I have a nose like this. I'm an American, all right."

"So am I," I says. "Not many of us left. What I'm talking

about is the fellows that sit up there in New York and trim the sucker gamblers."

The Jewish stereotype also differs from other stereotypes in its remarkable persistence, its deeply rooted position in the culture. The appearance of anti-Semitic tracings in the writings of men like Henry Adams and John Jay Chapman indicates how widely the stereotype has permeated American culture. Remembering the date of the Saratoga hotel incident, it is interesting to note that the stereotyped, the caricatured Jew had his "first night" on the American stage in the 1870's.[6] Theodore Dreiser's strange, frenetic outburst of anti-Semitism in the middle thirties is also a striking indication of how deeply the stereotype is embedded in American culture.[7] (It should be emphasized, however, that Dreiser later repudiated these unfortunate outbursts.) The Jewish stereotype appears in the novels of Robert Herrick; in a story by Willa Cather; and in the novels of Edith Wharton. It appears in a particularly offensive form in a sonnet by the distinguished American poet, John Peale Bishop;[8] and most significantly in the novels of Thomas Wolfe. All of the Jewish characters in Wolfe's novels are maladjusted or cruel or "queer," and in describing Abraham Jones in *Of Time and the River* Wolfe seems to have spewed out all of his hatred for the Jews.[9] There was not a little anti-Semitism in much of the writing of the 1920's, notably in the work of T. S. Eliot, Ezra Pound, and, in a less overt form, in the work of Scott Fitzgerald.[10] As Mr. Hindus points out, "there is a literary quality about it [the fashionable anti-Semitism of the 1920's] — as if the writers were not thinking of real, everyday, complicated, living Jews, but of an inherited image of them." Occasionally this fashionable literary anti-Semitism assumed, however, the crudest possible expression.[11]

To change the stereotype, therefore, the relationships which gave rise to it must be modified; the myth of anti-Semitism must be exploded. But it is shortsighted indeed to believe that through educational processes alone the stereotype can be uprooted. Education will certainly help to expose the illusory nature of the stereotype, but as long as the relationships out of which it arises exist, the illusion itself will persist. For as long as Jews occupy a special niche in the economy, it will appear as though they were "different" and the difference sensed will inevitably be rationalized. The source of this feeling, however, is to be found in social relationships; not in those outward manifestations of difference, real or imagined, which are seized upon to justify discrimination.[12]

To know what a majority group thinks of a minority, and to discover the image that the minority has formed of the majority, one needs to study in close detail the social and, above all, the economic relations between the two groups. For the image or stereotype will reflect or rationalize the relationship. This is not to say, of course, that *all* members of either group will accept the stereotype; there will always be individuals whose vision is not blinded by social illusions. While the pattern of relationships will determine what each group *thinks* of the other, as a group, it will not determine the extent of discrimination that is practiced, at any particular time, against the minority. This will vary in relation to many factors, social, economic, historical. The stereotype that the minority has formed of the majority will ordinarily not be deeply rooted, for the minority, by the nature of its position, has a clearer vision of the relationship. The myth that a majority develops about a minority that it is determined to subordinate serves two major functions: it rationalizes the relationship for the majority (that is, by attributing a false motive it makes the relationship seem fair, proper, and inherent in the nature of things); and it also serves to maintain the relationship. A basic element in all myths of this kind is that the minority is "incapable of assimilation," for this particular rationalization invests the relationship with permanence and inevitability. Closely examined, therefore, racial and other similar myths will be found to be masks for privilege. Myth, as Durkheim once said, imitates society, not nature.

CHAPTER VIII *The Function of the Crackpot*

To the average American, the mention of anti-Semitism sets off a chain reaction — the German-American Bund, Gerald L. K. Smith, William Dudley Pelley, Father Charles Coughlin — and brings to mind the lurid exposés of John Spivak and the more detailed and effective investigations of John Roy Carlson. In fact the proposition that "anti-Semitism is crackpotism" has now been thoroughly established in the public mind. Any number of cause organizations, promoting "tolerance" and "intercultural" understanding, have labored long and hard to establish this association. In some curious manner, however, the exclusionist policies of many of our social institutions and of particular American industries have always been tacitly excepted from the category of things anti-Semitic. These policies are "unfortunate" and "regrettable," but by implication have no direct relation to anti-Semitism. To a considerable degree, therefore, efforts to isolate and quarantine the crackpot anti-Semite have obscured his function in the development of an organized anti-Semitic movement. Generally speaking, this function is not understood even by those who make a business of denouncing anti-Semitism.

1. SAPPERS AND SHOCK TROOPS

Paralleling the efforts to isolate the rabid anti-Semite and to make anti-Semitism synonymous with obscenity (commendable efforts in themselves), a tendency has developed among American anti-anti-Semites to poke fun at the crackpot by exposing the absurdity of his arguments. The real function of the crackpot anti-Semite, however, is not to develop arguments but to encourage the open expression of anti-Semitism on the part of the latent anti-Semite. The crackpots function vicariously for their inarticulate listeners by doing and saying what the latter would like to do and say, but either cannot or dare not. The antics of the completely uninhibited anti-Semite are essentially aimed at releasing the inhibited anti-Semitism of his audience. Rationally and critically considered the various arguments advanced by American anti-Semites represent a collection of absurdities, fallacies, and lies; but viewed as propaganda these same arguments must be appraised in an entirely different light.

Crackpot anti-Semitic propaganda, as Dr. T. W. Adorno has pointed out,[1] aims at winning people to the open expression of anti-Semitism by playing upon their unconscious mechanisms rather than by presenting facts and arguments. Hence its personalized character; its consistent substitution of means for ends; and the emphasis upon propaganda as an end in itself. Anti-Semitic propaganda functions as a kind of wish-fulfillment. It attacks bogies rather than real opponents and systematically promotes "an organized flight of ideas." Intended to provide gratification rather than enlightenment, anti-Semitic meetings have a ritualistic character, as shown by the fact that the content of these meetings is invariably the same. Dr. Adorno has shrewdly observed that such meetings have a semireligious tone and quality in which the specific religious content is replaced by "a cult of the existent," an identification with and glorification of the *status quo* in politics, religion, social life, manners, the education of children, and so on. It is important, therefore, to note Adorno's conclusion that "the performance of the ritual as such functions to a very large extent as the ultimate content of fascist propaganda." [2]

Successful anti-Semitic propaganda is based, as Dr. Donald S. Strong has said, on an astute handling of the emotions of aggressiveness, guilt, weakness, and affection. The appeal to latent or potential aggressiveness is aimed at releasing the inhibitions normally placed on assertive impulses. Hence to be effective anti-Semitic propaganda must be extreme, violent, and highly provocative. Inhibitions are not released by arguments: they are released by bold and violent assertions. Similarly, in appealing to the emotion of guilt, the anti-Semitic propagandist seeks to depict an enemy who epitomizes evil and is the incarnation of vice and fraud, lust and violence. The picture which the anti-Semite draws of "the enemy" is not intended to convince by its plausibility and verisimilitude: it is intended to divert the emotional stress of guilt suffered by the persons to whom the propaganda is addressed. For this technique enables the guilty to project upon "the enemy" those impulses and half-sensed wishes which lie beneath the surface of their own natures. To overcome the feeling of weakness and impotence that so many of "the little people" experience in modern society, anti-Semitic propaganda is boastful, arrogant, and contemptuous; it struts and swaggers, it grimaces and screams. In appealing to the emotion of affection, the anti-Semite builds up the concept of the brave, unselfish, noble leader. Modesty is certainly not a characteristic of the crackpot anti-Semites, most of whom, as Adorno has said, are masterly salesmen of their own psychological defects. But the test of the effectiveness of their propaganda consists not in the degree to which it conforms to some objective standard of plausibility and truth, but in how it affects the persons to whom it is addressed. Nor can this effectiveness be appraised in terms of immediate reactions, for a delayed reaction may well be involved. A seed sown today may not ripen for months or years, but once planted in receptive soil it has the possibility of later growth.

The crackpot anti-Semitic propagandist is compelled, by the nature of his task, to exaggerate. As Strong writes, "the 'Red-Jew' menace is presented as so immediate and overwhelming that certain mores and inhibitions of conscience must be abandoned at once or the country will perish." Anti-Semitic propaganda is essentially and designedly negative, seldom bothering to project a long-range program in its appeal. According to Dr. Strong, its "anti" symbols outnumber its "pro-self" symbols in the ratio of ten to one. For America First, Nationalism, and Christianity, the anti-Semites are *against* everything else under the sun. To expose the emptiness of anti-Semitic propaganda and its lack of programmatic content is, therefore, a largely meaningless undertaking. At the same time, however, it would be extremely fallacious to assume that the case-hardened confirmed anti-Semites lack a program merely because they prefer to be vague. Their program is fascism and the blueprint is clear enough, although it is seldom clear to their followers.

Having in mind its aims and purposes, Dr. Strong drew some interesting conclusions about the effectiveness of anti-Semitic propaganda in the United States for the period from 1930 to 1940.[3] In general he found that this propaganda had been ingenious, adaptable, distinctive, and that its symbols were reasonably appropriate to its purposes. In fact, its one major weakness consisted in the assumption of an undifferentiated audience. Had the anti-Semites of this period analyzed the component parts of their large potential mass audience, they would have addressed special appeals and slanted their propaganda to different age groups, income groups, occupational groups, religious groups, sex groupings, and the like. In short, Dr. Strong concluded that the barrage of anti-Semitic propaganda in the thirties had been effective. Furthermore, he drew two collateral conclusions of considerable importance: that anti-Semitic propaganda had steadily increased in violence after 1936; and that "the anti-semitic movement in the United States can no longer be treated as if it were a transient phenomenon." Apropos the latter conclusion, he wrote: "About a dozen new anti-semitic organizations have been formed each year since 1933. This steady growth suggests that anti-semitism has taken root in the United States and will, even under the most unfavorable conditions, remain a minor ideology for some time." In appraising the significance of Dr. Strong's findings, one should recall that studies of the growth of anti-Semitism in Germany in the period from 1925 to 1935 have indicated that "the principal thing which changed during these ten years was the amount of anti-Semitic mass propaganda. The effectiveness of this propaganda was the chief thing which altered the attitude of the masses." [4]

The effectiveness of anti-Semitic propaganda has been minimized in the United States largely because it has not been related to the pattern of anti-Jewish discrimination which exists in our society. The anti-Semitic bias in the structure of the American economy is the reality upon which crackpot anti-Semitism is predicated. Some preliminary conditioning is always a prerequisite to the development of an organized anti-Semitic movement. Cunningly contrived, artfully constructed, this preliminary conditioning is primarily psychological in character. At this stage in the development of the movement, sappers must be deployed, booby traps must be built, and shock troops must be trained. The crackpot anti-Semites are the sappers, the shock troops. It is a foregone conclusion that they will be verbally abused, thrown into jail, and otherwise kicked around. But if they do their work well, they are easily expendable. Pre-Hitler Germany was full of crackpot anti-Semites, as mystical as Pelley, as absurd as Joe Jeffers, as corny as Smith, as noisy as Joe McWilliams. For years they were taken no more seriously than most Americans take their counterparts today. Patently absurd, their propaganda was nonetheless based upon a solid and powerful reality: the anti-Semitic bias in the culture of the German people. Over a period of many years, their activities were carefully linked with the politely concealed anti-Semitic plottings of powerfully placed persons and interests in Germany. Starting out as free-lance anti-

Semites, they eventually became the puppets of their upper-class sponsors and overlords.

While the evidence is necessarily skimpy and largely circumstantial, it is nevertheless apparent that our crackpot anti-Semites have long received the covert backing and support of powerful and respectable behind-the-scenes elements. A glance at the list of contributors to Harry Jung's American Vigilant Intelligence Federation — found to be contributors by a Congressional inquiry — certainly indicates that this particular anti-Semite had some powerful, wealthy, and influential backers.[5] The alibi invariably offered for these contributors is that they are "dupes" — that they do not understand the anti-Semitic character of the organizations to which they contribute. While this alibi is doubtless valid in some cases, it strains one's sense of the credible to believe that all such contributors are dupes.

In his detailed and elaborately documented study of eleven anti-Semitic organizations, Dr. Strong found that "a large percentage of the income of some of these groups" came from the wealthy classes.[6] The furtiveness with which upper-class elements have subsidized crackpot anti-Semitic movements in this country is the most telltale evidence that these elements have not been dupes. For the unwillingness to be publicly identified with openly anti-Semitic movements indicates the existence of a guilty conscience. The true dupe does not remain in the background and deal through an intermediary. In fact the furtiveness of the sponsors throws a great deal of light on the real function of the crackpot in the development of an anti-Semitic movement. It is his function to incur the public disapproval which his sponsor is reluctant to assume. While he is being booed and hissed, caricatured and lampooned, his sponsor is comfortably ensconced in an easy chair in some club exchanging anti-Semitic cracks with his fellow club members.

So far as the mores of American society are concerned, open identification with anti-Semitic organizations is neither sanctioned nor approved; but anti-Semitic slights and discriminations are obviously sanctioned. It is quite all right to draw a sharp line excluding Jews from important sectors of the economy and from a large domain of social life — even to tell defamatory stories about them — but it is not yet considered good form to bait Jews openly and those who do so still run the risk of being branded crackpots. In the eyes of his colleagues, Henry Ford's chief sin must have consisted in the clumsy way in which he revealed the existence of a strong anti-Semitic bias in the citadels of heavy industry. Whether the fault line of anti-Semitism which cuts across the American social structure will ever become "active" depends, of course, on many factors; but it is readily apparent that the crackpot has already performed his function and that the stage has now been set for larger and more significant developments.

2. THE ARMCHAIR ANTI-SEMITES

Antifascists long concerned over the growth of hate groups in America have consistently sought an answer to the question, Under what circumstances would it be possible for these groups to form a united front and make a joint appeal to an estimated potential audience of between ten and fifteen million Americans? Ideologically speaking, the leaders of the hate groups are a most heterogeneous lot: monetary reform addicts; Pope-baiters; mystics of the Pelley variety; pension plan schemers; professional God-killers; Bible-belt fundamentalists; West Coast sun worshipers and vegetarians; warped zealots of the John Rankin breed; Negro-haters and what not. It is not surprising, therefore, that these groups have experienced great difficulty in merging their ideological differences. To the extent that they have been able to work together at all, it has been by reason of their hatred of progressive political action, their strong antipathy to the trade-union movement, and their uniform and consistent anti-Semitism.

In the past, several attempts have been made to unite these crackpot legions of the gimlet eyes. One such attempt was made in 1934, when eleven of America's anti-Semitic leaders met in Chicago for the purpose of forming a coalition. This initial effort fell apart when the various leaders got to quarreling among themselves. A somewhat more ambitious scheme to form a coalition got under way in August 1936, when the American Forward Movement summoned the long-haired evangels of chaos to a conference in Asheville, North Carolina. Although it was aided by generous financing, this particular effort collapsed when the appearance of a gullible rabbi caused forty-five delegates to bolt the conference in horror of contamination. Still a third effort was made in August 1937, when George B. Deatherage, the Knight of the White Camellia, summoned the hate leaders to a conference in Kansas City called in the name of the American Nationalist Confederation. This effort likewise failed to produce the long-anticipated confederation.

Since so many of the hate groups are strictly personal promotions or rackets, Dr. Strong concluded that mutual suspicion and rivalry between the various leaders imposed an insuperable obstacle to confederation. Any general merger would necessarily result in the elimination of one or more leaders and, since anti-Semitism is the bread and butter of such gentry, proposals for confederation involving discipline and co-ordination have naturally been regarded with serious misgivings. Another barrier to confederation, noted by Dr. Strong, has consisted in the fact that most of the organized anti-Semitic groups in the thirties had a strong fundamentalist coloring and automatically opposed any move that might involve co-operation with Catholic anti-Semites of the Coughlin variety.

But a more basic explanation can be advanced for the failure of these bizarre groups to merge in the past — namely, that the bridge connecting these groups with their powerful armchair sponsors had not yet been built. Any attempt on the part of the crackpots themselves to form a confederation would necessarily be doomed to failure, since, at this level, anti-Semitism in the United States is a promotion of lunatics. One could more readily imagine a united front of the inmates of an insane asylum than a united front of crackpot anti-Semites acting on their own steam and initiative. But the chances of success in forming such a confederation steadily improve as the ties between the armchair anti-Semites and the crackpots become more intimate and regular, more open and normal. While the fringe groups reveal a bewildering variety of orientations, the armchair anti-Semites are men of substance, solid citizens, persons largely free of the neurotic taint and with a clear idea of what they want and how they propose to get it. Since all anti-Semitic movements are by definition undemocratic, it follows that unification can only come from the top, not the bottom, and that it must be based upon a strict authoritarian discipline. This conclusion finds general confirmation in the history of European fascist movements. In their early phases, as Ellis Freeman has pointed out, European fascist movements represented a peculiar combination of the wealthy, who provided the finances, and the very poor, who provided the manpower. It was only at a somewhat later date that the impoverished middle classes joined these movements.[7]

The America First movement represents, perhaps, the first attempt to form an open alliance between the armchair anti-Semites and their crackpot allies. Under its banner, the crackpot anti-Semites were united for the first time. While the movement could not be called anti-Semitic, it drew into its orbit most of the crackpot leaders and their variegated followings. It represented a center of power in what had previously been a vacuum. By refusing to repudiate, in any clear-cut or decisive manner, the anti-Semitic organizations and individuals that allied themselves with the movement, the leaders of America First showed a singular indifference to the use of anti-Semitism and a willingness to associate publicly with individuals with whom they had long been reluctant to be identified. The curiously halfhearted and unconvincing disavowal of Lindbergh's Des Moines speech is the best evidence that the leadership of America First was not averse to the use of anti-Semitism as a political weapon. Had the movement survived Pearl

Harbor, it is not improbable that the long-discussed merger of the crackpot groups would have been effected.

Immediately following the death of President Roosevelt in April 1945, the nationalist campaign was renewed under the sponsorship and direction of the former leaders of America First. In a series of articles which appeared in the Scripps-Howard newspapers, Eugene Segal demonstrated that former America First leaders were attempting once again to weld the dissident crackpot groups into a single mass movement. The manner in which the nationalist groups attacked the United Nations Conference in San Francisco, using the same themes, slogans, and appeals, clearly indicated that a high degree of co-ordination had been effected.[8] On July 26, 1945, the long-silent Lindbergh gave an interview to the press (the interview was held in the offices of the publisher of the *Chicago Tribune*), and other America First leaders began to speak out. What the fringe groups were saying at public meetings from coast to coast was echoed, almost verbatim, in speeches in Congress by Rankin, Bilbo, and Hoffman. Unquestionably the nationalist groups had carefully timed this renewed campaign, for the Roper polls in April 1945 had shown a definite increase in "anti" sentiment across the country with a sharp increase in anti-Semitism.

3. AMERICAN ACTION

Just as the name "America First" had echoed in crackpot circles for years before it was used as a rallying slogan by the armchair reactionaries, so the name "American

Action" stems directly from the fringe groups. An organization called American Action had been formed in 1939 to promote the formation of an American National Action Party. This particular group later merged its activities with those of the America First Committee. Early in 1945, Gerald B. Winrod announced the formation of American Action, Inc., which he said had been established to "uphold constitutional democracy as against the encroachments of un-American ideologies." But apparently Winrod got his wires crossed in making this announcement, for the real American Action Committee did not come into existence until midsummer 1945.

American Action, Inc., is an outgrowth of a meeting which took place in Chicago on July 30 and 31, 1945. According to Eugene Segal, this meeting was initiated by Salem Bader of Los Angeles, the author of a pamphlet entitled *Is America a Christian or a Jewish Civilization?* [9] The Chicago meeting was under the chairmanship of Merwin K. Hart, one of the founders of the America First Committee, once referred to by Justice Robert H. Jackson as "well-known for his pro-Fascist leanings." Among the individuals who attended the meeting were the following: John T. Flynn, active in America First; DeWitt Emery of Akron, active in the National Small Businessmen's Association; Maurice R. Franks, business agent of the Railroad Yardmasters of North America, a union not recognized by any branch of the American labor movement; William H. Regnery of Chicago, industrialist and banker, formerly active in America First and treasurer of Earl Southard's Citizens U.S.A. Committee; Samuel Pettengill, former chairman of the Republican National Finance Committee, a speaker for America First, and a trustee of the Committee for Constitutional Government; Colonel Charles Vincent of Chicago, head of the American Foundation; A. Dwight Nims of Los Angeles, formerly secretary of the National League of Mothers and Women of America; George Washington Robnett of Chicago, head of the Church League of America; Thomas N. Creigh, lawyer, head of the Chicago branch of Merwin K. Hart's National Economic Council; William A. Larner, Jr., and R. E. Minnis, of Topeka, both active in a committee that has sponsored meetings for Upton Close and Samuel Pettengill; and, of course, Upton Close.[10]

The next meeting of American Action took place in Los Angeles at the Clark Hotel, on August 28, 1945. Shortly prior to this meeting, ten thousand citizens of Los Angeles had participated in a great mass meeting at the Olympic Auditorium to protest Gerald L. K. Smith's activities in Southern California. Arousing much excitement in the community, this meeting had served to crystallize public opinion against Smith's anti-Semitic demagoguery. The Clark Hotel meeting was called in part for the purpose of countering the effect of the anti-Smith mass meeting. The principal speaker of the evening told the guests and members of American Action that the Jews, the international bankers, and Jewish Communist immigrants from Russia had acquired an almost complete control over American business, government, and labor. Following this talk, Howard Emmett Rogers, of the right-wing Motion Picture Alliance, took the floor, denounced the meeting as "nothing but another anti-Semitic enterprise," and walked out.[11]

Formal articles of incorporation were filed in Delaware for American Action, Inc., on January 8, 1946, and headquarters were established in Chicago. On May 23, 1946, a branch office was opened in Los Angeles with the announcement that American Action had been formed "to combat the inroads that have been made on the government by alien-minded pressure groups." The letterhead of American Action lists the following as officials of the new organization: Harold N. Moore, of Los Angeles, formerly active in America First; James H. Gipson of Caldwell, Idaho; Colonel Edward D. Gray; James E. McDonald, State Commissioner of Agriculture, Austin, Texas; Malcolm McDermott, professor of law at Duke University; and, as executive director, Captain Edward A. Hayes of Chicago, former national commander of the American Legion.

Announcing that it intended to purge 187 Congressmen, American Action took an active part in the 1946 campaign. The groundwork for this political activity had been laid, and its general purpose defined, in a strong editorial which appeared in the *Chicago Tribune* in midsummer 1946, mourning the passing of the America First Committee and urging the nationalists to reorganize. In a statement filed with the government, American Action acknowledged the receipt of contributions totaling $83,494.64 in the period between January 1 and October 15, 1946. While not taking an active part in all of the 187 congressional districts in which it had expressed an interest American Action did concentrate on twenty or thirty districts in New York, Illinois, Missouri, Oklahoma, Wisconsin, Washington, and California.

By the time of the November 1946 elections, the base of American Action had been greatly expanded. Listed among its contributors were the names of General Robert E. Wood, formerly head of the America First Committee; Colonel Robert R. McCormick of the *Chicago Tribune*; Robert M. Harriss, an ardent supporter of Father Coughlin and a founder of the American National Democratic Committee. Among those named as sponsors by James Reston in a story in the *New York Times* of October 10, 1946, are W. Homer Hartz of Chicago, former president of the Illinois Manufacturers' Association; Robert Christenberry of the Hotel Astor Corporation; Samuel Weldon, of the First National Bank; Ernest T. Weir of the Weirton Steel Company.

In an effort to avoid, so far as possible, the aroma of the America First movement, American Action has concentrated on domestic issues and has even disclaimed a direct interest in the international scene.[12] It is nevertheless apparent that the leaders of American Action are the former leaders of the America First Committee. While American Action has denied any connection with Gerald L. K. Smith, it is interesting to note that Smith regards the new movement with complete enthusiasm. In the issue of his newsletter for October 28, 1946, he urged all former members of America First to co-operate with American Action and to follow its lead. And this motion was, so to speak, quickly seconded by most of the other crackpot leaders. "Myriads of the smallfry bigots," reports the bulletin of the Friends of Democracy for September 30, 1946, "are fitting into the picture of American Action. . . . These are the people who will furnish the mass following for the new group's political action program; they will ring the doorbells, make house-to-house canvasses, bring out the vote for candidates endorsed by American Action."

American Action should be regarded, therefore, not as a new departure in American politics but as the end product of a long period of experimental work in the formation of an inclusive right-wing political alliance.

That American Action represents a new maturity or crystallization of reaction is shown by the emergence of intermediate figures who stand midway between the crackpots and the armchair reactionaries. The increasingly important role now being played by these intermediate types indicates that middle-class elements have begun to be involved and that the new movement aims to slough off some of the verbal crudities of the America First spokesmen. Since the crackpots have already discharged their preliminary softening-up assignment, the movement can now afford to modify its rhetoric, to disavow its more exuberant followers, and to refrain from open provocation. Part of this reorientation consists in pushing such intermediate figures as John T. Flynn and Upton Close into the foreground of the movement.

As a news analyst and commentator, Upton Close began to take a violently reactionary line after 1939. He was dropped for a time from the NBC staff following a broadcast on December 7, 1941, in which he had suggested that the attack on Pearl Harbor might have been a surprise to the Japanese government or that it could have been perpetrated by German ships or a fanatical portion of the Japanese fleet acting without orders. He was again dropped by the NBC circuit following a broadcast on July 9, 1944, in which he had implied that the death of John Bryan Owen, a friend of Tyler Kent, was part of an "international" scheme. Throughout the war, the crackpot groups had sought to use the Tyler Kent case as a means of attacking the Roosevelt administration, and also of imputing a variety of sinister motives to high officials in the State Department. The plot, however, had fallen rather flat when Joseph P. Kennedy, our Ambassador to Great Britain at the time of the Kent scandal, revealed that Tyler Kent had "built up a terrific anti-Semitic complex" while serving in the American Embassy in London. The intermediate role of Close is shown, in this instance, by the fact that he was repeating on a nationwide broadcast one of the favorite themes of the crackpot anti-Semitic organizations.

While insisting that he is not anti-Semitic, Close has used arguments in criticizing the Jews that cannot be distinguished from those used by anti-Semites. "The greatest sorrow of my career," he said in one broadcast, "and which may become America's greatest tragedy is the Communist control of the Jewish minority. . . . Hundreds of Jewish publications have become avowedly Communist. Also, the smart Jewish commentators on the radio put out the party line. Only in a few cases do the better minds among the Jews do anything about this menace."

In a recent bulletin, the Friends of Democracy call attention to the prominent role that Close has been playing in the "marriage between 'respectable' financiers and rabble-rousing Christian Fronters." Sponsored by John J. Raskob, John T. Flynn, and Ogden H. Hammond — one of Generalissimo Franco's admirers in the United States — the National Economic Council gave a dinner in honor of

Close at the Waldorf-Astoria Hotel in New York on November 1, 1946. "Flanked by Lammot du Pont and John J. Raskob," Close denounced the New Deal as "bastard Marxism." Prominent among the guests at this banquet, according to the *Friends of Democracy Bulletin*, were Colonel Edward D. Gray of American Action; Robert M. Harriss, the Coughlinite financier; Joseph Kamp, Edward A. Rumely, Mrs. Livingston Rowe Schuyler, and John A. Zellers. Tickets were distributed at the banquet for a rally of the Christian Front which was held at the Brooklyn Academy of Music a few nights later, at which Close was again the principal speaker. At this rally, May Quinn, the Coughlinite teacher who was recently fined two months' salary for "dereliction of duty," presided.

How these new intermediate types are being used to bridge the gap between the armchair reactionaries and their rabble-rousing followers may be clearly seen in a pamphlet by John T. Flynn called *The Smear Terror*. Originally published as a series of feature articles in the *Chicago Tribune*, the pamphlet develops the interesting thesis (a) that anti-Semitism has never been able to find reputable sponsors; and (b) that the danger of native fascist movements has definitely passed in the United States. It seems that anti-Semitism was never a real danger, anyway, since it was emphasized only "to frighten our unfortunate foreign populations and to induce contributions." Racial hatred will always be with us, according to Flynn, for "it is too much to hope that poor, weak human beings will be able to rid themselves wholly of some form of bias." Our aim, therefore, should be "to permit these poisonous infections to lie dormant and not by foolish or vicious procedures to develop them into a raging contagion." It is curious that Mr. Flynn should believe that a "poisonous infection" can safely be permitted to lie dormant. In one of the articles in this series, Mr. Flynn, by some amazing double talk, manages to convert a defense of Lindbergh against the charge of anti-Semitism into a frontal attack on the very groups who are fighting native fascism in the United States. That such shabby rationalizations should be advanced by a man like Flynn, who is certainly not a crackpot, only emphasizes the consolidation of reactionary tendencies now taking place in this country.

However I do share Mr. Flynn's dislike of the promiscuous use of smear words, such as "fascist," "anti-Semite," and, for that matter, "communist" and "red." Consequently I want to make it clear that I do not regard American Action, Inc., as either fascist or anti-Semitic; nor would I want an inference to be drawn that I believe its leaders are fascists or anti-Semites. Some of these leaders are men who have contributed to numerous Jewish causes and have, in other respects, demonstrated a friendly attitude toward the Jewish minority. American Action interests me because it illustrates the relationship between reaction and crackpotism. What is significant about the organization is this: that any strong center of power formed on the extreme right will nowadays attract anti-Semites as a magnet will pick up pieces of metal. The extreme reaction of right-wing industrial groups seems to have a natural attraction for these elements. Even if American Action were to disavow, more emphatically than it has done in the case of Gerald L. K. Smith, the following which it has attracted, the following would still be there. It is a truism that politics makes for strange bedfellows.

Overzealous antifascists in America have tried to make an
Alfred Hitchcock movie, with conspirators meeting at mid-
night in abandoned windmills, out of relationships that are
based on "affinities," not conspiracies. The question, therefore, is whether any extreme right-wing political movement
in the United States can *avoid* attracting anti-Semites and
uniting them by the mere force of this attraction.

Fascist movements never emerge out of thin air. "It is a
mistake to believe," writes Dr. Ellis Freeman, "that a European fascist party ever did, or an American ever will, spon-
taneously crystallize around a dramatic popular personality.
It has to be constructed from bed-rock up" (emphasis
mine). Certain elements, widely dissimilar in background
and interest, invariably collaborate in the early phases of
this construction. Their collaboration is quite frequently
of the unconscious variety suggested by the homely remark
of Gerald L. K. Smith that a Holstein cow in Wisconsin
gives much the same kind of milk as a Holstein cow in
New York. At the outset, leadership is frequently asserted
by a small group of crackpot zealots and fanatics. But these
elements would never be able to build a fascist movement
without the support of an elite group utterly immune, as
Freeman writes, "even to the minimum of mystical nonsense which the Fuehrer himself may be inclined to accept." In Germany such men as Thyssen and Krupp von
Bohlen did not pour vast sums of money into the Nazi
movement out of an enthusiasm for Aryanism any more
than Mussolini's behind-the-scenes backers were "infatuated with the beatitudes of Latinity." Both in Italy and in
Germany, these hard-boiled realists wanted a specific task

performed, namely, "the balking of social change which jeopardized their position."

In line with Huey Long's famous prediction that fascism would come to America in the guise of antifascism, one notices today a striking tendency on the part of organized reaction to twist democratic slogans and beliefs into profoundly undemocratic molds. Thus efforts to strengthen the position of minorities are denounced as an incitement of minorities against the majority. New York's antidiscrimination law is, in the view of Merwin K. Hart, "itself a discrimination against white Gentile Americans, who . . . bore the brunt of this terrible war." Exclusionist policies are defended in the name of "freedom of association," while monopoly becomes synonymous with "free enterprise." Efforts to combat the activities of anti-Semitic rabble rousers are described as attacks on "freedom of speech," while "freedom to hate" is advanced as a natural right. Through perverse rationalizations of this sort, antifascists become totalitarians and "red fascists" while native fascists emerge as the defenders of the American tradition!

Those who minimize the danger of native fascism should ponder the results of a study of the prevalence of attitudes favorable to fascism made by a social psychologist in 1936. Avoiding the use of the word "fascism," the attitudes of a fairly good sample of American citizens were tested in terms of seven basic concepts of European fascism. While 75 per cent of the sample professed strong opposition to "fascism," a disturbingly high percentage uniformly endorsed the characteristic pattern of fascist ideology.[18] "American culture," writes Dr. Jerome Himelhoch, "by creating personalities that need race prejudice in order to maintain their psychic balance, has created an enormous potential for fascism." [14] Whether prejudice will become sufficiently "salient," in Dr. Himelhoch's phrase, "to come out of the club and go into the streets" depends on many factors; but that the potential mass base for a fascist movement exists in the United States today can hardly be questioned. The nature of this potential mass base can be readily demonstrated by an examination of a recent "test tube" sample of American fascism.

CHAPTER IX *The Atlanta* Putsch

ON AUGUST 17, 1946, a corporate charter was issued in Atlanta, Georgia, to an organization calling itself Columbians, Inc. The petition for the charter filed in the Fulton County Superior Court listed the names of the incorporators as Homer L. Loomis, Jr., John H. Zimmerlee, Jr., and Emory Burke. According to the articles of incorporation, the new organization was formed "to encourage our people to think in terms of race, nation and faith and to work for a moral reawakening in order to build a progressive white community that is bound together by a deep spiritual consciousness of a common past and a determination to share a common future." From this insignificant beginning emerged the first fascist revolt in the United States — the Atlanta or "beer hall" *Putsch* of American fascism.

1. THE LEADERS

Who were the leaders of Columbians, Inc.? Of Zimmerlee little is known. Born in Montgomery, Alabama, Emory Burke was thirty-one years of age at the time of his arrest, a railroad draftsman by profession, a high school graduate. According to the Non-Sectarian Anti-Nazi League, Burke is a former member of one of Joe McWilliams's anti-Semitic hoodlum gangs in New York with a record of active participation in hate groups dating back to the middle thirties.

It was his boast that he had once shared an apartment with Ernest Elmhurst, a Nazi propagandist later indicted for sedition. From newspaper accounts, one can assume that Burke's background was lower middle class; but Loomis stems from a quite different background.

At the time of the Atlanta *Putsch*, Loomis was thirty-two years of age, having been born in New York on January 31, 1914. His father, Homer Loomis, Sr., is a successful admiralty lawyer, with a Park Avenue address and a listing in the *Social Register*. As a youngster Loomis attended such fashionable private schools as St. Bernard's School in Manhattan and, later, St. Paul's in Concord, New Hampshire. Entering Princeton University in the fall of 1932, he flunked out three years later. His first marriage, in 1935, culminated in a sensational action in the New York courts in which his wife won an annulment. In the trial of this action, Mrs. Loomis testified that her husband had forced her to read "A Mad Man's Manuscript" from the *Pickwick Papers* in a dimly lighted room — the story of a man who plotted his wife's murder. After she had finished reading the tale, Loomis asked her what she thought of it. To her reply that it was "practically impossible," he is reported to have said: "I disagree — I have thought about it often." Following this first adventure in notoriety, Loomis was involved in a typical playboy stunt: a sit-down strike in the Club Bali, where he and his companions slept on the banquette in pajamas, got themselves photographed, and otherwise made fools of themselves.

In the summer of 1937, Loomis remarried. With funds provided by his second wife, he then proceeded to fail in a business venture in Florida and, later, in a large-scale farming scheme in Virginia. It was apparently while living in Virginia that Loomis first became infatuated with Hitler and began to study the Nazi regime. According to Croswell Bowen's interesting account of Loomis in *PM* for January 12, 1947, the future *Führer* began to tell his neighbors and friends in 1940 that "Hitler has the right idea. He's not going to let the German race get mixed up with a lot of inferior races." Arguing endlessly that fascism was "inevitable" and "logical," Loomis was finally reported to the authorities and interviewed by the FBI. Inducted into the army in 1944, he served overseas with the 2nd Armored Division and was honorably discharged at Fort Meade in February 1946. It was shortly after his discharge that Loomis went to Atlanta for the express purpose of launching a fascist movement. "I had to leave New York," he said, "to discover America, to get close to the people." It was his intention, so he told a friend in New York, "to get just one congressman into Washington, then one from every state. . . . Then, I'm going to have a mighty army and we're going to march on New York. If I go to jail for a while, it'll give me a chance to think and to write a book, *Thunder in the South*. I'm going to be the Hitler of America."

In commenting on Loomis's ideas, the editor of the *Princetonian* suggests that he was motivated, perhaps, by ideas similar to those expressed under the heading of "Noblesse Oblige" in a recent article in *Hall-Mark*, the publication of Whig-Clio, Princeton's old and distinguished debating society. "Only if Americans can develop," to quote from this article, "a class which is fit to rule shall we have much hope for a prosperous future. Princetonians must develop a sense of duty equal to the privileges which have been bestowed on them. . . . If there might be developed a government of those fit to rule for the benefit of the masses, but without their assistance, we could look forward to a more prosperous future in our country and to more effective relations with other nations in a world at peace." It is interesting to note that in his interview with Bowen, Loomis had said that the people were "ignorant and underprivileged" and that they "craved leadership."

The most striking phase of Loomis's story is his Park Avenue background. As Max Lerner has pointed out in an editorial in *PM:*

Up to now the would-be *Fuehrers* have generally come from the rural regions, the small towns, the urban lower middle class. Loomis comes from a group which — fashioning a mongrel word suggested by the term *Lumpenproletariat* — I can only call the *Lumpen*-leisure-class. It is a world of emptiness, excesses, frustrations; a twilight world of functionless people who are the real wasteland of American life.

We have often thought of fascist leaders as the incarnation of hatred. But in Loomis' case it is clear that the hatred of Negroes and Jews is secondary — a convenient instrument, not a fanatic passion. Here was a man whose whole life was a succession of failures, in a group accustomed to success and rule. And so he cooks up a hotch-potch assortment of crazy ingredients drawn from the surrounding atmosphere — racial "purity," white supremacy, anti-Jewish myths, sexual asceticism, class-war, army discipline, the cult of violence. . . .

I find an alarming theme in the material Bowen has dug up from the Princeton paper, showing the conviction that many young men of the leisure-class have that they belong to an elite group; that, without doing anything useful in their nation, they are the natural rulers of the masses, by divine right

of property, race, breeding, leisure. From there it is only a
step toward the effort to manipulate the masses in order to
serve the power-lusts and the revenge-impulses of the self-
styled elite who are only empty-minded boys in an empty
world. What America contributes to the natural history of
fascism is this progression from night-club nuisances to street
political hoodlums. . . .

There is little question that the human material for fascism
is present in American life. . . .

2. THE BACKGROUND

That Loomis and Burke knew what they were about is
shown by their deliberate selection of Atlanta as the place
from which to launch a fascist movement. Beginning in
May 1945, strenuous efforts had been made in Georgia to
revive the K.K.K. Eugene Talmadge's victory in the Democratic primary a year later points to the conclusion that
these efforts had been largely successful. That racial tensions were mounting more rapidly in Georgia, perhaps,
than in any Southern state is shown not merely by the
revival of the K.K.K., which began in Georgia, but by the
frightful murder of four Negroes near Monroe, Georgia,
on July 26, 1946. Although neither Burke nor Loomis was
a native of Georgia, they had excellent reasons to believe
that here was the natural locale for a rehearsal of the fascist
plot in America. As a matter of fact, the formation of
Columbians, Inc., was directly related to the proceedings
to revoke the charter of the K.K.K. in Georgia. The Columbians received their charter only a few weeks after a
suit had been filed in the same court to revoke the charter
of the Klan. It has even been said that Columbians, Inc.,
was formed for the express purpose of taking over the

functions and activities of the Klan should its charter be revoked.[1]

According to a statement of the Non-Sectarian Anti-Nazi League, both Loomis and Burke appeared to be well-grounded in Nazi techniques.[2] While admitting that the Nazis had made mistakes, Loomis contended that the Columbians, by avoiding these mistakes, could build "a powerful force of reaction." A fairly careful plan of organization had been worked out for the Columbians. A captain and five lieutenants were designated for each section. Each of the lieutenants commanded ten sergeants. The captains acted directly on orders and instructions from the headquarters of the organization on Barstow Street in Atlanta. The timetable which Loomis and Burke had prepared called for control of the Atlanta city government in six months; of the Georgia state government in two years; of most of the Southern state governments and congressional delegations in four years; and of national control in ten years. While they really had no program, the stated objectives of the Columbians were: to make the United States into an "American nationalist state"; to deport all the Negroes to Africa; and to make America "a one-race nation."[3]

In a raid on the headquarters of the Columbians, the police later found a library of fifty volumes devoted to the Nazi movement and including, of course, Hitler's *Mein Kampf*, which Loomis referred to, appropriately enough, as his "bible." Shortly after its formation, Columbians, Inc., endorsed Gerald L. K. Smith's America First movement and aligned itself with the Gentile Army. Such anti-Semitic hate sheets as *X-Ray* and *Destiny* were regularly received at the headquarters. Among the first things the conspirators

did was to adopt an insignia for the new movement: the
thunderbolt or "flash" symbol copied from the Nazi Elite
Guard. A somewhat similar symbol had been used by the
Canadian fascist movement. Called the *Thunderbolt*, the
publication of the Columbians had a format patterned after
the official organ of the prewar Union of Canadian Fascists.
It has been suggested that there may well have been an
element of coincidence here, since Loomis said that he had
taken the flash insignia from the red bolt of lightning appearing in the shoulder patch emblem of the 2nd Armored
Division.

The headquarters of the Columbians consisted of a dingy
three-room suite in which some of the members lived,
sleeping on cots and mattresses on the floor so that someone
would always be present to answer emergency calls. White
persons were encouraged to telephone the headquarters
whenever a Negro attempted to move into a white or
mixed district; and to report "troublesome" Negroes. Members were given instructions in the gentle art of dragging
drunken Negroes into the homes of "nigger haters" where
the police could later arrest them on trumped-up charges
of burglary or attempted rape. When the police finally
cracked down on the Columbians, the organization had
approximately two hundred members, but eight hundred
application cards were found in the headquarters. Members
wore a brown-shirt uniform with the flash emblem on the
sleeves of their shirts and greeted their leader at meetings
with the cry "*Heil*, Loomis!" which was later modified to
"*Heil*, Columbia!" In soliciting new members, organizers
asked three simple questions: "Do you hate Negroes? Do
you hate Jews? Do you have three dollars?"

While at work on the morning of October 31, 1946, Arthur Weiss, Commander of Jewish War Veterans Atlanta Post No. 112, was told that Columbians, Inc., had issued a provocative anti-Semitic leaflet and were using a sound truck in the streets to drum up attendance for a meeting that evening. Carrying the lightning flash symbol in red ink, the leaflet charged that "the JEWS, who do the greatest part of advertising in newspapers, hate us because we had the courage to come out and tell the truth about how the JEWS are taking all the wealth and money in the nation. The JEWS and the newspapers are AFRAID of us because we are organizing the white people of the South." Sometime prior to the appearance of this leaflet, Loomis had told two students from Oglethorpe University that "the Negro would behave himself if it wasn't for the Jews. It's the Jews' fault that the Negroes are getting out of place."

That evening about 125 Jewish war veterans led by Weiss, who had served as a captain with the 1st Marine Division at Guadalcanal, appeared at the hall and interrupted the meeting with shouts of "Lies!" when Loomis said, "I hate the Jews because they have never become part of the American way of life," and went on to charge that "Jews were the original Nazis" who had conspired for world domination. "The Jew," he said, "will die for what he believes in, but I've never seen one die for the American world." At this point, the police intervened and Loomis announced that the remainder of the meeting would be closed to the public. The Jewish war veterans then left the hall.

Following this meeting, Loomis and three other uniformed members of Columbians, Inc., were arrested on November 2 for intimidating, by threats of violence, a Negro from moving into a home in a semi-white neighborhood. Before appearing at the scene of the picketing, Loomis had granted a two-hour interview to Tom Ham of the *Atlanta Journal*.⁴ The interview took place in the headquarters of the organization, with Loomis sitting at a desk placed in front of a wall decorated with a large purple curtain containing the red flash emblem. During the course of this interview, Loomis poured out "a torrent of impassioned words," denouncing Negroes, Jews, and Communists, and castigating the rich who exploit the masses. He impressed Ham as "tense, high-strung"; a man who used good English and who displayed oratorical talent. "We're political," Loomis told Ham; "we're going to show them [the white people] how to take control of the government — first a neighborhood, then the whole city, then the state government, and finally the national government." While the interview took place, Loomis was busy directing by phone the squads who were picketing the home of the Negro. "Just stand around," Ham heard him say. "Don't budge. If the Negro tries to move in, just stand there on the doorstep and don't give ground. But if the police order you directly to let him move in, let him. That will put the burden on the police." Remarks of this character demonstrate, clearly enough, that Loomis knew something about Nazi tactics in handling police and had studied their skillful use of provocation. "This police trouble," he said, "is purging out the weaklings. It's good for us."

3. THE DENOUEMENT

Prior to the picketing incident of November 2, the Atlanta police had investigated the bombing of a home at 333 Ashby Street, occupied by a Negro, Goldsmith Sibley, and his grandmother, sister, and niece. A blast of dynamite had ripped off a portion of the porch and about ten square feet of weatherboarding. One of the members of Columbians, Inc., has described in an affidavit what occurred on November 2:

When we got out there [to the Negro's home] there were not many people. The niggers came over on the truck with their furniture. Jack Price [a Columbian] walked up and said: "Niggers, you can't move in here. This is a white section. I am telling you, you had better not move in here. If you do, we will blow you out."

The nigger said, "Boss man, I bought this here house. They told me this is a colored section. I got my money in it. It is my house and I got a right to move in."

Price then said: "This is not a nigger community. The niggers who live here are going to move out. If they don't move out, we are going to blow up everyone just like we are going to do to you. If you don't believe I'll stop you, just get that furniture in. I'll stop you right here." [5]

It was at this point that the police arrested the pickets. A day or so later, however, Loomis ordered two Columbians to return to the home and told them "to shoot any colored man who comes out." One of the pickets who returned has said in an affidavit: "I had a rifle, Jimmy had a rifle, and the others had three pistols. When we got there, however, the police were sitting out front." One of the

informers also charged that Loomis had once taken him to
a shack three miles from Atlanta where he saw Loomis
exchange two K.K.K. membership cards for five sticks of
dynamite. Stored in the shack was "a mess of ammunition"
including about twenty-five rifles, shotguns, and pistols.
The riot indictment subsequently filed against Loomis and
Burke charged them with responsibility for beating a
Negro into a state of hysteria on the night of October 28.[6]

At one of the street meetings conducted by the Columbians, a uniformed member appeared holding his sixteen-
months-old daughter in his arms (ostensibly to demonstrate
the "peaceful" character of the demonstration). It was later
established that this storm trooper had, for more than a
year, been sending his daughter to a free child clinic maintained in Atlanta by the B'nai B'rith organization.[7]

"Everybody in America is free to hate," Loomis shouted
at a meeting on November 22. "Hate is natural. It's not
un-American to hate. Why does the Jew think that he
alone is above criticism and being hated?" Returning from
a money-raising trip to New York, Loomis told his followers: "I talked to some of the rich folks I know in
New York. The kind who have escutcheons hanging on
their walls and are so proud of their blood lines and ante-
cedents. They're all for me in what I'm trying to do, but
they don't like your kind of people — the people I'm working with. They made their money exploiting common
people and they don't want to see you organized and put
in a position to help yourselves. Sure, I got a little money
in New York; but I had to get it from poor folks." [8]
According to Ellis Arnall some outside money was unquestionably involved in the promotion of Columbians, Inc. "I

know," he said, "that such organizations as the Columbians, and such peddlers of hate as the hundreds of slimy little racial and class sheets that are distributed and broadcast throughout our common country, cost a great deal more money to support than the riffraff that front for such groups can raise from deluded and neurotic followers."

The Columbians had prepared a list of the organizations and individuals that they intended to purge from Southern society. Both CIO and A. F. of L. unions occupied conspicuous places on the list. Loomis and Burke had made it quite clear that they wanted labor organizers, "particularly Negro organizers, kicked off the streets, leaving the field clear for a Columbian Gentile union." [9] Shortly after Ralph McGill, editor of the *Constitution*, launched a vigorous editorial campaign against the Columbians, he was visited by two men who threatened to "fix" him if the campaign were not dropped immediately. When a suit was brought by the Attorney General of Georgia to revoke the charter of the organization, Burke, in a fit of anger, tore up the charter and mailed the pieces to the Attorney General with his compliments. "We don't care a mouthful of snuff spit," he said, "what the papers say or think. That's how much we care about them."

In an official report to Governor Arnall, the Attorney General charged that Columbians, Inc., had:

1. Systematically planned to intimidate and injure members of minority racial and religious groups;
2. Conspired to bring about the arrest of innocent Georgia citizens on false charges;
3. Unlawfully arrested citizens of Georgia;
4. Assembled a private arsenal of deadly weapons;

5. Bombed the home of a Negro in the City of Atlanta;
6. Corruptly influenced the behavior of minors by inciting them to the commission of criminal offenses; and
7. Restrained home owners in Fulton County from the full and proper enjoyment of their property by force, threats, duress and intimidation.

In this same report, the Attorney General outlined the plans which the Columbians had formulated for spreading the movement to other states. The tactics of the campaign, he reported, involved incitement against the Negro in the South, the Jews in the big cities, the Mexicans in the Southwest, and the Orientals on the West Coast. In fact Loomis had boasted to the Columbians that he had arranged for offices in various cities in the Middle West and that, once organized there, the Columbians would "go into these cities like storm troopers, parading, smashing windows of Jewish stores and scaring people. We will start street fights. After a week or so of this, we will hold a mass meeting and work from there on."

Here is Albert Deutsch's description of some of the personality types to be found in this test-tube sample of American fascism:

A real estate man reputed to be buying up white homes cheap and selling them high to Negroes in "tension areas" at the very time he was egging on his fellow-Columbians to fight off the "nigger invasion.". . .

A salesman who had signed a contract with the leaders to sell memberships at $3 each, pocketing $2 on each card. . . .

A fugitive from a mental hospital. . . .

A 21-year-old youngster, who had spent his youth in a Georgia orphanage and who had served with the Marines on Guadalcanal and Bougainville. Asked why he had joined Columbians, Inc., he said "To tell the truth, I had no place to go. I wanted to be with other fellows and get into something. Besides, I don't like niggers.". . .

A youngster, 17 years of age, who had run away from his Georgia home when he was 13. He had bummed around Chicago, worked as a bellhop in the Morrison Hotel, and had then returned to Atlanta to work in a hamburger joint when he joined the Columbians.

Concluding his revealing account of the personality types to be found in the membership of Columbians, Inc., Deutsch writes:

There are great numbers of young people like these with poor moorings or no anchorage, who feel like outcasts, who feel that they have nothing to look forward to, whose natural craving for adventure is not socially directed into constructive channels, who have been poisoned by regional and national prejudices, who don't feel that they belong, who wish desperately to latch on to something concrete with the colorful overtones that youth yearns for. *They are duck soup for fascist demagogues.*[10]

On February 15, 1947, Loomis was sentenced to serve a year in a public works camp following his conviction of incitement to riot. He was defended at his trial by his father, who, in a two-hour speech to the jury — "my fair-skinned brothers" — had argued that his son was being "crucified like Christ by the Jews." Given a three-year sentence a week later, Emory Burke announced that "a few court cases are not going to stop this movement." And thus ended the Atlanta *Putsch* — thanks to the effective work of the Non-Sectarian Anti-Nazi League and the prompt and courageous action of Governor Ellis Arnall.

But the idea upon which this abortive *Putsch* was based is not dead by any means. On December 17 the FBI revealed that application cards, soliciting membership in Columbians, Inc., had been distributed in Austin, Texas. On November 18, a grand jury in Asheville, North Carolina, indicted a group of men for incitement to riot, the indictment charging that the leaders of this conspiracy had formed a "protective association" to take over the function of law enforcement in the community. On November 25, several policemen in Tacoma, Washington, were stripped of their badges for having participated in a vigilante movement aimed at usurping the functions of the regularly constituted law enforcement officials. The K.K.K. is still very much alive in Georgia and the Klan is the parent of Columbians, Inc. The Columbians, reports Assistant Attorney General Dan Duke, were simply "the juvenile delinquents of the Klan."

It is significant that the Atlanta *Putsch* should have been launched at a time when World War II had not yet been formally terminated (the President's proclamation was not issued until December 31, 1946). While the Columbians have been crushed and their leaders imprisoned, their movement went one step further than any native American fascist movement has yet dared to travel along the road which Hitler and Mussolini moved to dictatorial power. Even such groups as the Klan have consistently functioned as secret, conspiratorial organizations; but the Columbians, recognizing the value of provocative tactics, swaggered through the streets in broad daylight and intimidated their victims without attempting a disguise. The revolt which the Columbians attempted to organize in Atlanta was a fascist revolt — the first real *Putsch* attempted in America. "Tendencies to dismiss the Columbian order as just another crackpot, hoodlum movement," writes Deutsch, "are off the beam. With just a little more effective timing or balance, this movement might have clicked and thrown not only Georgia but the country into chaos."

With the incorrigible egotism of the playboy, Loomis had not even attempted to gear Columbians, Inc., into the larger scheme of things. Acting prematurely, on his own, he had given little thought to securing pledges of support and assistance, as well as advice, from the real leaders of American fascism. He went about the organization of Columbians, Inc., much as he had gone about organizing the pajama strike in the Club Bali. If he had not been so anxious to make the headlines, the launching of Columbians, Inc., might have coincided with the present red-baiting crusade and received the blessing, temporary though it would have been, of Herman Talmadge. But daring has its own rewards and the Atlanta *Putsch* has unquestionably left its imprint on the fascist mind in America. Patterned after this ludicrous precedent, who knows what structures of power will be built on some troubled tomorrow when the chips are really down and the final hand has been dealt? Is this the collapse of a playboy's fantasy or perhaps an intimation of things to come? [11]

CHAPTER X *No Ordinary Task*

TODAY there is no excuse for the smug suburbanite who would refuse to live next door to Einstein, for the Nazis have exposed every excuse, every alibi, every shabby rationalization underlying such conduct. "At no time in the past 2,000 years," to quote from *The Black Book*, "has anti-semitism been unmasked and discredited in the eyes of the people as it is today." But the showing of newsreels based on the Nazi atrocities will not rid the world of anti-Semitism. A searchlight must be thrown, not on the victims, but on the nature of the disease, on the social atmospheres conducive to its spread, on the means by which it is communicated and the purposes for which it is used. For anti-Semitism is the most treacherous, deceptive, and tenacious of social prejudices; the most difficult to isolate or to define; the most resistant to enlightenment and therapy. Related to much larger issues, its eradication will prove no ordinary task.

1. DRAIN THE SWAMPS

The campaign to eradicate anti-Semitism must be organized on two levels: a general attack on the socio-economic conditions which breed the disease; and a special campaign to eliminate all forms of discrimination based solely on race, color, or creed. The general attack demands, as Joshua

Trachtenberg once said, that "we drain the swamps of our social life where the Anopheles of anti-semitism breed." This is a task of a large order which it is not my purpose to outline, even if I felt competent to do so. But it should be apparent from the preceding chapters that what the task involves is the creation of a society in which production is organized on some basis other than individual self-aggrandizement. Since most of the various forms of discrimination have long since become institutionalized in our society — part of the framework of society itself — their elimination will require important modifications in the social structure. To eliminate discrimination, our acquisitive economy must be brought under conscious democratic controls and must be made to serve a major purpose of all social organization — namely, to enlarge the areas in which co-operation rather than competition is the norm.

In this sense, "draining the swamps" of our social life involves issues not directly related to the type of economy in which we function. The larger issue, perhaps, is: how can we fashion an industrial society in which full provision is made for basic human needs? For it is all too obvious that many of the frustrations of modern life can be traced to the kinds of work that people are required to perform, quite apart from the conditions under which these tasks are currently performed or the incentives, individual and social, now offered for their performance. Socially speaking, the function of work should be to orientate the individual to reality. But what judgment must be passed on a society in which work has been robbed, in many areas, of any semblance of meaning, purpose, or human dignity?

"It is interesting to speculate," writes Dr. Edward A.

Strecker, "on what the mental patient might say in his own defense if he had his day in the Court of Mental Hygiene. Should the schizophrenic patient argue the matter of reality versus unreality . . . he might ask some rather embarrassing questions. Is it not possible that in the individuality of the mental patient . . . there is an unconscious protest and in that protest a lesson? Perhaps a segment of that protest is against a scheme of standardized, industrial civilization, so efficiently standardized that tens of thousands of human beings are counted among the fortunate because they are given an opportunity to push a piece of tin under a machine which will punch a few holes in it or perhaps the chance to attach a small part to something destined to become a motor car, as it passes before them on a revolving belt?" [1]

Since it is generally recognized today that most prejudice is socially conditioned, the problem of eradicating anti-Semitism obviously involves much larger issues than the proponents of "intercultural" understanding would seem to imply. "Freedom from fear," Dr. Clyde Kluckholn said in a recent speech, "is the best way to cure group prejudice. This means freedom from the fear of war, from the fear of economic insecurity, from the fear of personal unworthiness. . . . The frustrations of modern life are sufficient to breed any number of latent and unconscious prejudices. In the larger sense these are more threatening than any specific overt manifestations that have yet occurred. *For 'race' prejudice is not isolated* — it is a part of a chain of tendencies." [2] It is certainly no accident that the number of lynchings in fourteen southern states in the years from 1882 to 1930 correlated with the annual per acre value of cotton to the extent of — .67. The conditions that breed racial antagonisms will not be exorcised by avowals of eternal brotherhood pronounced in unison once a year during Brotherhood Week.

Today there is a dangerous tendency to narrow the inquiry into so-called "group tensions" by focusing attention exclusively upon the minutiae of the problem, upon the oddities and quirks of prejudice, on the fascinating pathological detail. In the last few years, I have attended dozens of "intercultural workshops" and "interracial conferences" where the problem of prejudice was discussed much as a group of theologians might discuss original sin. We need to be reminded, as Dr. Frederic Wertham puts it, "that the soap produced in Nazi death factories was not a by-product of sadism to be understood in individual psychological terms. It was produced as a commodity."

2. REMOVE THE BARRIERS

The problem of democracy is so to perfect the organization of society that every man and every group may have the freest possible opportunity to realize and perfect their natures, and to attain the excellence appropriate to their kind.

— HORACE KALLEN

Granted that anti-Semitism and related issues can never be divorced from the larger problems of which they are a part, what is most needed in the United States today is the development of a concept of functional equality. Such a concept should be based on several obvious assumptions: (a) that individuals are not responsible for the color of their skin, the place where they were born, or for their ancestry; (b) that in point of scientific fact as well as moral theory all individuals should be regarded as equals since they differ in capacity, intelligence, and human worth not as groups but as individuals; (c) that nowadays a measure of equality must prevail if individuals are to function as responsible citizens of a democracy and if democratic government is to function effectively in a highly industrialized mass production economy; (d) that to be fully effective such a concept should be universally recognized and (e) that the mere recognition of human rights, however adequately defined, will not in itself guarantee their free exercise.

Such a conceptualization of human rights is being evolved today by the Commission on Human Rights of the United Nations. It has been proposed to the commission that such a code should affirm the obligation of all member states to insure equality before the law of all inhabitants "without qualification or distinction as to race, sex, language, or religion"; that all member states be requested to enact without delay such legislation as will be necessary to implement the code; that member states should take positive and continuous action to insure the full and effective application of the code through agencies set up for this purpose; and that provision be made for appeal from any decision of the commission to the General Assembly.[3]

In the United States the problem is one not of securing the recognition of certain basic human rights, but of insuring their application; of spelling out, in some detail, just what is embraced within the broad guarantees of the Constitution. What we need is a program of social and political action aimed at bringing about, in the phrase of Justice Harlan, "a state of universal civic freedom." Embraced in such a concept of functional equality would be equal educational opportunities for all; equal economic opportunities regardless of race, creed, or color; equal access to good housing; equal access to health and medical facilities; equal access to publicly supported recreational, cultural, and civic facilities of all kinds; equal access to common civic conveniences, such as hotels, restaurants, common carriers, and places of public accommodation; equal enforcement of the law; equal protection of civil and political rights; and, as a variant of the concept of religious freedom, a degree of equality in personal relations (for example, the right of individuals to marry regardless of racial differences). In the implementation of some such concept is to be found the best answer to the problem of anti-Semitism.

What the achievement of these objectives requires is the formation of "a great, special camp" of all the democratic forces in the United States. Progress has been made in this direction, but the movement itself is still embryonic. Today there are some 700 separate organizations actively interested in some phase of the problem, usually on behalf of a particular minority. At the local level some unification of these forces has been achieved and there are now two state-wide organizations (in California and Colorado); but as yet their activities have not been unified on a national scale. This is the obvious next step. For the power to carry such a program into effect exists today in the United States, if it were properly organized. It is to be found in the churches — Jewish, Catholic, and Protestant; in the labor unions; in the minority groups; in literally hundreds of civic, social, and fraternal organizations; and, above all, in the strong appeal which the American tradition of "equal opportunity" has for most of the American people. Where these groups have been united, as in the campaign to enact the Quinn-Ives Bill in New York, they have generally prevailed; but for lack of a common objective — a unifying and dynamic concept — they more often function in a kind of splendid isolation. The problem of implementing a concept of functional equality poses not a question in techniques or know-how, nor a question of power; the problem is really one of leadership and organization.

Fortunately we now have in the report of the President's Committee on Civil Rights a specific program in support of which public opinion can be organized. Here, for the first time, the federal government has taken an inventory of civil rights, noting the areas of weakness and pointing out how and by what means the exercise of these rights can be strengthened. Here, at long last, is a clear recognition that merely to declare certain rights is not to insure their exercise; that a laissez-faire attitude toward civil rights is nowadays inadequate and anachronistic; that the main threat to the exercise of these rights comes from so-called "private groups" and that, in consequence, an affirmative approach must be projected. All of this represents a new departure in American thinking. When *Brothers Under the Skin* was published in 1943, I was taken to task by *liberal* editors for suggesting that the power and the prestige of the federal government could, and should, be used to prevent discrimination. I finally got so annoyed with editorial reminders that "the law follows the mores" and that "legislation cannot prevent discrimination" that I wrote a pamphlet to prove that, in one sense, just the reverse of these propositions is true — namely, that the mores are often shaped by

the law and that discrimination creates perhaps more prejudice than it reflects.

While the report of the President's committee has certain
weaknesses and skirts certain issues, nevertheless if its
recommendations were adopted they would go a long way
toward the creation of a real functional equality in American life. Here, then, is a summary of the recommendations:
(1) The committee proposes to strengthen, in a number of
ways, the Civil Rights Section of the Department of Justice
(an excellent recommendation). (2) To amend and supple-
ment Sections 51 and 52 of the United States Code so as
to clarify the right of the federal authorities to intervene
where rights secured by the Constitution are violated.
(3) To protect the right to vote in federal elections by the
elimination of the poll tax and the adoption of laws protecting the right of all qualified persons to vote in federal
primaries and elections. (4) The enactment by Congress
and the states of legislation requiring groups which attempt
to influence public opinion to disclose pertinent facts about
themselves through a systematic registration procedure.
(5) The elimination of segregation based on race, color,
or creed, including the enactment of a Fair Employment
Practices Act (here the report is weak since it throws the
whole issue, with the exception of fair employment practices, back to the states, whereas it might have recommended
a new federal civil rights act, or, as I suggested in *Brothers
Under the Skin*, a fair racial practices act); nevertheless
this section does contain many excellent suggestions on
how segregation can be eliminated in education, housing,
and other fields. (6) A recommendation that public opinion
be rallied in support of this program by a long-range educa-

tion effort. This, of course, is only a summary of the high lights of the report. By and large, the report is a document of great historic significance for it constitutes an official recognition of the great error which was made in 1876 when by a series of court decisions and legislative acts we permitted the Civil War amendments to be robbed of their original meaning and intention.

The dynamics for achieving such a program are to be found in the obligations of the United States under the United Nations Charter. Under Article 55(c) of the Charter, we are obligated to promote "universal respect for, and observance of, human rights and fundamental freedoms for all without distinction as to race, sex, language, or religion." Under Article 56 we are obligated "to take joint and separate action in co-operation with the organization for the achievement of the purposes set forth in Article 55." In the Act of Chapultepec, signed in Mexico City on March 6, 1945, the United States agreed, in concert with the other signatory nations, "to make every effort to prevent in their respective countries all acts which provoke discrimination among individuals because of race or religion." Ratified as treaties, the United Nations Charter and the Act of Chapultepec define a federal responsibility in the clearest possible terms.

If it be asked, then, where the line is to be drawn between the right of voluntary associations to exclude and the right of the state to protect citizens against discrimination, the answer is to be found in a distinction between those actions which directly affect a person's rights — to a job; to live in whatever residential district he desires and can afford; and to enjoy, on a basis of equality, such amuse-

ment, educational, recreational, and cultural facilities as
may be available — and those exclusions which have no relation to civic or functional rights. Such a concept of functional equality enlarges rather than narrows the right of
individuals to associate on a basis of complete freedom of
choice. There is certainly nothing authoritarian in the suggestion that all voluntary associations in a democracy should
be encouraged to set up standards of membership and
eligibility that are consistent with the premises upon which
democracy rests, however arbitrary or exacting they may
be in other respects.

The importance of this issue of "private governments"
can be grasped if two historical considerations are kept in
mind: that the original American conception of freedom
and equality was that of freedom *from* governmental controls and equality *before* the government (that is, its courts
and such); and, second, that we have always allowed an
extraordinary and largely unrestricted freedom to private
associations and groups (what I call "private governments"). With the government playing a laissez-faire role
in relation to civil rights and the "private governments"
growing in power, the most serious inroads have been
made on the conception of democratic citizenship. It took
a Civil War to get "due process" and "equal protection"
clauses which would limit the power of state governments;
but we are still in a twilight zone so far as recognizing that
the "private governments," in a limited sense, must also be
made to comply with certain constitutional policies.

Admittedly there is much to be said for the pluralistic
philosophy which would allow great scope and freedom to
"private governments," for this is one way of offsetting

the tendency toward concentration of power in the federal government. But a trade-union, a "private" school, an industry, a company town, a corporation, a political party, can, by various discriminatory practices, make a mockery of rights secured by the Constitution. Many of these associations are in effect "governmental instrumentalities" and on this theory alone, should be subject to certain regulations; then, too, many of their functions are essentially governmental and should be brought into compliance with constitutional requirements; frequently the rule or regulation of the private government is enforced by recourse to the state courts and thus, in effect, represents "state action" within the meaning of the construction that the courts have placed on the Fourteenth Amendment. It should also be pointed out that many private governments enjoy governmental support in one form or another, such as tax exemption.

The question, therefore, is where does one draw the line between the legitimate freedom which should be allowed private governments and the point at which the federal government must intervene to prevent their regulations from impinging on civil rights? Now, no one has suggested that a Jewish boy should be able to penetrate a restricted fraternity by a sheriff's writ, although public opinion, in a democracy, should constantly seek to induce *all* associations to abandon voluntarily discriminations based solely on race, color, or creed. The line is not to be drawn arbitrarily but by balancing the interest of the community in the preservation of democratic values against such rights as freedom of contract. It is not every ethnic discrimination, therefore, that would warrant intervention. The right impinged may be of slight social value. But where the private association discriminates in the area of what I have called "functional" rights — health, housing, education, employment, and so forth — then the government should intervene.

On this point the report of the President's committee is quite clear and what the report has to say about education indicates the basis on which we should "draw the line":

> The Committee is absolutely convinced of the importance of the private educational institution to a free society. It does not question the right of groups of private citizens to establish such institutions, determine their character and policies, and operate them. But it does believe that such schools immediately acquire a public character and importance. Invariably they enjoy government support, if only in the form of exemption from taxation and in the privilege of income-tax deduction extended to their benefactors. Inevitably, they render public service by training young people for life in a democratic society. Consequently, they are possessed of a public responsibility from which there is no escape. (p. 66)

ॐ

The Committee is not convinced that an end to segregation in education or in the enjoyment of public services essential to people in a modern society would mean an intrusion upon the private life of the individual. In a democracy, each individual must have freedom to choose his friends and to control the pattern of his personal and family life. But we see nothing inconsistent between this freedom and a recognition of the truth that democracy also means that in going to school, working, participating in the political process, serving in the armed forces, enjoying government services in such fields as health and recreation, making use of transportation and other public accommodation facilities, and living in specific communities and neighborhoods, distinctions of race, color, and creed have no place. (p. 87)

Nor does the concept of functional equality in any manner interfere with what has been called "the right to be different." For example, the Central Conference of American Rabbis at its 58th annual convention affirmed its stand against "mixed marriages between Jews and non-Jews without conversion." [4] The right to make this affirmation is in no manner inconsistent with the position that miscegenation statutes constitute an arbitrary interference with the personal rights and privileges of individuals and should, therefore, be repealed. "If," says Dr. Kluckholn, "individuals of all backgrounds will accept persons of all other backgrounds not 'in their place,' not as exotics but as individuals, then we shall have created something new in the world." If it be said, as it always is said, that a broad policy aimed at eliminating all forms of discrimination would tend to obliterate "differences" and thereby rob America of its cultural diversity, the answer is that a false emphasis upon diversity can come dangerously close to a type of separatism basically inconsistent with the patterns of democracy. The right to be different should not be confused with the artificial preservation of differences. "The United States," to quote Dr. Kluckholn again, "must be made safe for differences, so long as these are not a threat to a certain minimum of national solidarity. But this does not mean that differences should be artificially resuscitated or their preservation demanded. . . . Any culture is, more than anything else, a set of solutions, a delicate adjustment, to a particular set of environmental problems.

When situations change, culture changes. Designs for living that make a great deal of sense in Swiss mountain valleys make very little sense when the same people try to continue them in Chicago or on the plains of Kansas. Respect for cultural variation must begin at home. But this means respect for those variations that are appropriate and not a threat to the social order. It does not mean that we must try to make the United States into a cultural museum."

3. PREJUDICE IS INDIVISIBLE

While the discrimination against Jews is neither as visible nor as severe as that against racial minorities, it is quite apparent that their stake in the achievement of a functional equality for all citizens is as great as any other minority. In the key areas of housing, education, and employment, they are directly involved. A surprisingly large number of subdivisions in American cities are restricted against "persons of Jewish or Hebrew descent." Quite recently public attention was directed to two new subdivisions in Austin, Texas, that were advertised as being restricted against Jewish occupancy. Asked for an explanation, the subdivider put it this way: "One of my best friends is Jewish, but this is a cold-blooded free enterprise business." [5] A restriction in Roanoke is aimed at Negroes, Greeks, Assyrians, "or any person who belongs to any race, creed, or sect which holds, recognizes or observes any day of the week other than the first day of the week to be the Sabbath . . . or any corporation or clan composed of or controlled by any such group"! That such a case should have arisen in Virginia —

the cradle of religious liberty in the United States — is an ironic commentary on our schizoid culture.

A study of Jewish residential settlement in any large or medium-sized American city will reveal that external pressures have played an important role in restricting the area of settlement. As Louis Wirth demonstrated in *The Ghetto* (1928), Jews have generally settled in a primary area, a kind of modified ghetto district, from which they have moved, not into the contiguous or adjacent districts, but into districts usually far removed from the original area. This outward movement has usually been made "in jumps and spurts" and has been motivated, in part, by a desire "to escape into anonymity," a flight which tends to be cumulative, for the ghetto keeps following the Jew. "Unwittingly," writes Wirth, "the deserters from the ghetto have become the founders of a new ghetto." This pattern has been particularly noticeable in hotels and apartments, types of residence that offer the promise of anonymity. Since Gentiles have been known to move out when the first Jew moves in, the process tends to be repeated. It is thus absurd to contend that clannishness alone can account for the clusters of Jewish settlement to be found in most American cities.

The stake that Jews have in the fight against discrimination in employment is so obvious that little comment is required. While all minorities have an equal concern with fair employment practices, the issue should be of greater concern to Jews today than ever before. Wherever bureaucracies have developed, whether in business or in government, the feasibility of excluding Jews has been enhanced. "At a time," writes Nathan Reich, "when ever-increasing numbers of young Jews will have to seek employment in large corporations or government agencies; when the opinion of personnel managers may decide the fate of thousands of job-seekers, the 'social' prejudice of those in charge of employment policy acquires a new and menacing significance." [6]

So far as Jews are concerned, no form of discrimination should be opposed more vigorously than the quota system. It has been said that educational quotas are democratic since it is their purpose to ration educational opportunities in rough approximation to the size of the various racial and ethnic groups. Since we have a certain number of Jews, Catholics, and Negroes, so the argument runs, we should have a certain number of Jewish doctors, Catholic lawyers, and Negro dentists. But this contention, as Dr. Robert Redfield has pointed out, is tantamount to a denial of "the American assumption that men of all religious and all ethnic origins may come to acquire the capacities for carrying on the common life." [7] It assumes, furthermore, that Jewish doctors will only serve Jewish patients. The hypocrisy of the argument is best demonstrated by its inconsistency. Quoting Yves R. Simon, Dr. Redfield says that he will believe with Pascal in the sincerity of those witnesses who allow themselves to be martyred. Until the advocates of the quota system urge quotas for white, Protestant, Anglo-Saxon students, one is justified in questioning the sincerity of their position.

It is also said that quotas are necessary to preserve some special quality of a college or university, as being primarily "Christian" or "Baptist" or "nonurban." But this assumes that private educational institutions should not be responsive to changing needs in a democratic society. Since these institutions insist that their "special quality" contributes to the total affirmation of American values, they can hardly defend, in good conscience, a practice which violates one of the most basic tenets of American democracy, namely, "that nothing granted to one citizen is to be denied another by reason solely of his membership in a racial or religious group."

Frequently this argument is used in reverse. To be thoroughly representative of American democracy, it is contended that institutions must impose restrictions against certain racial or religious groups. But which institution is the more thoroughly representative of American values: the one that arbitrarily seeks a "cross-sectional" representation or the one that firmly adheres to the American principle of equality in educational opportunities? Again it is argued that quotas are necessary to minimize anti-Semitism. If Jews urged this argument upon non-Jews, it might have some validity. But, as Dr. Redfield asks, "is there not something disingenuous in one, not a Jew, who contends that the Jew is his own worst enemy and that to keep him from injuring himself by pushing his case too far, he, the non-Jew, should limit the enrollment of Jews, when it is remembered that it will be the self-appointed protector's own group that will do the threatened damage to the Jew?"

The quota system can be successfully attacked along three lines: through the pressure of lawsuits and protests aimed at eliminating the tax-exempt status of quota institutions unless these institutions agree to adhere to a nonquota system; through legislative enactments designed to compel adherence to such a policy; and through the development of an organized public opinion against quotas. Some years ago, for example, the presidents of twelve American universities asked President Roosevelt to appoint a Fair Educational Practices Commission. The suggestion has great merit and should be adopted. If, through pressure of public opinion, all educational institutions agreed to abandon quotas, and were to do so at the same time, no one institution would suffer any temporary disadvantage, real or imagined, by comparison with any other.

The fight against the quota system needs to be correlated with the fight against segregated schools, for quotas are merely a polite form of segregation. The movement to abolish quotas should also be closely correlated with the campaign for fair employment practices. Any number of vocational guidance clinics can be set up to advise young Jews not to enter the free professions, but they will continue to do so as long as they encounter discriminatory employment practices in American industry. While much progress has already been made in the effort to abolish quotas, a strong opposition has of late been voiced against the movement in the name of "freedom of educational institutions." [8] It should be observed that in these three key areas of housing, employment, and education, the opposition to Jews has been stiffening for the last two or three decades.

The method of combating racism outlined in this section — the "law and social action" approach — is one of the most effective methods in use today. Here legal techniques are fused with social science insights in concerted campaigns to break down the pattern of discrimination in education, employment, housing, and related fields. Campaigns of this sort have great educational value, both for the organizations which conduct them and for the general public. They also have the merit of focusing attention upon specific aspects of discrimination, of high-lighting the facts, of setting people in motion. Remarkable headway has been made in this field of recent years and one might well rest the case for the effectiveness of this approach by calling attention to some of the excellent work of the Law and Social Action Commission of the American Jewish Congress.

4. DEFINE A REAL SCAPEGOAT

It goes without saying that anti-Semitism must be combated through education: at every level and by every proved means and technique, particularly through mass education in political and social action. A vast amount of money is currently being spent on educational programs to combat racism in general and anti-Semitism in particular. But it has only been of recent years that these programs have been subjected to scientific tests to determine their effectiveness. It is apparent from these studies that a great deal of money has been wasted, and is being wasted, in large-scale educational projects of one kind or another. Other studies in the social sciences have demonstrated the kinds of educational programs that have proved their efficiency.[9] Generally speaking, educational programs to combat racism, both in and out of the schools, should be more closely related to research in the social sciences, and the effectiveness of particular programs should be constantly checked by scientific tests.

Granted the maximum effectiveness, however, there are limits to what can be accomplished solely through education. "If you want my watch," writes Maurice Samuel, "or my job, you will find it much easier to set about getting it if the action is accompanied by a process of self-propaganda: that is, if you first prove to yourself that I killed your God, or violated your culture, or that I eat soup noisily and fail to salute your flag. It will then do me no good to prove that the Romans killed your God, or that your God is nine-tenths myth, that I contribute to your culture, that I eat soup quietly and am extremely patriotic. The better my arguments, the angrier you will get; in the last analysis, you will relieve me of my watch for being too clever in defending my possession of it." [10] Since stereotypes rationalize relationships, it is apparent that the relationships must be changed, in some respects, before the re-education of the individual can be complete.

A major weakness of most educational programs to combat racism is that they fail to define a legitimate scapegoat — that is, they fail to define the real sources of frustration. Such an effort should be directed toward interpreting, particularly to the middle class, the nature of the social forces operating in our society. The interpretation should be accompanied, of course, by a statement of realizable goals and of the various steps by which these goals might be achieved. The weakness of most "antifascist" political and educational activity has consisted in its defensive character. It is not enough that fascist trends should be opposed, for much of this activity is directed at symptoms rather than at causes. Starting with some emergency of the moment, the prodemocratic elements exhaust themselves in defeating a particular drive only to discover that the same effort must be repeated a week later. What is so obviously needed is a strong and sustaining mass movement with goals that could fire the imagination of people above and beyond a concern for the petty interests of the moment and the purely short-range objectives.

In periods of social crisis, fascist demagogues take skillful advantage of the tendency, as Ellis Freeman puts it, "to cling to the falsehoods and frauds of good repute, not necessarily through congenital stupidity or any other innate predispositions but because of deficient opportunities to learn better." In other words, fascism thrives on social bewilderment. Almost every study of fascist movements has emphasized that the mass following of such movements has been made up of people who have been overwhelmed by the social confusion of the times. Unable to understand this confusion and not receiving an acceptable explanation of its causes, they have taken refuge out of desperation in the dogmatic certainties of fascism.

Perhaps the least effective educational method in use today consists in the distribution of what is termed "tolerance propaganda." Here an enormous amount of money is being wasted. It is fairly well established, for example, that more than $1,000,000 a year is now being spent on well-intentioned propaganda campaigns of this sort. The idea behind these campaigns is that it is possible to sell "tolerance" as one would sell tooth paste. But as Dr. Paul F. Lazarfeld demonstrated in a memorandum submitted to the President's Committee on Civil Rights, tests have shown that this propaganda is often of dubious value and that it frequently has a "boomerang" effect. As he points out, "people have a remarkable ability for assimilating propaganda to their existing attitudes so that these attitudes remain intact." While something is to be gained by propaganda methods, the propaganda should be pretested for its effect and there should be some follow-up to determine its results.

Research in the social sciences can provide a scientific basis for experiments in mass education. That anti-Semitism is so often found as part of an interconnected "system of ideas" should prompt, for example, additional research on the techniques by which this system can be changed. Which parts of the system are most vulnerable to attack? What are the interconnections which hold these ideas together in a single complex? Is it possible to direct an educational attack at the entire system?

Where social scientists have made their greatest contribution is in the field of child training and personality formation. Early childhood experiences and parent-child relationships have been found to have a bearing — how important has yet to be determined — on the development of attitudes hostile or friendly toward groups other than the one into which the child is born. Part of the long-range problem, therefore, is "to modify our institutions, particularly our child-rearing institutions, the home and the school, in such a manner that secure and loving, rather than insecure and hate-ridden, personalities are produced." [11] But since these institutions never function in a vacuum, the real scrutiny must always be focused upon the larger social pattern.

To be effective, education against racism should emphasize the real causes of fascism. At the end of a nationwide speaking tour, devoted to exposing fascist trends in the United States, O. John Rogge recently said that he had found "an appalling lack of information and a desperate need for education. Many of the people to whom I spoke were hearing a speech about fascism for the first time. Some of them had already accepted parts of a fascist program, completely unaware that their prejudices and attitudes were antidemocratic. Too many of them would not recognize a fascist if they heard him speak or if they read his propaganda — provided he didn't have a thick German accent and kept a swastika off his printed material." Nothing points to the danger of fascism more clearly than the fact that, although a congressional committee on un-American activities has been in existence since the middle thirties, we have yet to have a thoroughgoing investigation of fascist intrigue in the United States. As a postscript, one notes that the Rogge report was suppressed by the Department of Justice and that Rogge was fired from his position as Assistant Attorney General under the most curious circumstances.

Education should also expose the bogus countertradition that has developed in the United States. A pattern of prejudice against certain groups has been interwoven in American culture; but this culture also contains the conflicting pattern of equality. The resolution of this "American dilemma" must involve a frank recognition of the conflict and an effort to uproot the spurious countertradition. Confused by the presence of two traditions, many Americans seem to experience great difficulty in distinguishing between the real tradition and its bogus counterpart. When Senator McKellar suggests that the chairmanship of the Atomic

Energy Commission should be limited by law to "a second-generation native American," he is appealing to this bogus countertradition. One must acknowledge with shame that the fight against David Lilienthal was motivated, in part, by the circumstance that he is of Jewish descent. Comparing this fight with the earlier fight to confirm the nomination of Brandeis, Marquis Childs pointed out that "the same poison of racism colors not a little of the prejudice against Lilienthal. It is whispered in the Senate cloakroom and proclaimed when lobbyists and special pleaders meet." [12] When Senator Bilbo charged that "Jewish and Negro minorities are trying to destroy our freedom and the American way of life," and when Congressman Rankin interrupts the testimony of William Bullitt to inquire if it isn't true that most Jews are Communists, it is the false, the un-American tradition that echoes in the halls of Congress.

Still another education method for combating racism involves an attempt to change the attitude of *groups* by creating new group experiences, more particularly by creating new institutions with new patterns of human relations. In our society, individual prejudices are fortified by, and often coerced by, the attitude of the group to which the individual belongs. To educate the individual to the folly of racism it is often valuable to create a new group relationship. Studies have shown, for example, that most "white" Americans are in favor of residential segregation for Negroes; but few of them have ever lived in the same neighborhoods with Negroes and know nothing about Negroes as neighbors. The experience of public housing projects where mixed occupancy prevails demonstrates that prejudice tends to break down under the impact of the new pattern of relationships. Here the re-education of the individual is likely to be real, for it is based upon a new experience, a new relationship, and not upon the assimilation of certain factual information in a pamphlet. While "organized group experiences" of this sort are often of real value, it too frequently happens that the new institution — the school, the housing project, the summer camp — is isolated in the larger community like an island in the ocean. The importance of creating new relationships, however, cannot be overemphasized. Most "white" Americans know Negroes in only a few relationships: landlord and tenant; seller and buyer; master and servant. These are not relationships likely to make for mutual understanding and appreciation. Much better relationships are those of fellow classmates, neighbors, membership in the same trade-union, fellow employee, and so forth.

∽

The campaign to combat racism in America demands that every individual American citizen accept full and conscious responsibility for his public and private acts. "The mores," writes Dr. Robert Redfield, "are not extrahuman pressures, like the weight of the atmosphere or the pull of gravity. They are not something external to the wishes and the sentiments of men. They *are* the wishes and the sentiments of men (so far as imbued with a sense of rightness), and men change their wishes and their sentiments in response to what other men do and in response to what they themselves do. If one man or one institution takes a public position against racial prejudice so as to make effective an equality as among racial groups that was before denied, that act gives encouragement to all others whose attitudes inclined toward equality and justice but who were held from acting in accordance with their inclination by uncertainty or timidity or other causes. . . . Whether we like it or not, our every act of discrimination or of equal treatment as between ethnic groups is an influence upon the general attitudes of the community. If we act so as to bring about just treatment of all citizens, the people of our community will, on the whole, tend to uphold that justice; if we act unjustly, then men will be helped to excuse their unjust attitudes. We are not helpless to reduce discrimination in the community."

Without waiting for the millennium, any individual American citizen can do certain things to combat racism, and I know of no better advice on what he can do than that recently offered by Dr. Clyde Kluckholn:

We can treat people as people rather than as representatives of ethnic groups. We can show our friends how absurd it is to think of whole segments of the population as "all bad" or "all good." We can discredit the sadists in our own circle of acquaintances. We can ridicule and deflate demagogues and rabble rousers. We can circulate jokes that bring out the American virtues of fair play and tolerance at the expense of Jew-baiters. We can do our part to see to it that newspapers and radios represent those in the process of assimilation as enjoying general support rather than as weak and isolated. In our own talk we can emphasize the facts of assimilation and adjustment as much as the facts — both "desirable" and "undesirable" — of differences. We can insist that our leaders continue to express their disapproval of attempts to arouse ethnic strife. We can expose the attempts of the unscrupulous, whether in government, industry or labor, to turn the hatred of the citizenry from their real enemies upon innocent scapegoats. We can raise children who are more secure and freer so that they do not have an inner need to hurt and to attack. We can increase, each of us, our own self-understanding, winning greater freedom and a higher degree of responsible behavior, as we gain deeper insight into our own motives. . . .

If we can do these things within our own country — if we can treat assimilation as something other than a one-way process, if we can feel the pride we ought to feel in the diverse origins of our ideas and customs, then we shall be able to take leadership in world acceptance of cultural diversity. We shall also need to alter situations — perhaps the structure of our economy. For under certain arrangements of the social order, respect for others cannot become general — no matter how fine the ideals.

Men do very difficult things, if they are thoroughly realized as being profoundly necessary, more adequately than they do easy things. The people's capacity must be believed in, and the present and permanent task of democracy is to affirm that capacity and to seek the ways to enable it to prevail. It is the challenges which seem to be little — not the ones recognized as big — to which people do not rise. They can rise to the challenge of peace, as they did to the challenge of war. The strength of a democratic world order will be, not merely that it will allow the individual an enjoyment procured through security and through conveniences, but that it will call upon him for greatness.

Americans determined to accept this type of individual responsibility might well start, at this time, by advocating a liberal policy of immigration and the removal of discriminatory bars, racial and otherwise, from existing immigration and naturalization laws.

5. TAKE AWAY THE WHIP

When I see a driver abusing his weary horse so mercilessly with his whip that the beast's veins and its nerves quiver, and one of the passive if compassionate bystanders asks me: what can be done? I must tell him: first take the whip away from that savage.

— JACOB WASSERMANN

One of the reasons that minority groups perform a scapegoat function is simply that they are weak. By strengthening the position of minorities, the temptation to use them as whipping boys can be minimized if not eliminated. Needless to say, this does not involve conferring special rights or group privileges upon minorities. For the protection offered, say, by an FEPC statute applies to *all* individuals; not to any particular group. There is one facet of the issue, however, which does have a special relation to the problem of anti-Semitism.

As its history universally confirms, anti-Semitism is a formidable weapon. The organized use of this weapon should not be countenanced in a civilized society. If society can outlaw physical instrumentalities of destruction, it should be able to protect individuals against the systematic use of a social weapon which universal experience has shown to be no less dangerous and destructive. Using new means of mass communication, fascist groups have perfected the weapon of systematic defamation. In its early stages, a fascist movement uses verbal violence as the precursor for the physical violence that will come later. Systematic defamation has the effect of welding the profascist elements into a unified force by concentrating their hatreds and aggressions against a particular minority. Provocative by intention, these verbal assaults can reach a pitch of violence that a democratic society cannot afford to ignore. By fastening the charge of violating civil liberties on their opponents, fascist demagogues cleverly demoralize public opinion. Through a fantastic perversion of the real issues, they emerge as the defenders of law, order, and free speech while systematically undermining respect for law and order and deliberately corroding the concept of free speech.

The division of opinion that exists today on this issue constitutes the best proof that a reconsideration of our traditional laissez-faire attitude toward civil liberties is needed. Faced with the difficult task of rethinking certain concepts, many liberals have preferred to take refuge in "the certainties of inaction." Being chronic perfectionists, they have been reluctant to experiment with new tactics and strategies simply because these measures cannot be regarded as perfect solutions to particular problems. Nevertheless one can detect a gradually developing awareness of the limitations of the laissez-faire attitude toward civil liberties. In one of the best studies of the constitutional issues, David Riesman has suggested that the law of civil libel should be reframed to permit actions for group defamation; [13] while the late A. H. Pekelis urged that groups defamed should defend themselves by taking the issues directly to the public by such means as picket lines, demonstrations, and public meetings. The essence of his proposal consists in the suggestion that minorities should *assert a right* — namely, the right to be free of systematic vilification and organized abuse. [14]

The key to the problem, it seems to me, is to be found in the distinction between unorganized and organized defamation; between individual slander and conspiracies to violate the rights of citizens of the United States. Government cannot assume the formidable task of supervising propaganda; but it should be able to protect citizens against an organized assault upon their rights, as citizens, just as it protects them against physical violence. It is rather absurd to contend that a modern government can protect a Jewish merchant against vandalism but that it is powerless to protect him against an organized campaign to violate his civil rights. Our real concern should be not so much with anti-Semitic propaganda as with organized racism. *Mein Kampf* is a good example of anti-Semitic propaganda; but it should be read and carefully studied by those who believe in democracy.

It was this distinction between private opinion and organized agitation that Heywood Broun once sought to define. "Where, then," he asked, "does one draw the line across which the legal right changes into a moral wrong? It might be placed at the point where personal feeling denies to others the right to earn a living; it becomes a social menace *where a concerted understanding* saddles onto a class a burden of economic disability" (emphasis added). As Dr. Milton Steinberg has said, "The state cannot enact affection between Gentiles and Jews. What non-Jews think about their Jewish fellows is legally their business. But how non-Jews behave in this respect is another matter, and one of more than private concern. Not only the welfare of the Jews, but the tranquility of the community and perhaps ultimately the peace of the world may be involved. In the teeth of these considerations it is arrant nonsense to contend that the state has no interest in restraining agitation against racial, cultural or religious groupings in our midst." [15]

Hard as this line may be to draw — and it should be drawn with great care — the effort should not be abandoned merely

No Ordinary Task 253

because of the difficulties involved. For there is such a line
to be drawn and we are gradually drawing it in practice.
When efforts were launched in 1945 to revive the K.K.K.,
public opinion demanded action. Under the leadership of
Robert W. Kenny, then Attorney General of California,
actions were brought in a number of states to revoke the
corporate charters of K.K.K. groups. Did this type of action represent an interference with the right of certain
citizens to be Klansmen? If it did, then the interference
was justified, for what a Klansman thinks and says and
writes is one thing; what he does, in concert with other
Klansmen, is an entirely different thing. Most observers
agree that these actions have arrested the growth of the
Klan.

Following Father Coughlin's notorious anti-Semitic radio
speech of November 20, 1938, group pressure finally forced
him off the air. Was this an interference with free speech
when his major purpose was to attack a minority group?
Coughlin's speech was not an isolated statement; he was
the head of the Union of Social Justice which was then con-
ducting a systematic campaign against Jews and his speech
was part of that campaign. When Jewish war veterans
appeared at a meeting of the Columbians and protested
Homer Loomis's defamatory statements, they were clearly
acting within their rights. Who will contend that Governor
Arnall was unlawfully interfering with "the right to hate"
— which Loomis asserted — when he caused his arrest for
incitement to riot?

The same issue was involved in the successful effort
of the American Jewish Congress to induce the Federal
Communications Commission to deny the application of

the *Daily News* for a permit to operate a radio station. By the use of the most rigorous scientific techniques, the Congress demonstrated that in the period from 1938 to 1946 the *Daily News* developed an image of the American Jew which was far from flattering. Since the air is a natural monopoly, government has been forced to regulate broadcasting; and, in doing so, it has set up certain standards of public service. One of the FCC regulations is that radio stations shall "treat all races, colors and creeds fairly, without prejudice or ridicule." Is this an unreasonable requirement? Were the groups that caused disciplinary action to be instituted against a teacher in the New York schools who had made remarks indicating a sharply biased attitude toward minority groups guilty of an interference with "academic freedom"? What these and similar issues indicate is that the general public can no longer afford to take a laissez-faire attitude; that the public must find means of expressing its disapproval of organized defamation.

Without a single addition to the statute books, law enforcement officials can protect citizens against most discriminatory actions organized by private groups — if public opinion demands that such protection be afforded. Every American city has ordinances that could be used to suppress various manifestations of organized anti-Semitism, such as recent acts of vandalism which caused $20,000 damage at the Oak Woods Cemetery in Chicago.[16] In a brief period in 1946, some eighteen or twenty acts of vandalism were reported in the city of Los Angeles, including the desecration of Temple Israel and the destruction of an ancient Torah that Rabbi Max Nussbaum had managed to bring from Berlin when he sought refuge in America. None of these acts was punished. In most communities, law enforcement officials simply do not recognize manifestations of prejudice, even those that involve a clear violation of existing ordinances, as being criminal in character. What is needed is an informed public opinion that will demand enforcement of all existing laws that could be used to protect minorities against organized assaults upon their rights.

In federal legislation affirmatively safeguarding civil rights is to be found the best means, not of outlawing anti-Semitic propaganda, but of outlawing organized racism. "In a democracy which knows its own mind," writes Dr. Ellis Freeman . . . "it would be difficult for a Fritz Kuhn to claim that any suppression of his Nazi storm troopers was also a blow at the right of the Boy Scouts to parade. When a democracy allows freedom of development to groups, it is realizing a principle of liberty and consummating itself. When it extends the same opportunity to forces conducive to mobs, it is frustrating that principle and slowly strangling itself." [17]

Just as a democracy must distinguish between groups and mobs, between private opinions and organized racism, so it may be forced to distinguish between "speech," in the sense of communicating ideas, and speech as a weapon of abuse. Should this necessity arise, the basis for the distinction has been clearly set forth in Mr. Justice Murphy's opinion, for a unanimous court, in *Chaplinsky* v. *New Hampshire* (315 U.S. 568):

Allowing the broadest scope to the language and purpose of the Fourteenth Amendment, it is well understood that the right of free speech is not absolute at all times and under all circumstances. There are certain well-defined and narrowly limited classes of speech, the prevention and punishment of which has never been thought to raise any constitutional problem. These include the lewd and obscene, the profane, the libelous, and the insulting or "fighting" words — those which by their very utterance inflict injury or tend to incite an immediate breach of the peace. It has been well observed that such utterances are no essential part of any exposition of ideas, and are of such slight social value as a step to truth that any benefit that may be derived from them is clearly outweighed by the social interest in order and morality. Resort to epithets or personal abuse is not in any proper sense communication of information or opinion safeguarded by the Constitution, and its punishment as a criminal act would raise no question under that instrument.

It will be argued, of course, that such distinctions as I have tried to draw in this section can be appropriated by undemocratic groups and used, with reverse effect, against democratic groups. It is obvious that such a risk exists; but we live in a dynamic society and the social forces operating in this society will not remain static merely because we hope that they will. The fascist threat to democracy is a real threat and the real risk consists in minimizing this threat. While I see no objection to group libel statutes and think they might serve a good purpose (and the same holds for ordinances prohibiting the distribution of anonymous material), I also believe that it is a mistake to place too much confidence in techniques of this sort. Not only are serious constitutional issues involved, but it is doubtful if even the most carefully drawn group libel statute would reach many of the defamations that one currently encounters. In short, I would give this particular approach to the problem a low priority rating.

The unmasked and undisguised mob that murdered four Negroes near Monroe, Georgia, on July 26, 1946, was psychologically conditioned to commit any crime in the calendar of Nazi atrocities. Three of the victims were not suspected of criminal behavior or even of any wrongdoing. The Nazis who stoked the crematoriums could at least offer the specious defense that they acted under orders; but no one ordered the murder of Roger and Dorothy Malcolm, of Willie Mae and George Dorsey. No callow sophistries such as Westbrook Pegler's statement that "bigotry and intolerance are not un-American," and therefore presumably not manifestations of fascism, can possibly obscure the reality of fascist trends in American life today. The occurrence of such acts and the brief minor revolt of the Columbians should be a sufficient warning that "fascism is a global disease, a universal shame, fermenting in the soil of this century, breaking out to mutilate the brains and limbs of mankind everywhere." [18]

6. "WHEN THE DEMAGOGUE COMES TO TOWN"

That the issues raised in the foregoing section are real issues demanding real answers is shown by the confusion created by the resumption of fascist agitation which began in the spring of 1945. Lack of basic agreement on questions of strategy and tactics spread confusion, demoralization, and dissension in community after community. In far too many instances, the appearance of Gerald L. K. Smith precipitated an ideological civil war among his opponents.

Out of this experience two sharply divergent points of

view have emerged. As generally formulated, the issue is made to turn on a choice between the so-called "silent" versus the "noisy" treatment. The silent treatment policy has been most plausibly argued by Solomon Andhil Fineberg in a pamphlet entitled *Checkmate for Rabble-Rousers or What to Do When the Demagogue Comes to Town.* Dr. Fineberg makes a distinction between "prominent" anti-Semites and the garden variety of native fascist rabble rousers. While the former cannot be ignored, he argues that the latter must be dealt with by a policy of planned silence. Rabble rousers like Smith, so the argument runs, would be inconsequential were it not for the opposition which their provocative tactics arouse. In other words, they thrive on publicity. Therefore communities should ignore the rabble rouser while attempting to immunize the people against the virus of his propaganda.

Is it really true, however, that rabble rousers thrive on opposition? Obviously some types of opposition are catnip to a man like Smith, but he certainly does not relish all types of opposition. On July 20, 1945, ten thousand citizens of Los Angeles attended a rally at the Olympic Auditorium to protest Smith's activities in Southern California. The meeting was called for the same evening on which Smith was scheduled to address a rally at the Shrine Auditorium. With a miserable attendance at his meeting, Smith spent most of the evening denouncing the individuals who had organized the counterdemonstration. Obviously this was one type of opposition he did not relish.

This same experience demonstrates why the silent treatment cannot be applied, as a uniform policy, under all circumstances. Smith's highly provocative speeches had aroused a section of Los Angeles opinion to a high pitch of excitement. Had the counterdemonstration not been organized, this feeling of indignation might have assumed a less constructive form of expression. As a member of the committee that organized the demonstration, I have a vivid recollection of the state of community opinion at the time. The people not only wanted something done, but they wanted it done publicly so that it could be seen and heard and felt in the community. If demonstrations of this sort are planned and carefully organized, the form of expression can be controlled; but an unchannelized community indignation is likely to assume dangerous modes of expression.

As a result of the anti-Smith mass meeting, a movement was launched to recall a city councilman who had become enamored of America First doctrines. The recall of this councilman had a most tonic effect on official attitudes. Yet there were liberals in the community who insisted that the recall movement constituted an improper interference with the councilman's right to hold views similar to those of Gerald L. K. Smith! As part of the recall movement, opinion polls were taken which revealed that the voters who knew about Smith were, generally speaking, opposed to him; but that a high percentage of the voters in the district — around 45 per cent to be exact — had never heard of Smith. Before the recall campaign was successfully concluded, however, this situation had been corrected. On the other hand, not much in the way of mass education can be achieved by the wire-pulling or clever maneuvers of a few top leaders working behind the scenes.

Closely related to the "silent treatment" philosophy is the emphasis that has long been placed by certain Jewish organizations on "anti-defamation" work, that is, the investigation of subversive, organized anti-Semitism. Today it is generally estimated that more than $250,000 a year is being spent by private organizations for this type of work. It would be my guess that this sum is probably in excess of the total budgets of the subversive groups. While much of this anti-defamation work is of undeniable importance, in the past little use has been made of the information so laboriously and expensively accumulated. A well-organized Civil Rights Division in the Department of Justice might, one would think, well take over this activity.

The dispute over what to do when the rabble rouser comes to town involves a fundamental division of opinion on the nature of fascism. Advocates of the silent treatment seem to regard fascism as a form of social measles, spread by exposure to fascist propaganda. Fascist tendencies, however, represent a diseased growth in a contradiction-laden society and, as such, they will not be overcome by trick formula or magical incantations. "Fascist groups flourish or decline," writes Irving Howe, "because of much deeper social reasons than the wise or foolish tactics of their opponents. They can be defeated, but they cannot be hushed into insignificance, for they feed on more substantial food than noise." [19] Fascist groups will never, in fact, permit their opposition to ignore them. If one form of provocation fails, they will try another and still another until a point is inevitably reached where the forces opposing them must take an open, public stand. The real question, therefore, is whether the opposition should be open or secret, organized or unorganized.

The form the opposition to fascist tendencies should

take, in any particular situation, is purely a question of
tactics, to be determined by the facts of each case, the time,
the place, the general political situation, and so forth. It is
impossible to say, as a matter of formal predetermined
policy, that picket lines are desirable or undesirable: it depends on the circumstances. While there is room for difference of opinion on the question of tactics, there should
be no division whatever on the basic proposition that fascist
tendencies must be opposed in an organized manner, openly,
publicly, democratically. Public demonstrations build up
a sense of confidence in the democratic groups which becomes of great importance in offsetting the intimidation
and coercion that inevitably accompany the rise of such
movements. The side that is able to rally the strongest support at the outset is the side most likely to win the support
of the undecided, the indifferent, and the uninformed.

CHAPTER XI *The Yellow Myth*

The Jew is a myth, the myth of German impotence. There is no more useful myth.

The Jew exists because I have failed. Every time I fail, it is the fault of the Jew. Each of my failures shows the pattern of the Jew and all these patterns make up "international Jewry."

A German has a nightmare. On awakening it is a Jew that he accuses.

"He wanted to ruin me, to soil me, to kill me."

"Who?"

"The Jew that hovered over my bed last night. That one, I recognize him."

"That cannot be he, he was elsewhere."

"Then that one. All of them, for if it was not he, it was one of his."

— DR. CHARLES ODIC in *"Stepchildren" of France*

To PLACE anti-Semitism in its proper niche in the scheme of prejudice, one must distinguish between its use as a weapon — its social function — and its function in the personality of the bigot. To demonstrate the social function of anti-Semitism does not explain the predisposition toward anti-Semitism in the individual. The key to this riddle is to be found in the existence of certain fairly well delineated anti-Semitic "types" or personalities. In some obscure manner, anti-Semitism seems to serve a function in these personalities that closely approximates its larger social function.

While social scientists have made marked progress in

isolating certain characteristics of the anti-Semitic types, it has remained for Jean-Paul Sartre, the French philosopher, to give us a really satisfactory portrait of the anti-Semite.[1] Sartre starts with the proposition that anti-Semitism cannot be regarded in the category of mere opinion; on the contrary, it is a passion. When the moderate or latent anti-Semite argues that "there must be something about the Jews" that accounts for the feeling against them, he is using logic dictated by passion. It is as though he were to say, "There must be something about tomatoes because I can't bear them." This quality of the anti-Semitic statement indicates to Sartre that anti-Semitism represents "a syncretic totality," that it serves to integrate conflicting tendencies in a certain type of personality.

The anti-Semitic attitude, as Sartre points out, is not provoked by personal experiences with Jews nor is it based upon an observation of Jews as Jews. When a woman says, "I've had a terrible row with furriers, they've robbed me, they've burned the furs I entrusted to them. Well, they were all Jews" — why, asks Sartre, does she hate Jews rather than furriers? The answer, of course, is that she possessed a predisposition to anti-Semitism. But this predisposition is not created by what the Jew does or fails to do; nor by what he is or is not. If Jewish "differences" were a real factor, why did the Nazis feel compelled to make the Jews identify themselves by wearing the Star of David? Sartre gets to the root of the psychological riddle when he says that the anti-Semitic passion *"precedes the facts which should arouse it,* it seeks them out to feed upon, it must even interpret them in its own way in order to render them really offensive"* (emphasis added). The anti-Semite, as

Sartre shrewdly points out, *grows* angry because he has already consented to become angry; because he has willed in advance "to exist on the passionate level."

The anti-Semite has chosen to reason falsely because he feels or experiences "the nostalgia of impermeability." The rational man seeks the truth gropingly. Never knowing where his investigations will carry him or what conclusions he will finally reach, he is hesitant and doubtful; his conclusions are tentative and provisional. But there are people, writes Sartre, who are attracted by the durability of stone; who want to be massive and impenetrable *because they do not want to change*. It is the very form of truth that frightens them, for its contents they do not even suspect. Not wanting to live a life of reason, they insist that reason be relegated to a subordinate position in the scheme of things. "They do not want acquired opinions, they want them to be innate." If the anti-Semite deigns to defend his point of view, "he lends himself without giving himself; he simply tries to project his intuitive certainty onto the field of speech." Often he is completely aware of the absurdity of his position, but it amuses him to defend it. The anti-Semites "like to play with speech because by putting forth ridiculous reasons, they discredit the seriousness of their interlocutor; they are enchanted with their unfairness because for them it is not a question of persuading by good arguments but of intimidating or disorienting. If you insist too much they close up, they point out with one superb word that the time to argue has passed." Thus if the anti-Semite is impervious to reason and experience, it is not because his reasons are strong but because he has chosen to be impervious. A reading of the superb short story by John

Berryman to which I have already referred will show how perfectly this analysis accounts for the damnable situation in which Berryman once found himself when he engaged in an argument with a member of the Christian Front. As a matter of fact, Sartre's analysis parallels very closely the findings made by American social scientists who have studied the personality of the anti-Semite.[2]

Since the passion of the anti-Semite has not been provoked from the outside, he is able to keep it well in hand, letting himself go as much as he wants. He has chosen, in other words, to be terrifying. Thus he controls the situation vis-à-vis the anti-anti-Semite. The disquieting picture that he reads in the eyes of the nonprejudiced person dictates his own strategy and tactics. "This external model relieves him of the necessity of seeking his own personality within himself; he has chosen to be all outside, never to examine his conscience, never to be anything but the very fear he strikes in others: he is running away from the intimate awareness that he has of himself even more than from Reason."

Thus the anti-Semite is essentially a mediocre person, a person well aware of his own mediocrity. "There is no example," writes Sartre, "of an anti-Semite claiming individual superiority over the Jews." The anti-Semite knows and readily admits that he is a mediocre person; in fact, he glories in his mediocrity and seeks out the kinship of other mediocrities. "If he has become an anti-Semite, it is because *one cannot be anti-Semitic alone*." The statement "I hate Jews," writes Sartre — and how true it is! — is one that is always said in chorus. By saying it, the anti-Semite connects himself with a tradition and a community: that of the

266 A Mask for Privilege

mediocre man. Sensing his own mediocrity, the anti-Semite seeks to take possession of some concrete aspect of his life — his being 100 per cent American or native born — as a means of rationalizing his essential mediocrity and of investing it with importance.

The hatred of French for Germans, of Poles for Russians, is not like the hatred of the anti-Semite for the Jew, for it is not colored by sadism. "It is amusing," writes Sartre, "to be anti-Semitic." It is notorious that the sadist persecutes the weak and defenseless not merely because it is safer but because it is somehow more pleasurable than to persecute the strong. The Nazis did not immediately set about the extermination of the Jews: they wanted to exterminate them in a piecemeal fashion, to prolong the pleasure derived from the process. Thus the confirmed anti-Semite is, in the depths of his soul, a criminal. For the measures that he advocates from time to time against the Jews are but the preliminary steps to the final act of murder: they are "symbolic murders."

The latent anti-Semite is a somewhat different type. He would not harm the Jews nor would he act to prevent violence against them. The latent anti-Semites, in Sartre's analysis, "are nothing: they are no one." To them anti-Semitism is "an enormous affirmation" which must be respectable because they have borrowed it from respectable people. "It presents, too, a serious advantage for those people who recognize their profound instability and who are weary of it: it allows them to assume the appearance of passion and . . . to confuse passion with personality."

While Sartre's analysis of the anti-Semitic personality is brilliant and shrewd, it is subject to one important qualification. It could be inferred from this analysis that individuals are born into the world with the types of personality in which prejudice serves a psychic function. Obviously this is not the case; prejudice is overwhelmingly a product of social conditioning. It is only in a sick society that certain types of individuals feel the need to scapegoat; or, if not a sick society, one in which the social side of man's nature cannot find adequate satisfactions. It is only in such a society that prejudice can be said to have a personal and a social function. The frustrations which are displaced, projected, and rationalized, as outlined in an earlier chapter, are induced by society, not by some irreducible core of sin, hatred, or animus in human nature. It is debatable if a false feeling of racial superiority brings any real satisfaction to the individuals and groups that seem to crave this feeling as a solace to their egos. But from a short-range point of view, it is true that *a few* individuals profit from group dominance and it is also true that in a society riddled with social contradictions prejudice does have a function.

Here, then, is Sartre's final portrait of the anti-Semite:

He is a man who is afraid. Not of the Jews of course, but of himself, of his conscience, of freedom, of his instincts, of his responsibilities, of solitude, of change, of society and the world; of everything except the Jews. He is a coward who does not want to admit his cowardice to himself; a murderer who represses and censures his penchant for murder without being able to kill except in effigy or in the anonymity of a mob; a malcontent who dares not revolt for fear of the consequences of his rebellion. By adhering to anti-semitism, he is not only adopting an opinion, he is choosing himself as a person. He is choosing the permanence and impenetrability of rock, the total irresponsibility of the warrior who obeys his leaders — and he has no leader. He chooses to acquire nothing, to deserve nothing but that everything be given him as his birthright — and he is not noble. He chooses finally, that good be ready made, not in question, out of reach; he dare not look at it for fear of being forced to contest it and seek another form of it. The Jew is only a pretext; elsewhere it will be the Negro, the yellow race. The Jew's insistence simply allows the anti-semite to nip his anxieties in the bud by persuading himself that his place has always been cut out in the world, that it was waiting for him and that by virtue of tradition he has the right to occupy it. *Anti-semitism*, in a word, *is fear of man's fate*. The anti-semite is the man who wants to be pitiless stone, furious torrent, devastating lightning: in short, everything but a man.

This is the type of personality to which the professional anti-Semite addresses his strictures of hate and envy; this is the underlying predisposition upon which he builds his structures of blind fury. Anti-Semitism is a fear of one's self — the sweat of fear, the fever of inadequacy — that, in moments of crisis, breeds havoc and social panic. As a weapon in social conflicts, anti-Semitism is a menacing reality; as a deep-seated psychological fear of one's self, it is likewise an incontestable reality; but anti-Semitism as a doctrine, as an ideology, is a scurrilous yellow myth, a swamp fever exhaled by sick people in a sick society.

This yellow myth must be dispelled. If men will think, they can ferret out the real evils of this world; and if they will act, they can correct these evils. But the yellow myth that obscures their personal inadequacies also blinds them to the inadequacies of the world in which they live. For it is a myth with a hidden meaning, a perverse reflection of reality. This hidden meaning is revealed in the history of the Protocols of the Elders of Zion. The book which the forgers of the Protocols pirated was a fantasy written by Maurice Joly as a means of satirizing and exposing the dictatorial regime of Napoleon III. It might best be described as a vivid and imaginative foreshadowing of fascism, a kind of blueprint for the fascist conspiracy. By picturing this conspiracy as a Jewish conspiracy, the Czarist agents who committed the forgery succeeded in creating one of the most persistent and dangerous myths of all time. For subsequent world happenings seemed to confirm the prophecy of the Protocols; in fact, the delusion was almost perfect.

What more clever stratagem could be imagined than for a man, bent on committing a crime, to project his criminal intention on an innocent victim by charging the victim with having organized a conspiracy which is, in fact, his own? Then, while the circumstantial evidence mounts against the victim, the real criminal commits his crime in full view of a public whose attention is so riveted upon the scapegoat that it does not even see that a dagger is being driven in its back. Those who charge the Jews with a conspiracy to dominate the world are themselves the real conspirators and their conspiracy is the reality hidden in the fable.

Anti-Semitism is one of the greatest barriers to self-knowledge and social understanding of our times because it masks a reality — the reality of social, economic, and political injustice. "The Jew in the Thorn," a folk tale which dates from 1500 A.D., tells of a manservant who, having been swindled out of his wages, feels absolutely justified in stealing the money from a Jew. The fact that he has been robbed is the meaning hidden in the yellow myth of anti-Semitism.

When men come to understand this meaning, they will recognize that anti-Semitism is a universal injustice, born of injustice, fostering injustice, kept alive by injustice. Man's ability to live in peace with his fellow men, his capacity to see justice done, his humanity, all can be measured by his freedom, as an individual and as a member of society, from the blinding effects of this ancient yellow myth.

Since this chapter began with a parable, perhaps it can close on another. Milton Hindus, substituting quotation marks for James Joyce's system of dashes and indentations, has provided a fine parable from *Ulysses*. The dialogue is between Mr. Deasy, the anti-Semite, and Stephen Dedalus:

"Mark my words, Mr. Dedalus," [Deasy] said, "England is in the hands of the jews. In all the highest places: her finance, her press. And they are the signs of a nation's decay. Wherever they gather they eat up the nation's vital strength. I have seen it coming these years. As sure as we are standing here the jew merchants are already at their work of destruction. Old England is dying. . . ."

"A merchant," Stephen said, "is one who buys cheap and sells dear, jew or gentile, is he not?"

"They sinned against the light," Mr. Deasy said gravely. "And you can see the darkness in their eyes. And that is why they are wanderers on the earth to this day. . . ."

"Who has not?" Stephen said.

"What do you mean?" Mr. Deasy asked. . . .

"History," Stephen said, "is a nightmare from which I am trying to awaken."

Notes

CHAPTER I

1. See *Jewish Encyclopedia*, Vol. XI, p. 169, where it is referred to as "the first incident of this kind that occurred in the United States"; and also the comments of Dr. Joshua Bloch, the *Protestant*, November 1943, p. 16, where it is described as "the beginnings of this obnoxious and alas now widespread form of social prejudice."

2. See *Organizing American Jewry* by Bernard G. Richards, pp. 12–13.

3. See comments of George William Curtis, *Harper's*, July 1877, p. 300.

4. *The Politicos*, 1939.

5. *The Wild Seventies*, 1941.

6. *The New Nation* by Frederic L. Paxson, 1927, p. 72.

7. *The Beginnings of Critical Realism in America*, Vol. III, p. 48.

8. *Jews and Judaism*, 1906.

9. *Anti-Semitism* by Bernard Lazare, 1903, pp. 352, 355, 362.

10. *The Jews*, 1922, pp. 201–203.

11. *The American Rich* is not the only book in which Hoffman Nickerson has given expression to what might be called a kind of medieval anti-Semitism. See *Arms and Policy* (1945); and *The New Slavery* (1947).

CHAPTER II

1. See the *American Magazine* for December 1914.

2. *Harper's Weekly*, November 13, 1915.

3. *The Conquering Jew*, 1916.

4. *The Rise of the Jew in the Western World* by Uriah Zevi Engelman, 1944, p. 118.

5. *Foreign Influences in American Life*, 1944, p. 95.

6. *American Journal of Sociology*, January 1939.

7. *Foreign Influences in American Life*, p. 50.

8. *Tom Watson: Agrarian Rebel* by C. Vann Woodward, 1938.

9. See *The Tragedy of Henry Ford* by Jonathan Leonard, 1932, p. 208.

10. See *Anti-Semitism in the United States* by Lee J. Levinger, 1925, p. 9; and *Encyclopedia of the Social Sciences*, Vol. II, p. 119.

11. See *Jews in the Contemporary World* by Abram Leon Sachar, 1939, where the effect of the act upon American Jewish life is discussed in detail.

12. "The Jewish Problem," *Century*, 1921.

13. *Nation*, June 22, 1921.

14. See the articles by Norman Hapgood in *Harper's Weekly*, January 15, 22, and 29, 1916.

15. *Nation*, November 14, 1923, and February 13, 1924.

16. *New York Times*, December 16, 1937.

17. *The Jews Come to America*, 1932.

18. *Harper's*, November 1933.

19. *Common Ground*, 1938.

20. Vol. 37, p. 155.

21. *Anti-Semitism: Yesterday and Tomorrow*, 1936, p. 141.

22. *Jews in a Gentile World*, 1942, p. 111.

23. See *It's a Secret* by Henry Hoke, 1946, Chaps. IV and V.

24. On the subject of Mr. Rankin's attitude to the Jews, see *Congressional Record*, April 24, 1941, p. 327960; June 4, 1941, p. 4726; March 29, 1943, p. A–1585; April 24, 1941, p. 327980; April 7, 1943, p. A–1817; December 18, 1943, p. 10999; January 26, 1944, pp. A–446 and A–447.

25. See *The Home Front*, published by the American Jewish Committee, March 15, 1947; and the report of the Anti-Defamation League, *New York Times*, May 7, 1947, and *PM* for the same date.

CHAPTER III

1. *Nation*, March 21, 1923.

2. *The Jewish Problem in the Modern World* by James Parkes, 1946.

3. Vol. 54, p. 421.

4. See *Race: A History of Modern Ethnic Theories* by Louis L. Snyder, 1939, p. 230.

5. *Atlantic Monthly*, December 1908.

6. *Race and National Solidarity*, 1923.

7. See *Literary Digest*, September 13, 1913, p. 428.

8. See also *The New Barbarians* by the famous historian Dr. Wilbur C. Abbott, 1925.

9. *Up Stream; An American Chronicle*, 1922.

10. *The Education of Henry Adams*, p. 344.

11. *The Jew in Our Day*, 1944.

CHAPTER IV

1. *Jews in a Gentile World*, p. 156; emphasis mine.

2. *Jewish Experiences in America*, 1930, p. 148.

3. *Political Science Quarterly*, Spring 1942.

4. *Anti-Semitism: A Social Disease*, 1946, p. 12.

5. *Jewish Encyclopedia*, 1925, the article on "Anti-Semitism" by Gotthard Deutsch.

6. See the *Home Front*, March 14, 1947.

7. *Jews in a Gentile World*, p. 157.

8. *Anti-Semitism: A Social Disease*, 1946, pp. 96–125.

9. *Journal of Psychology*, 1944, Vol. 17, pp. 339–370.

10. See, in particular, *The Rise of the Jew in the Western World*, 1944, by Uriah Zevi Engelman.

CHAPTER V

1. From the article on "Clubs" by Dr. Crane Brinton, *Encyclopedia of the Social Sciences*, Vol. 3, p. 576.

2. *Civilization and Group Relationships*, 1945, p. 96.

3. *How Odd of God*, 1934, p. 116.

4. See *A Social and Religious History of the Jews*, by S. W. Baron, 1937, p. 285; and *Anti-Semitism: A Social Disease*, 1946, p. 5.

5. *Public Opinion Quarterly*, Spring 1942, p. 48.

6. *Kenyon Review*, Autumn 1945.

7. *Menorah Journal*, Spring 1946, p. 139.

8. *All in the Name of God*, 1934.

9. See, for example, my article comparing the pattern of discrimination in Minneapolis with that in the twin city of St. Paul. *Common Ground*, Autumn 1946.

10. *Catholics, Jews, and Protestants*, by Silcox and Fisher, 1934.

11. See *Where Hope Lies,* by Leo Schwarz, 1940, pp. 31–33, for General Moseley's views on anti-Semitism.

12. *Nation,* February 28, 1923, emphasis mine.

13. See "Jewish Teachers" by Samuel Tennenbaum, *Jewish Experiences in America,* 1930, pp. 75–80.

14. *Who Shall Be Educated?* 1944, by Warner, Havighurst, and Loeb, p. 60.

15. See *PM,* August 8 and 28, 1945, and the *New Republic* of August 20, 1945.

16. *New York Post,* August 7, 1945.

17. See the report of Dr. Frank Kingdon, placed in the *Congressional Record,* October 18, 1945; "College Quotas and American Democracy" by Dan W. Dodson, the *American Scholar,* Summer 1945.

18. *American Mercury,* July 1946.

19. *New York Times,* January 23, 1946.

20. *PM,* February 21, 1946, p. 13.

21. See *PM,* October 23, 1946, *New York Times,* October 23, 1946. Nineteen of 23 nonsectarian colleges in New York State ask applicants about their race or religion or national background — *New York Times,* March 8, 1947.

22. *Congress Weekly,* November 22, 1946.

23. See *Quotas,* a pamphlet published by Dr. Harry Cimring, Los Angeles, 1946.

24. *New York Post,* November 22, 1946.

CHAPTER VI

1. See the article by David Riesman, *Public Opinion Quarterly,* Spring 1942, p. 41.

2. *Jews in a Gentile World,* p. 396.

3. *The American Jew,* 1942, p. 161.

4. See *Jews in a Gentile World,* p. 409.

5. *The Social System of Ethnic Groups,* 1945, p. 203.

6. *Jewish Experiences in America,* p. 121.

7. *Jewish Frontier Anthology,* 1945, p. 220.

8. *Jews on Approval,* 1932.

9. *Congress Weekly,* December 27, 1946, p. 8.

10. See *PM,* September 23, 1946.

11. *New York Times*, May 8, 1946.

12. See, for example, "Whittling Away Religious Freedom" by Milton R. Konvitz, *Commentary*, June 1946.

13. *Christian Century*, June 9, 1937.

CHAPTER VII

1. *Anti-Semitism: A Social Disease*, p. 9.

2. See *Essays on Anti-Semitism*, 1946, p. 146.

3. *Political Science Quarterly*, March 1919.

4. *Jews in a Gentile World*, p. 388.

5. *Jews on Approval*, pp. 217–218; emphasis added.

6. See "Minority Caricatures on the American Stage" by Dr. Harold E. Adams in *Studies in the Science of Society*, 1937.

7. See the *Nation*, April 17, 1935, and October 10, 1935; also the *New Masses*, April 23, 1935.

8. See "This Is the Man" in *Now with His Love*, 1933, p. 36.

9. See "Of Jews and Thomas Wolfe" by Harold U. Ribalow, *Congress Weekly*, January 24, 1947.

10. See "F. Scott Fitzgerald and Literary Anti-Semitism" by Milton Hindus, *Commentary*, June 1947, pp. 508–516.

11. See two articles by Albert Jay Nock which appeared in the *Atlantic Monthly* for June and July, 1941; and an article by Ernest Boyd in *Scribner's* for October 1933.

12. For an interesting and penetrating discussion of "marginal trading peoples" see the section entitled "The Stimulus of Penalizations" in *A Study of History* by Arnold J. Toynbee, 1947, pp. 125–139.

CHAPTER VIII

1. *Anti-Semitism: A Social Disease*, p. 131.

2. For other studies of fascist propaganda techniques, see *The Fine Art of Propaganda* by Alfred McClung Lee and Elizabeth Briant Lee, 1939, an excellent study of the fancy techniques of Father Coughlin; and also *Conquering the Man in the Street*, 1940, by Ellis Freeman, a brilliant analysis of fascist propaganda and of the cultural factors which make for its acceptance.

3. *Organized Anti-Semitism in America*, 1941, Chapter XIV.

4. *Anti-Semitism: A Social Disease*, p. 13.

5. See Strong, *op. cit.*, pp. 97–98.

6. *Organized Anti-semitism in America* by Dr. Donald S. Strong, American Council on Public Affairs, 1941, p. 176.

7. *Conquering the Man in the Street,* 1940, p. 319.

8. See the series of articles by Tom O'Connor in *PM* for May, June, and July, 1945.

9. For background on Bader, see *The Plotters* by John Roy Carlson, 1946, pp. 145–146.

10. For further details on the meeting, see *Pittsburgh Press,* March 6, 1946.

11. *Pittsburgh Press,* March 7, 1946.

12. *New York Times,* October 10, 1946.

13. *Journal of Social Psychology,* Vol. VII, pp. 309–319.

14. *Commentary,* March 1947, p. 284.

CHAPTER IX

1. *New York Times,* December 1, 1946.

2. *New York Post,* December 13, 1946.

3. *New York Times,* November 5, 1946.

4. See the issue of November 3, 1946.

5. *New York Post,* December 12, 1946.

6. *New York Herald Tribune,* December 11, 1946.

7. A picture of the child appeared in the *National Jewish Monthly,* a publication of the B'nai B'rith organization, in the issue for October 1946.

8. *New York Post,* November 22, 1946.

9. *Atlanta Constitution,* November 3, 1946.

10. *PM,* December 13, 1946; emphasis added.

11. On July 1, 1947, the acting director of the Anti-Defamation League announced that Loomis, on bond pending an appeal of his conviction, was organizing a new "hate" group.

CHAPTER X

1. Quoted in *Anti-Semitism: A Social Disease,* p. 45.

2. From a speech before the Institute of Ethnic Affairs, Washington, May 29, 1946; emphasis added.

3. For one of numerous proposals made to the commission, see *Civil Liberties News,* Chicago, July 11, 1947, Vol. 3, No. 28, based

upon the proceedings of the first International Consultative Conference on Human Rights held in London, June 13–16, 1947.

4. *New York Times*, June 29, 1947.

5. *PM*, April 3, 1947, p. 4.

6. *The American Jew*, 1942, p. 179.

7. "Race and Religion in Selective Admission," *Journal of the American Association of Collegiate Registrars*.

8. See statement of the Catholic Welfare Committee, *New York Times*, February 27, 1947.

9. See *Journal of Social Issues*, August 1945.

10. *Jews on Approval*, 1932, pp. 214–215.

11. *Commentary*, March 1947, p. 284.

12. See also the comments of Cabell Phillips in the *New York Times* of February 16, 1947.

13. *Democracy and Defamation*, 1942.

14. *New Republic*, October 29, 1945.

15. *A Partisan Guide to the Jewish Problem*, 1945.

16. *Civil Liberties News*, May 23, 1947.

17. *Conquering the Man in the Street*, p. 326.

18. Martin Gumpert in the *Nation*, May 12, 1945.

19. *Commentary*, November 1946, p. 464.

CHAPTER XI

1. *Partisan Review*, Spring 1946, p. 163.

2. *Commentary*, March 1947, p. 284.

Acknowledgments

For helpful comments, criticisms, and suggestions I wish to thank Dr. Bruno Lasker; Mr. Will Maslow and Mr. Henry Silberman of the American Jewish Congress; Mr. Hyman Edelman; Mr. and Mrs. Joseph Aidlin; and Dr. Frederick Pollock of the Institute of Social Research, who made available certain manuscript material, including a paper by Dr. Paul Massing which is referred to in Chapter IV. For assistance in preparation of the manuscript, I am indebted to Margaret O'Connor and Ross B. Wills.

Portions of the manuscript appeared in article form in *Common Ground*, *Jewish Life*, and *Commentary* and I am indebted to the editors of these publications for assignments of rights.

I also wish to acknowledge a deep indebtedness in the preparation of this and other books to Mrs. Thelma Jackman of the Sociology Department of the Los Angeles Public Library and to her always courteous and most helpful assistants: Adalea Haass, Dorothy Smith, Mary Beth Otis, and Anne Mueller.

My thanks, also, to the editors of *Partisan Review* for permission to quote from Jean-Paul Sartre's article "Portrait of the Antisemite" which appeared in the Spring 1946 issue of that publication; to The Viking Press, Inc., for permission to quote from *The Theory of the Leisure Class* by Thorstein Veblen; to Harcourt, Brace and Company, Inc., for permission to quote from *The Beginnings of Critical Realism in America* by Vernon Louis Parrington; to Random House, Inc., for permission to quote from *The Sound and the Fury* by William Faulkner; to Houghton Mifflin Company for permission to quote from *John Jay Chapman and His Letters*, edited by M. A. DeWolfe Howe, from *The Letters of Henry Adams*, edited by Worthington Chauncey Ford, and from *The Education of Henry Adams* by Henry Adams; to The Macmillan Company for permission to quote from *Jews in a Gentile World* by Graeber and Britt (Copyright, 1942, by The Macmillan Company and used with their permission); to Oxford University Press for permission to quote from *The Jewish Problem in the Modern World* by James Parkes (Copyright 1946 by Oxford University Press, New York, Inc.); to Liveright Publishing Corporation, New York, for permission to quote from *Jews on Approval* by Maurice Samuel, and to Roy Publishers for permission to quote from *"Stepchildren" of France* by Charles Odic.

Index

Index

ADAMS, HENRY, 75–77, 181; quoted, 18, 70

Adams, Herbert Baxter, 67

Adler, Cyrus, quoted, 52

Adorno, Dr. T. W., quoted, 185, 186, 187

Advertising, position and influence of Jews in, 146

Agriculture, position and influence of Jews in, 144, 152

Ahlwardt, 98

Alexander II, Czar, assassination an excuse for expelling Jews, 25

Altman, Benjamin, 61

America First Committee, 194–196, 198, 199

American Action, Inc., 195–200, 202, 203

American Association of Dental Schools, 139

American Federation of Labor, 218

American Forward Movement, 192

American Foundation, 197

American Israelites, 3

American Jewish Congress, 253; Law and Social Action Commission of, 241

American Legion, 198

American National Action Party, 196

American National Democratic Committee, 199

American Nationalist Confederation, 192

American Protective Association (A.P.A.), 28, 81

American Vigilant Intelligence Federation, 190

Amusements, position and influence of Jews in, 146, 148

Anglo-Saxons, apotheosis of, 69

Anti-Defamation League, 24

Anti-defamation work, evaluated, 260

Anti-Semites, latent type of, 266; personality types of, 262; psychological analysis of, 263–269; sadism of, 266; subordination of reason by, 264; symbolic murder concept of, 266. *See also* Anti-Semitism; Crackpots

Anti-Semitism, absence of, in American political institutions, 51–52; American and European, compared, 48; antisocial uses of, 88, 106–107; as escape from reality, 109; as rationalization of undemocratic social order, 50; as social disease, 105–112, 267–268; as symbol of fascist groups, 42; as symptom of social change, 107–109; as universal social injustice, 269–270; as yellow myth, 268–270; based on alleged resistance to democratic process, 160; character of, defined by social context of use, 89; Christian influences as factor, 49; combating of, through education, 241–247; through governmental protection, 251–255; through individual action, 241–247; compared with other group prejudices, 174; conflicting traditional background of, 49–50; correlated with fear of social change, 103; anti-demo-

Hill, James J., 18, 69
Hillman, Sidney, 45
Himelhoch, Dr. Jerome, quoted, 205–206
Hindus, Milton, quoted, 181, 270
Hitler, Adolph, 57, 204, 209, 221
Hoellering, Franz, quoted, 72
Hoffman, 195
Hopkins, Dr. Ernest M., defends quota system at Dartmouth College, 134
Horkheimer, Dr. Max, quoted, 169–170
Horner, Dr. Harlan H., quoted, 139
Hotel Astor Corporation, 199
Hotels, exclusion of Jews by, 3–7, 24, 38, 114, 118, 125. *See also* Seligman, Joseph
Howe, Irving, quoted, 260
Huguenots, 174
Human rights, defining and application of, 227–228. *See also* Functional equality
Huntington, Collis P., 18
Hyde, James Hazen, 150

ILLINOIS MANUFACTURERS' ASSOCIATION, 199
Immigration, as threat to native American stock, 67–68; factors in, 12–13, 15–17; increase in Jewish, 18; Jewish and non-Jewish, in relation to status of Jews, 149, 152–154; Jewish, stimulated by American protection, 54–55; selective, 69
Immigration Act of 1924, 16, 21, 58, 164, 169; condemned by leading Jews, 35–36; effect on anti-Jewish prejudice, 81; on Jewish life and institutions, 36; later social effects, 43; viewed as culmination of antialien movement, 35–36
Indian minority problem, 14, 17, 21
Indians, American, 12, 63
Industrial revolution, 8–13; bigotry and intolerance in, 17; growth of

anti-Semitism from, 94–102; minorities question in, 13 ff.; race prejudice and anti-Semitism in, 11–22; social and cultural effects of, 9–13; status distinctions in, 13; triumph of bourgeoisie in, 8–11
Industrial society, refashioning of, to eliminate discrimination, 223–224
Industrial tycoons, rise and social influence of, 9–11, 18
Industry and finance, position and influence of Jews in: advertising, 146; agriculture, 144, 152; amusement, 146, 148; automobile, 144; aviation, 144; banking and finance, 143; boots and shoes, 145; chemical, 144; clothing, 145; coal, 144; commerce and trade, 151–152, 157; construction, 151; dairy farming, 144; department stores, 145; drugstore chains, 145; fields of greatest concentration, 147–149; fields of negligible influence, 142–147; food-distribution chains, 145; food processing, 144; furniture, 145; heavy machinery, 144; general merchandising, 145; insurance, 143; law, 148; light and power, 144; liquor and distilling, 145, 148; lumber, 144; mail-order, 146; manufacturing, 151–152; marginal fields, 147–151, 171; meat-packing, 144–145; mining, 144; motion pictures, 146, 150; needle trades, 154; personal services, 151; petroleum, 144; printing and publishing, 146; radio, 146, 150; railroading, 144; scrap, 145; shipbuilding, 144; shipping, 144; stock exchanges, 143; telephone and telegraph, 144; textiles, 144; tobacco, 145; transportation, 144, 151
Industry and trade, limitations on Jews imposed by, 48
Insurance companies, limitation on

Treitschke, Heinrich von, quoted, 104

Tripoli, treaty of 1796 with, 51

Truman, President Harry S., 51

Turkey, Jewish persecution in, opposed by United States, 53

"UNDER MEN" of Lothrop Stoddard, 63–67

Undesirability, myth of, 60–63

Union for Social Justice, 42, 253

Union of Canadian Fascists, 213

United Nations, 195, 227; attacked by anti-Semites, 195

United States Army, anti-Semitism in, 125–126; exclusion of Jewish ministers from, defeated, 3

United States Government, foreign pronouncements in behalf of Jewish freedom, 53–54

University of Berlin, revival of Jewish quota demanded at, 39

VALENTIN, HUGO, quoted, 49, 50, 107

Vanderbilt, Cornelius, 18

Vassar College, anti-Jewish discrimination in, 136

Veblen, Thorstein, quoted, 12, 172–173

Vincent, Col. Charles, 197

von Bohlen, Krupp, 204

von Holst, Hermann, 67

WALKER, EZEKIEL, lynching of, 73–74

Warburg, Felix M., 19, 35

Warner, Dr. Lloyd, quoted, 116, 152–153

Washington, George, quoted, 51

Wassermann, Jacob, quoted, 249–250

Watson, Tom, 31–33, 74

Weber, Max, 165

Weir, Ernest T., 199

Weiss, Arthur, 214

Weitzenkorn, Louis, quoted, 37

Weldon, Samuel, 199

Wellesley College, anti-Jewish discrimination in, 136

Wertham, Dr. Frederic, quoted, 226

Western Golf Association, exclusionist policy of, 125

Wharton, Edith, 181

Wheeler, Senator Burton, 46

Whitman, Walt, 11, 72

Whitman, Willson, quoted, 78–79

Wilson, Woodrow, 33

Winrod, Gerald B., 196

Wirth, Louis, quoted, 237

Wise, Dr. Stephen S., quoted, 132

Wolfe, Thomas, 181

Wood, Gen. Robert E., 199

"YANKEE CITY" investigations, 152–153

Yellow myth, 268–270

Yellow peril, 69

ZELLERS, JOHN A., 202

Zimmerlee, John H., Jr., 207